Contesting Governing Ideologies

Michael A. Peters is Professor of Education at the University of Waikato, New Zealand, and Emeritus Professor in Educational Policy, Organization, and Leadership at the University of Illinois at Urbana–Champaign. He is the executive editor of the journal *Educational Philosophy and Theory*.

Marek Tesar is a Senior Lecturer in Education at The University of Auckland, New Zealand, with a focus on philosophy of education and childhood studies. He is a member of the editorial board of *Educational Philosophy and Theory*.

Educational Philosophy and Theory: Editor's Choice

Series editors:
Michael A. Peters, University of Waikato, New Zealand;
Marek Tesar, The University of Auckland, New Zealand.

The EPAT Editor's Choice series comprises innovative and influential articles drawn from the *Educational Philosophy and Theory* journal archives, spanning 46 volumes, from 1969. Each volume represents a selection of important articles that respond to and focus on a particular theme, celebrating and emphasizing the heritage and history of the work, as well as the cutting edge contemporary contributions available. The series will create a rich vertical collection across five decades of seminal scholarship, contextualizing and elevating specific themes, scholars and their work. The EPAT editors, Michael A. Peters and Marek Tesar, introduce each volume, the theme, and the work selected within that volume.

Titles in the series include:

Beyond the Philosophy of the Subject
An Educational Philosophy and Theory Post-Structuralist Reader
Edited by Michael A. Peters and Marek Tesar

In Search of Subjectivities
An Educational Philosophy and Theory Teacher Education Reader
Edited by Michael A. Peters and Marek Tesar

Contesting Governing Ideologies
An Educational Philosophy and Theory Reader on Neoliberalism
Edited by Michael A. Peters and Marek Tesar

Troubling the Changing Paradigms
An Educational Philosophy and Theory Early Childhood Reader
Edited by Michael A. Peters and Marek Tesar

Contesting Governing Ideologies

An Educational Philosophy and Theory Reader on Neoliberalism

Volume III

Edited by Michael A. Peters
and Marek Tesar

LONDON AND NEW YORK

First published 2018 by Routledge

2 Park Square, Milton Park, Abingdon, Oxfordshire OX14 4RN
52 Vanderbilt Avenue, New York, NY 10017

Routledge is an imprint of the Taylor & Francis Group, an informa business

First issued in paperback 2018

British Library Cataloguing-in-Publication Data
A catalogue record for this book is available from the British Library

Library of Congress Cataloging-in-Publication Data
A catalog record for this book has been requested

ISBN: 978-1-138-09638-7 (hbk)
ISBN: 978-0-367-18196-3 (pbk)

Typeset in Galliard
by Apex CoVantage, LLC

MIX
Paper from
responsible sources
FSC   FSC™ C013985
www.fsc.org

Printed in the United Kingdom
by Henry Ling Limited

Contents

Citation Information

The following chapters are reprinted by permission of Taylor & Francis, Ltd, http://www.tandfonline.com, on behalf of © Philosophy of Education Society of Australasia:

Chapter 2

Neo-Liberal Education Policy and the Ideology of Choice
John A. Codd (1993)
Neo-Liberal Education Policy and the Ideology of Choice, *Educational Philosophy and Theory*, 25:2, 31–48

Chapter 3

Varieties of Neo-Liberalism: a Foucaultian Perspective
James D. Marshall (2001)
Varieties of Neo-liberalism: a Foucaultian perspective1, *Educational Philosophy and Theory*, 33:3–4, 293–304

Chapter 4

The Labouring Sleepwalker: Evocation and Expression as Modes of Qualitative Educational Research
Paul Smeyers (2005)
The Labouring Sleepwalker: Evocation and expression as modes of qualitative educational research, *Educational Philosophy and Theory*, 37:3, 407–423

Chapter 5

The Learning Society, the Unfinished Cosmopolitan, and Governing Education, Public Health and Crime Prevention at the Beginning of the Twenty-First Century
Thomas S. Popkewitz , Ulf Olsson and Kenneth Petersson (2006)

The Learning Society, the Unfinished Cosmopolitan, and Governing Education, Public Health and Crime Prevention at the Beginning of the Twenty-First Century, *Educational Philosophy and Theory*, 38:4

Chapter 6

What Were You Thinking? A Deleuzian/Guattarian Analysis of Communication in the Mathematics Classroom
Elizabeth De Freitas (2013)
What Were You Thinking? A Deleuzian/Guattarian analysis of communication in the mathematics classroom, *Educational Philosophy and Theory*, 45:3, 287–300

Chapter 7

(Re)Visioning the Centre: Education Reform and the 'Ideal' Citizen of the Future
Linda J. Graham (2007)
(Re)Visioning the Centre: Education reform and the 'ideal' citizen of the future, *Educational Philosophy and Theory*, 39:2, 197–215

Chapter 8

Biopolitical Utopianism in Educational Theory
Tyson Lewis (2007)
Biopolitical Utopianism in Educational Theory, *Educational Philosophy and Theory*, 39:7, 683–702

Chapter 9

A Place Pedagogy for 'Global Contemporaneity'
Margaret J. Somerville (2010)
A Place Pedagogy for 'Global Contemporaneity', *Educational Philosophy and Theory*, 42:3, 326–344

Chapter 10

Antonio Gramsci and Feminism: The Elusive Nature of Power
Margaret Ledwith (2009)
Antonio Gramsci and Feminism: The Elusive Nature of Power, *Educational Philosophy and Theory*, 41:6, 684–697

Chapter 11

Foucault, Educational Research and the Issue of Autonomy
Mark Olssen (2005)
Foucault, Educational Research and the Issue of Autonomy, *Educational Philosophy and Theory*, 37:3, 365–387

Contesting Governing Ideologies

Contesting Governing Ideologies is the third volume in the *Educational Philosophy and Theory: Editor's Choice* series and represents a collection of texts that provide a cutting-edge analysis of the philosophy and theory of performances of neoliberal ideology in education. In past decades, philosophy of education has provided a critical commentary on problematic areas of neoliberal ideology. As such, this collection argues, philosophy of education can be considered as an intellectual struggle that runs through the contemporary ideological landscape and has roots that go back to the Enlightenment in its traditions.

This book covers multiple philosophical and educational theoretical perspectives of what we know about the ideology of neoliberalism and many of its practices and projects. Neoliberalism is difficult to define, but what is certain is that it has significantly matured as a political doctrine and set of policy practices. This collection covers questions of ideology, politics and policy in relation to the subject and the institution alike. The chapters in this book provide rich and diverse reading, allowing readers to rethink established discourses and contest ideologies, providing a thorough and careful philosophical and theoretical analysis of the story of neoliberalism over the past decades.

Contesting Governing Ideologies will be key reading for academics, researchers and postgraduate students in the fields of philosophy of education, philosophy, education, educational theory, post-structural theory, the policy and politics of education and the pedagogy of education.

Chapter 1

Philosophy and Performance of Neoliberal Ideologies
History, Politics and Human Subjects

Michael A. Peters and Marek Tesar

> "Neo-liberalism is not Adam Smith; neo-liberalism is not market society; neo-liberalism is not the Gulag on the insidious scale of capitalism."
>
> (Foucault, 2008, p. 131)

The Theory and Philosophy of Neoliberal Ideology

The assertion above in the opening quote means to distinguish positionings towards this governing ideology through three approaches to neo-liberalism. The political and economic theory behind neoliberal ideology is one of the main architectural and philosophical features of the educational policy paradigm in the Western world since the late 1970s and early 1980s. The notion of 'policy enactments' means to consider some of the 'lived effects' of neoliberal policy on our contemporary educational discourses and on lived experiences and narratives that occur in education settings and that testify to these changes.

The neoliberal restructuring of state education systems, and particularly of higher education in many Western countries in recent decades, has become a new paradigm that has been positioned, historically, as a series of important shifts and turns. Some of these have been the move from public, state and free education into private and somewhat personalized education, which is the move away from the notion of 'equality of opportunity' that historically many countries were defined as (a good example is New Zealand). The other shift that has been significant in determining these changes was the move away from an emphasis on policy and administration towards the importance, and rise, of management. This idea should be considered in context with the rise and contemporary prevalence of neoliberalism as the predominant ideology of globalization.

The theory of neoliberalism and its practice differs quite radically (Peters & Tesar, 2016b). The theory takes the view that individual liberty and freedom are the paramount goals of human subjects in the civilization, and that they can be achieved, and protected, for that matter. This achievement is driven by the idea of structures of institutions, which are made up of strong private rights, property rights, free markets, and free trade. It is the civilization in which a human subject – an individual – can flourish. So the implication of such positioning of human subjects is that the state should not be involved much in navigating the economy, but that it should utilize its influence and power to preserve human subjects' rights to private property, and to support the institutions of the free market, and promote them on the global stage where needed. The theory of neoliberalism includes the radical policies that have been systematically embedded, such as the market liberalization and free trade, limited government, narrow monetarist policies, a deregulated labour market, and fiscal restraint, and have become common sense and beyond challenge.

Neoliberal ideology is united by the strong belief that state intervention, which promotes egalitarian social goals, has been responsible for economic decline (Peters & Tesar, 2016a). In addition, in neoliberalism such state intervention represents a violation of individual rights, self-reliance and initiative of human subjects. In that sense, the neoliberal ideology is clear in that equality and freedom are incompatible notions to human subjects' existence within the institutions and structures of the globalised world. In such thinking, freedom is then construed in individual and negative terms (such as freedom from intervention), and is thus indispensable for economic vitality and individual well-being. Theoretical underpinnings for this view are located, in part, in a contemporary rejuvenation of neoclassical liberal economic theory that privileges both the free market as an institution above all others and market values over all other values that human subjects can encounter. In this sense, from the late 1970s, a combination of anti-statist critiques and public sector deficits has contributed to a climate of fiscal retrenchment. Neoliberal ideology and its political forces have argued that the constant enlargement of social welfare undermines stable economic growth, and therefore is detrimental to political legitimacy, traditional community and family values.

What are the specific features of the liberal art of government, as they were outlined in the 18th century? What crisis of governmentality characterises the present world and what revisions of liberal government has it given rise to? This is the diagnostic task addressed by Foucault's study of the two major 20th century schools of neo-liberalism: German ordo-liberalism and the neoliberalism of the Chicago School. In Foucault's work (lectures), the discussion of contemporary economic theory and practice culminates in an analysis of the model of *homo economicus* (Besley & Peters, 2007). He argued in *The Birth of Biopolitics*, "the analysis of biopolitics can only get under way when we have understood the general regime of this governmental reason I have talked about, this general regime that we can call the question of truth, of economic truth in the first place, within governmental reason" (Foucault, 2008, p. 22).

The Neoliberal History of Human Subjects

When examining the histories of present neoliberalism, Harvey (2005) traces the intellectual roots of neoliberal thought back to the Austrian political philosopher Friedrich von Hayek, who authored *The Consititution of Liberty* in 1960. As Harvey argues, neoliberalism is a form of utopian thought, the dangers of which were first examined by Hayek's contemporary Karl Polanyi in 1957, a Hungarian economic philosopher and historian. As Harvey (2005) works through Polanyi's thinking, he concludes the following:

> The idea of freedom 'degenerates into a mere advocacy of free enterprise', which means 'the fullness of freedom for those whose income leisure and security need no enhancing, and a mere pittance of liberty for the people, who may in vain attempt to make use of their democratic rights to gain shelter from the power of the owners of property'. But if, as is always the case, 'no society is possible in which power and compulsion are absent, nor a world in which force has no function', then the only way this liberal utopian vision could be sustained is by force, violence and authoritarianism. Liberal or neo-liberal utopianism is doomed, in Polyani's view to be frustrated by authoritarianism, or even outright fascism.
>
> (p. 37)

When examining the historical effects of neoliberalism, it is clear that some of the late 1970s and 1980s politics were strongly linked to the idea of rising neoliberalism. Ronald Reagan argued that, "[i]n this present crisis, government is not the solution to our problems; government is the problem." And under his administration, Reaganomics became the prevalent way to operate, to implement policies based on supply-side economics and his governance emphasized and advocated a classical liberal and laissez-faire philosophy, seeking to stimulate the economy with large, across-the-board tax cuts (Peters, Paraskeva & Besley, 2015). In China, in the late 1980s, it was the leadership of Deng Xiaoping, as the chairman of the Communist Party (1978–92), who was the reform Communist to lead China on a path to a version of the market economy, stating that it was "to learn knowledge and truth from the West in order to save China" (Stewart, 2001, p. 23). In this way, since the 1980s, the economic reforms in China have accelerated towards a Western capitalist model, while his main rhetoric had a Communist-style flavor. The leader – Deng – advanced China in regards to what became known as the 'four modernizations' of China: economy, agriculture, scientific and technological development. Merged with national defense, these ideas came to be known as 'socialism with Chinese characteristics'. As Deng Xiaoping argued, "Planning and market forces are not the essential difference between socialism and capitalism. A planned economy is not the definition of socialism, because there is planning under capitalism; the market economy happens under socialism, too" (Hou, 2013, p. 1).

At a similar time, in the 1980s, in the United Kingdom, the longest serving prime minister, Margaret Thatcher, was strongly influenced by the economic philosophy of Hayek and Friedman. Her administration had a persuasive agenda of lowering direct and increasing indirect taxation, systematic attacks on labor unions, and favoured the privatisation of state assets. This statement from Margaret Thatcher (1987) represents the fundamental performance of this ideology:

> I think we have gone through a period when too many children and people have been given to understand "I have a problem, it is the Government's job to cope with it!" or "I have a problem, I will go and get a grant to cope with it!" "I am homeless, the Government must house me!" and so they are casting their problems on society and who is society? There is no such thing! There are individual men and women and there are families and no government can do anything except through people and people look to themselves first. It is our duty to look after ourselves and then also to help look after our neighbor and life is a reciprocal business and people have got the entitlements too much in mind without the obligations.

As Harvey (2005) argues, it is necessary to perceive neoliberalism not only through the policies and administrations of Reagan and Thatcher, but through developments in China, Chile and elsewhere around the world, as neoliberalism was conceived as a worldwide doctrine, albeit performed in different countries in different times and in very diverse ways. These developments since the 1970s and 1980s are the fundamental conditions which have shaped human subjects' lived experiences and foregrounded contemporary policy landscapes to create fertile soil for particular global economic, political, and social history, where financial politics determine the course of all state sectors including education. "From these several epicentres, revolutionary impulses seemingly spread and reverberated to remake the world around us in a totally different image . . . [These leaders] plucked from the shadows of relative obscurity a particular doctrine that went under the name of 'neoliberalism' and transformed it into [a] central guiding principle" (p. 3), argues Harvey. Harvey thus constructs a framework, not only for analyzing the political and economic dangers of the contemporary landscape, but also for assessing the prospects for the turn to more socially just alternatives, as they are being advocated by many resistance and oppositional movements.

Neoliberalism is thus the doctrine, an ideology, which argues that free market – and the market exchange – is an ethic in itself, constantly capable of re-inventing itself and acting as a guide for all human subjects' actions. These ideas have become dominant in thought and practice since the rise of neoliberalism. The way this doctrine has been elevated and spread was in line with, and at the same time depended upon, a reconstitution of policies and state powers that included the privatization of state assets, and the way financial markets processes were emphasized in policy making. In this doctrine, state interventions into the economy are limited, and the obligations of the state to provide for the welfare of its citizens are mini-mized, if not diminished (Hood, 1991).

Neoliberal Account of Personal Responsibility

Neoliberal ideology has been focused on the rising and apparently irreversible tide of welfare expectations, arguing that the notion of the welfare state evaded both investment and work incentives. From the neoliberal viewpoint, the welfare state has directly contributed to the economic recession that Western countries have been encountering since the 1970s. According to neoliberal ideology, the combined effects of social policies, which included guaranteed minimum wages, superannuation, and the exponential growth of the health and education sec-tors, have also strengthened organised labour *vis-a-vis* capital, augmented wages as against capital goods, and increased state borrowings from itself, leading to a decline of profitability and capital shortage (Peters & Marshall, 1996). Accord-ing to the neoliberal ideology, the effects of this welfare state led to greater state interventionism in both social and economic terms: however, the more this wel-fare state helps, the more it will support the regression of capital and diminish the effectiveness that the free market thrives on (Hood, 1992). The neoliberal critique of increasing levels of intervention that led to the so-called crisis and imbalance between state receipts and expenditure, thus leading to the neolib-eral ideology long-term removing liberalism of its vitality: "it sounds the death knell of the market economy, of competition – in a word, of private enterprise" (Delcourt, 1985, p. 36). To the neoliberal ideology, the effects of economic and social intervention represent a fundamental threat to human subjects' political, economic and democratic freedom. The neoliberal policy to redeem this situation is the revival of faith in the philosophy of economic liberalism, and thus a return of the privatization of public assets aimed at capital accumulation, and the eleva-tion of the principles of a free market economy.

Through this powerful critique, neoliberal ideology has emerged as the domi-nant paradigm of public policy in the globalized world. Human subjects have been re-configured as individual consumers of very competitive public services that have been significantly re-structured, downsized and rationalized. Their management has been delegated or devolved while executive power has been further concentrated at the top levels of institutions. In social welfare, this has, for example, represented a shift from universality to a 'modest safety net' (Peters & Tesar, 2016c). The values of the welfare state of participation and belonging have been weakened, and human subjects are being charged for social services that have been introduced across the board. Similarly, substantial cuts in benefits and other forms of income support have accompanied this shift, as eligibility cri-teria have been re-thought and new measurements and targets introduced. Social assistance has become the new social philosophy, and there is a greater policing of the welfare state, aimed at reducing benefit fraud. Neoliberal ideology argues for the release of human subjects from the dependency of state welfare, since, in their argumentation, the policies of the welfare state discourage effort and self-reliance. It also argues that strong government and state monopolies in the delivery of social welfare services has encouraged the growth of 'dysfunctional families', and the problem with the educational and health sectors is that they are monopoly public services run by the state. Neoliberalism targets them, arguing that these services need the discipline of free market forces, as rightful benefits, which has led to a loss of personal responsibility (Power, 1997).

Perpetual Neoliberal Restructurings

In the past decades, the restructuring of state education systems, and in particular of higher education, has, in many Western countries, involved a very significant shift away from an emphasis on administration and policy, to an emphasis on management, which is referred to as 'new managerialism'. In its theory, it has relied theoretically, on the one hand, on the model of corporate managerialism and private sector management styles and, on the other, on public choice theory and new institutional economics, such as agency theory and transaction cost analysis. These theoretical underpinnings cannot, however, be seen without the rise of neoliberalism as a predominant ideology of globalisation (Kascak & Pupala, 2014).

The theories and models of the new public management and new institutional economics have been used both as the legitimating basis and instrumental means for redesigning state educational bureaucracies, educational institutions, and even public policy processes. This has had a tremendous impact on the education sector. Most importantly, there has been a decentralization of management control away from the individual institution – sometimes referred to as the doctrine of self-management – which was coupled with forms of a new accountability and introducing new funding structures (Peters, 2005). This shift has in many cases been accompanied by a disaggregation of large state bureaucracies into autonomous agencies, leading to the clarification of organizational objectives, and a clear separation between functions of implementation and policy advice (Peters, 2005). This form of 'new managerialism' has also involved a shift from input controls to quantifiable outputs that should be measurable and comparable, and to the introduction of performance targets to raise the desired productivity agenda. Alongside these measures, these changes include short-term performance contracts for chief executive officers and senior managers, and their key performance indicators. To achieve this productivity agenda and productivity efficiency, the provision of educational services has been made contestable, and state education has been marketized and privatized to increase so-called allocative efficiency.

The central notions that neoliberalism occupies are the spaces of the self-interested individual as a self-interested economic subject, where a human subject optimizes and activates his interests and needs (Olssen & Peters, 2005). This occurs within a range and prevalence of free market economics, where resources and opportunities are activated through the market, and where the market becomes an extremely efficient mechanism of governance and the existence of human subjects. However, because the free market is a self-regulating mechanism and ideology, the government needs to practise laissez-faire order as it believes that it can regulate itself better than the government or any other outside force. There is thus a fundamental and distinct distrust of governmental power and a strong argument for limiting state power to reduce its role to the protection of individual rights.

Neoliberalism performs what can be perceived as accountability regimes. There are different contemporary forms that this accountability takes, and they may operate as hybrids. A state-mandated agency regulates activity or performance according to standards or criteria laid down at state or national level and is often associated with the devolution of management (though not necessarily governance) and the development of parallel privatization and the quasi market in the delivery of public services. Professional accountability tends to operate through ideas around collegiality, peer review and the control of entry and codes of practice that are struck by professional associations, including education. Consumer accountability is the accountability through the market, where consumer organizations have been strengthened in relation to the development of public services delivered through markets (Kuttner, 2015). Furthermore, democratic accountability is premised on the demand for both internal and external accountability, such as requests for the accountability of a politician to parliament or governing organization and accountability to his or her electorate.

Professional accountability may be perceived to be a form of democratic accountability. Both proceed from Kantian assumptions about autonomy, self-regulation, duty and responsibility for one's actions whether this is considered in institutional (such as parliament or university) or individual terms. There has been a tendency in Western liberal states to emphasize both agency and consumer forms at the expense of professional and democratic forms of accountability, particularly where nation-states engage in large-scale shifts from traditional Keynesian welfare state regimes to more market-oriented and consumer-driven systems. The criticism that has emerged is that the agency/consumer couplet instrumentalizes, individualizes, standardizes, marketizes and externalizes accountability relationships at the expense of democratic values such as participation, self-regulation, collegiality, and collective deliberation that are said to enhance and thicken the relationships involved. There is also a hybrid version of accountability that runs across these couplets rather than consolidating policies. The new hybrid form is a citizen–consumer hybrid accountability regime which acts as a dialectic in that it can be constructed either way with different emphases (Peters, 2006).

In classical liberalism, the human subject is characterized as having an autonomous human–individual nature that practices its freedom. In neoliberalism the state seeks to create an individual – in other words, to produce a human subject – that is both an enterprising and competitive entrepreneur. As Graham Burchell (1996) argues, while for classical liberalism the basis of government conduct is in terms of private-interest-motivated conduct of free market exchanging individuals, for neoliberalism "the rational principle for regulating and limiting governmental activity must be determined by reference to artificially arranged or contrived forms of free, entrepreneurial and competitive conduct of economic-rational individuals" (pp. 23–24). The end goals of freedom, choice, consumer sovereignty, competition and individual initiative, as well as of compliance and obedience, are constructions of the state and government that act through the development of auditing, accounting and management techniques. These techniques, as Barry, Osbourne, and Rose (1996) put it, "enable the marketplace for services to be established as 'autonomous' from central control. Neoliberalism, in these terms, involves less a retreat from governmental 'intervention' than a re-inscription of the techniques and forms of expertise required for the exercise of government" (p. 14). The new managerialism then functions as an emergent and increasingly rationalized and complex neoliberal technology of governance that operates at a number of levels: the individual ('self-managing' technologies), the classroom ('classroom management techniques'), the academic program (with explicit promotion of the goals of self-management), and the educational institution (self-managing institutions) (see Olssen & Peters, 2005 and Peters, Fitzsimons & Marshall, 2000, for further details.).

The new public management took the form of performance management including the use of incentives to enhance performance at both the institutional and the individual level. These are also present in the education sector, including short-term employment contracts, performance-based remuneration systems, promotion systems and other systems that govern human subjects. So-called 'contractualism' introduced the extensive use of contracts to specify the nature of performance required and the respective obligations of agents and principals (including performance and purchase agreements). There was an increase in strategic planning and emulation of private sector management styles throughout the public sector. In addition, multiple accountability relationships within the public sector, and the avoidance of joint central and local democratic control of public services became prevalent. Competitive tendering and contracting out became strongly encouraged, but were accompanied by only a few mandatory requirements for market testing or competitive tendering (Boston et al., 1996; Boston, 1996).

Neoliberal Governmentality

Neoliberal ideology is permeated by neoliberal governmentality, where the hierarchy of management chains substitute delegated power to become hierarchical forms of authoritatively structured human working relations. These relations then erode, and thus prohibit, an autonomous space from emerging and a particular form of governance takes place. This is a structural turn that governs the professional. It has changed the fields of academia and teaching, and transformed the role of teachers and academics. Neoliberalism cuts across the spaces of classical liberalism, as the institutionalization of principal–agent chains of line management inserts a hierarchical mode of authority by which the free market and state pressures are instituted. For professionals and for academic staff this carries with it the effect of de-professionalization that can be understood as a shift from collegial or democratic governance in flat structures, to hierarchical models based on dictated management specifications of job performance in principal–agent chains of command (Hood, 1990).

Traditional conceptions of professionalism involved an ascription of rights and powers over work, in line with classical liberal notions of intersections of freedom and of the individual. Free market pressures increasingly redesign these traditional understandings of rights, as institutions and human subjects need to adapt to market trends. Under neoliberal governance, a strong implementation of restructuring initiatives in response to the free market and state demands the maximization of profits and involves, in teaching and academic professions, increasing workloads and governance of course content specifications by management (Aucoin, 1990). Such hierarchically imposed specifications erode and destabilize traditional conceptions and establishments of professional autonomy over work in relation to academic labour in teaching, research and service. In such a sense, neoliberal governance systematically deconstructs the space in terms of which professional autonomy is exercised.

Contractualism involves a specification, which is fundamentally at odds with the notion of professionalism. Professionalism conveys the idea of a human subject directed power based on the liberal conceptions of autonomy, rights and freedom. The human subject under such an ideology harnesses a power, and utilizes a human subject's ability to make professional and ethical decisions in the workplace (Tesar, 2016). The professional human subject has the terms of their practice and conduct shaped by their peer groups and determined by structural levers that are outside of their control. As a particular production of power, professionalism is systematically in tension with neoliberalism, as in neoliberal ideology the professional human subject is seen as a self-interested group (Peters & Besley, 2006).

Quality, Performance and Performativity

The neoliberal ideology has also created the proliferation of quality initiatives and quality units, and the ever-more-frequent use of the term 'quality' in institutional discourse is evidence that state control over universities is substantially achieved by some version of quality assurance auditing. As with accountability, the effectiveness of this form of managerial discourse depends upon the rhetorical device of switching between general and technical meanings of the word. Quality assurance is used for the purpose of auditing as a technical managerial term and is focused on systems and processes, rather than outcomes (Charlton, 2001). Quality assurance is built on the assumption that institutions or organizations should have auditing systems and processes in place. Quality assurance auditing has become closely identified with other, traditional managerial approaches that have included the word 'quality' – such as Total Quality Management (TQM), and the awarding of quality assurance systems of organizations with particular sets of standards (Feigenbaum, 1983; Perigord, 1990). Quality assurance auditing therefore is linked to quality enhancement strategies, which are based upon creating a particular culture, centred on 'quality' understandings and measurements that usually recognize the production of reliable processes and systems that consist of checking and feedback.

Criteria to measure the notion of 'excellence' or 'quality' of teaching, education and particularly tertiary teaching are not agreed upon, and the notion of the 'quality' of teaching has been re-defined by the Quality Assurance Agency for Higher Education in terms of documented compliance with an approved quality assurance system. The attribute that has become key in this exercise is that the approved system of teaching is auditable, so it can be comprehensively and self-consistently documented. Therefore, 'high quality' teaching becomes an explicit set of systems that is characterized by different mission statements, aims and objectives, flow-charts, ghent charts, monitoring, feedback and formal procedures for all imaginable contingencies. So quality becomes only what is documented, in neoliberal language auditable, is it is deemed to count as legitimate teaching activity and performance (Charlton, 2002).

Jon McKenzie (2001) argues that "performance will be to the 20th and 21st centuries what discipline was to the 18th and 19th centuries, namely, an onto-historical formation of power and knowledge" (p. 176). In this sense, the genealogies of 'performance' reveal multiple and disparate sources in performance studies. However, it is Lyotard's (1984) use of 'performativity' and particularly 'the logic of performativity' that is pertinent to the field of educational studies. The logic of performativity that was developed in his work *The Postmodern Condition*, theorized a philosophical interpretation of the knowledge and its changing state, including science and education in the Western world. Lyotard synthesized research on contemporary science within the broader context of the sociology of postindustrial society and studies of postmodern culture. Furthermore, he brought together diverse threads and notions that were previously separate in literatures and an analysis that clearly signaled an epochal break not only with modernity, but also with what were seen as traditionally 'modern' ways of viewing and being in the world. Lyotard's (1984) major thesis was that "the status of knowledge is altered as societies enter what is known as the postindustrial age and cultures enter what is known as the postmodern age" (p. 3). He uses the term 'postmodern condition' to describe the state of knowledge and the problem of its legitimation in the most highly developed societies. Lyotard (1984) argues that science and technology are falling under the sway of "another language game, in which the goal is no longer truth, but performativity – that is, the best possible input/output equation" (p. 37).

The move from a discipline to a performance marks the notions of 'effectiveness' and 'efficiency' as they are growing in power, as new conventions defining the basis for measuring what is right, true, and good. McKenzie (2001) positioned the argument as follows, and in this sense, the notion of 'performance' has emerged as a crucial term in at least three different areas of social life (economics, technology and art):

> For better or for worse, I have come to think that we are entering an age of global performance. We can understand performance as a stratum of power/ knowledge by extrapolating from Foucault's well-known genealogy of discipline. While disciplinary mechanisms produce unified subjects through a series of institutions (school, factory, prison, hospital), each with its own discrete archive of statements and practices, performative power blurs the borders of social institutions by connecting and sharing digital archives. Financial information, criminal records, medical files, and school transcripts once stored in separate metal file cabinets are now being uploaded to silicon databases and electronically networked.
>
> (p. 6)

Performance as a Transgressive Cultural Praxis

Performance is not only perceived as a transgressive cultural praxis and phenomenon and as a formation and production of power and knowledge, but also as the one that challenges us on how to perform. Performance moves beyond, and thus displaces and also extends, the disciplinary power used and analysed by Michel Foucault (1991) in his work *Discipline and Punish*. The actual politics of performance are far more post-colonial than just traditionally colonial, the infrastructures are far more digital than electronic and industrial, and economies are dominated by the provision of services rather than manufacturing. Factory labour and tradeoff commodities have not become obsolete, but instead they have been digitally coded into new modes and forms of mostly immaterial production, that are fully recognized and found in communications, finance, healthcare, social work and increasingly in education. This digital labour has produced a new version of software.

Performance management does not provide a version of itself as scientific but rather, adopting the paradigm of cultural performance, it re-describes itself as an *ars poetica* of organizational practice, which is evident in texts like *Corporate Renaissance: The Art of Reengineering* (Cross et al., 1994), *Jamming: The Art and Discipline of Business Creativity* (Kao, 1998) and *Cultural Diversity in Organizations* (Cox, 1993). This new, what may be called 'soft power' of management theory and practice, recognises performance as having acquired a normative force.

In education, it is higher education that is a crucial sub-sector where these types of performative power intersect and play out, especially when framed by the policy template of the knowledge economy. This is the very idea behind the new form of economy which is no longer based on raw materials but is rather focused on the transformation of ideas and symbolic resources of intellectual, human and social capital. It is this environment where increasingly the economic, technical and cultural spheres are brought into a close assemblage, as performative power combines the rational calculation of (something perhaps of a 'high performance') technical systems and databases with the domain of affective management based around personal experience and social interaction (Perigord, 1990).

Performance management is an ideal system for knowledge management especially where one of the main aims for the knowledge manager is to extract knowledge from human subjects and to embed it within the intellectual systems or processes as soon as possible, both protecting it as intellectual property and putting it into service to make a profit (Peters, 2002). This performance management is concerned with the appropriation of the knowledge surplus, and in combination with simple counts, computer and/or accounting methodologies (including the weighting and the arithmeticization of soft variables like 'reputation') to produce departmental, faculty, and institutional performance 'profiles', and institutional, national and international league tables.

New public management is a systematic programme of corporatization, privatization and commercialization, it has a greater reliance on competitive tendering and contracting out and the devolution of human resource management to the chief executives of individual departments and agencies. It is a move from cash-based to accrual accounting, into an improved system of budgetary control, a greater reliance on financial incentives, and major changes in institutional design that include the placement of many service delivery functions in separate, and non-departmental agencies. It also means the fragmentation and proliferation of agencies, and their subsequent reduced trust and cooperation between them, which may, as it happened in some countries such as New Zealand, result in punitive economic and social policy, and consequent social and ethical inequality (Peters, 2003).

Evidence-Based Practice

Evidence-based practice is an interdisciplinary approach to mainly clinical practice that originated in medicine, utilizing randomized controlled trials that emerged from the field of clinical epidemiology in the late 1980s, but that have been utilized recently in psychology and education under the neoliberal ideology. The premise of evidence-based practice is that all practical decisions should originate from scientific studies and that studies are interpreted based upon standards and norms. Introducing 'current best evidence' and 'five levels of quality evidence', including statistical validity and risk prediction, meta-analysis, systematic review, clinical relevance, currency and peer-review, it was developed as a framework for public health policy in the 1990s with the establishment of the Cochrane Collaboration in 1993 and the Centre for Evidence Based Medicine. The same evidential model has since been generalized and applied to other areas of public policy, including education (Bridges, Smeyers, & Smith, 2009).

The history of evidence-based policy has evolved from evidence-based medicine, in which research findings are used to support clinical decisions, and evidence is gathered by randomized controlled trials (RCTs). In 1993, the Cochrane Collaboration was established in the UK. It works to keep all RCTs up to date and provides Cochrane reviews of health policy. Research and policy advocacy pushed for more evidence-based policy-making, leading to the formation of the Campbell Collaboration in 1999, which conducts reviews on best evidence, analyzing the effects of social and educational policies and practices. *Campbell Systematic Reviews* is a peer-reviewed online monograph series of systematic reviews, prepared under the editorial control of the Campbell Collaboration. Campbell systematic reviews follow structured guidelines and standards for summarizing the international research evidence on the effects of interventions in crime and justice, education, international development, and social welfare. More recently, it has been developed in a UK Cabinet policy paper (Haynes et al., 2012) *Test, Learn, Adapt: Developing Public Policy with Randomised Controlled Trials* published in collaboration with Ben Goldacre and David Torgerson, arguing that RCTs should be used much more extensively in public policy. In March 2013, Teach First in the UK launched 'a new vision for evidence-based practice in education and teaching', attended by Secretary of State for Education Michael Gove and introducing Ben Goldacre, author of *Bad Science* (2008), who presented 'Building Research into Education'.

The purpose of a systematic review is to sum up the best available research on a specific question. This is done by synthesizing the results of several studies. A systematic review uses transparent procedures to find, evaluate and synthesize the results of relevant research. Procedures are explicitly defined in advance in order to ensure that the exercise is transparent and can be replicated. This practice is also designed to minimize bias. Studies included in a review are screened for quality, so that the findings of a large number of studies can be combined. Peer review is a key part of the process; qualified independent researchers control the author's methods and results. A systematic review must have: clear inclusion/exclusion criteria, an explicit search strategy, systematic coding and analysis of included studies and meta-analysis (where possible). Campbell reviews must include a systematic search for unpublished reports (to avoid publication bias). Campbell reviews are usually international in scope, a protocol (project plan) for the review is developed in advance and undergoes peer review, study inclusion and coding decisions are accomplished by at least two reviewers who work independently and compare results.

Davies (2003) develops a critique of new managerialism and of its implications for the professional work of scholars and teachers, and then critiques 'evidence-based practice' as it is being developed for schools. Davies argues that it is only possible to make sense of the policies and practices of the evidence-based practice movement within the framework of new managerialism, and also explores some of the tensions and contradictions between managerialism and gender reform in educational contexts. Davies ends with a challenge to begin the work of generating the collective story through which we can dismantle the hegemony of new managerialism and engage in the transformative work that will afford us a different future. On the other hand, Clegg (2005) argues that a critical realist perspective can contribute to a critique of evidence-based practice, while at the same time not abandoning the idea of evidence altogether. Her paper is structured around a number of related themes: the socio-politics of 'evidence-based'; epistemological roots and a critical realist critique; the debate in action, based on the recent systematic review of personal development planning; and theory-to-practice gaps. The advocacy of evidence-based practice is currently being used to undermine professional autonomy and to valorise the 'gold-standard' of randomised controlled trials. However, her work proposes that evidence can properly be claimed for critique and emancipatory projects, and that its current discursive location at the core of New Labour thinking is not the only kind of thinking available.

Biesta (2007) provides a critical analysis of the idea of evidence-based practice and the ways in which it has been promoted and implemented in the field of education, focusing on the tension between scientific and democratic control over educational practice and research. He examines three key assumptions of evidence-based education: first, the extent to which educational practice can be compared to the practice of medicine, as the field in which evidence-based practice was first developed; second, the role of knowledge in professional actions, with special attention to what kind of epistemology is appropriate for professional practices that wish to be informed by research; and third, expectations of the practical role of research implicit in the idea of evidence-based education. Evidence-based practice provides a framework for understanding the role of research in educational practice that not only restricts the scope of decision making to questions about effectivity and effectiveness, but that also restricts the opportunities for participation in educational decision making. He argues that we must expand our views about the interrelations among research, policy, and practice, to keep in view education as a thoroughly moral and political practice that requires continuous democratic contestation and deliberation under the neoliberal umbrella.

Concluding Comments

Neoliberalism represents a struggle between two forms of welfare or social policy discourses based on the opposing and highly charged ideological metaphors of 'individualism' and 'community'. The one form posits the sovereign individual or family with an emphasis on its primacy over community and State; the other, what might be called a rejuvenated social democratic model, inverts the hierarchy of value to emphasize community or 'the social' over the individual. As such, it is an intellectual struggle that runs through the contemporary ideological landscape and allows the rise of a range of subjects, with roots going back at least to the Enlightenment in different native traditions. Neoliberalism is a class-based project that benefits the rich and leads to ever-increasing inequalities both within, and between states.

As Foucault (2008) argued, "the problem of neo-liberalism is rather how the overall exercise of political power can be modeled on the principles of a market economy . . . to discover how far and to what extent the formal principles of a market economy can index a general art of government' (p. 131). What we do know about neoliberalism is that many of its practices, most notably the ideology of 'market fundamentalism', have failed. They have failed as a political doctrine of neoliberal market fundamentalism that served multiple interests and was not really supported by economic theory or any kind of historical experience. The market and debt crises of recent years have testified to this notion: the imposition of market fundamentalism runs in complete opposition to neoliberalism's own libertarian premises and emphasis on negative freedom. Neoliberalism is thus not easy to define, but it is very subtle, complex and dynamic, changing its disciplinary and historic forms and shapes. What is certain is that over the past decades it has significantly matured as a political doctrine, international activist movement and set of policy practices.

References

Aucoin, P. (1990). Administrative Reform in Public Management: Paradigms, Principles, Paradoxes and Pendulums, *Governance: An International Journal of Policy and Administration* 3(2), 115–37.

Barry, A., Osborne, T., & Rose, N. (1996). *Foucault and Political Reason: Liberalism, Neo-Liberalism and Rationalities of Government.* Chicago, IL: University of Chicago Press.

Besley, T. A. C. & Peters, M. A. (2007). *Subjectivity & Truth: Foucault, Education, and the Culture of Self.* New York, NY: Peter Lang Publishing.

Biesta, G. (2007). Why 'What Works' Won't Work: Evidence-Based Practice And The Democratic Deficit In Educational Research, *Educational Theory*, 57(*1*), 1–21.

Boston, J., Martin, J. Pallot, J. & Walsh, P. (1996) *Public Management: The New Zealand Model.* Melbourne, Australia: Oxford University Press.

Boston, J. (1996). Origins and Destinations: New Zealand's Model of Public Management and the International Transfer of Ideas. In P. Weller and G. Davis (Eds.), *New Ideas, Better Government*, pp. 107–31. Sydney, NSW: Allen & Unwin.

Bridges, D., Smeyers, P., & Smith, R. D. (Eds.). (2009). *'Evidence Based Policy': What Evidence? What Basis? Whose Policy?* Oxford, UK: Blackwell.

Burchell, G. (1996). Liberal Government and Techniques of the Self. In A. Barry, T. Osborne & N. Rose (Eds.), *Foucault and Political Reason: Liberalism, Neo-Liberalism and Rationalities of Government*, pp. 19–36. Chicago, IL: University of Chicago Press.

Charlton, B. G. (2001). Clinical Governance: A Quality Assurance Audit System for Regulating Clinical Practice. In Andrew Miles *et al.* (Eds), *Clinical Governance: Encouraging Excellence or Imposing Control?* London, UK: Aesculaepius Medical Press.

Charlton, B. G. (2002) Audit, Accountability, Quality and All That: The Growth of Managerial Technologies in UK Universities. In Stephen Prickett and Patricia Erskine-Hill (Eds.), *Education! Education! Education! – Managerial Ethics and the Law of Unintended Consequences.* London, UK: Imprint Academic.

Clegg, S. (2005). Evidence-Based Practice in Educational Research: A Critical Realist Critique of Systematic Review, *British Journal of Sociology of Education*, 26(3), 415–428.

Cox, T. (1993). *Cultural Diversity in Organizations: Theory, Research and Practice.* San Francisco, CA: BerrettKoehler.

Cross, K. F., Feather, J. J. & Lynch, R. L. (1994). *Corporate Renaissance: The Art Of Reengineering.* Cambridge, MA: Blackwell Publishers.

Davies, B. (2003). Death to Critique and Dissent? The Policies and Practices of New Managerialism and of 'Evidence-Based Practice', *Gender and Education*, 15(1), 91–103.

Delcourt, J. (1985). Social Policy – Crisis or Mutation. In R. Girod, A. Gladstone, & P. de Laubier (Eds.), *Social Policy in Western Europe and the USA, 1950–80*, pp. 27–55. London, UK: Palgrave Macmillan.

Feigenbaum, A. V. (1983). *Total Quality Control,* 3rd edition. New York: McGraw Hill.

Foucault, M. (1991). *Discipline and Punish: The Birth of the Prison.* London, UK: Penguin Books.

Foucault, M. (2008). *The Birth of Biopolitics.* New York, NY: Palgrave Macmillan.

Goldacre, B. (2008). *Bad Science.* London, UK: Fourth Estate.

Harvey, D. (2005). *A Brief History of Neoliberalism.* Oxford, UK: Oxford University Press.

Haynes, L., Service, O., Goldacre, B., & Torgerson, D. (2012). *Test, Learn, Adapt: Developing Public Policy with Randomised Controlled Trials.* UK Cabinet Policy Paper. Retrieved from https://www.gov.uk/government/publications/test-learn-adapt-developing-public-policy-with-randomised-controlled-trials

Hood, C. (1990). De- Sir Humphreyfying the Westminster Model of Bureaucracy: A New Style of Governance?, *Governance: An International Journal of Policy and Administration* 3(2), 205–14.

Hood, C. (1991). A Public Management For All Seasons?, *Public Administration* 69, Spring: 3–19.

Hood, C. (1992). The New Public Management Model and its Conceptions of Performance Engineering. In *The Public Sector Challenge: Defining, Delivering and Reporting Performance*, pp. 35–50. Wellington, NZ: New Zealand Society of Accountants Public Sector Convention.

Hou, X. (2013). *Community Capitalism in China: The State, the Market, and Collectivism.* Cambridge, UK: Cambridge University Press.

Kao, J. (1997). *Jamming: The Art and Discipline of Business Creativity.* London, UK: HarperCollins.

Kascak, O., & Pupala, B. (2014). Towards Perpetual Neoliberalism in Education, *Human Affairs*, 24(4), 545–563. DOI: 10.2478/s13374-014-0248-3

Kuttner, R. (2015) *Debtors' Prison: The Politics of Austerity Versus Possibility: the Politics of Austerity versus Possibility.* New York, NY: Vintage.

Lyotard, J-F. (1984). *The Postmodern Condition: A Report on Knowledge.* Minneapolis: University of Minnesota Press.

McKenzie, J. (2001). *Perform or Else: From Discipline to Performance.* London, UK: Routledge.

Olssen, M. & Peters, M. A. (2005). Neoliberalism, Higher Education and the Knowledge Economy: From the Free Market to Knowledge Capitalism, *Journal of Education Policy*, 20(3), 313–345.

Perigord, M. (1990). *Achieving Total Quality Management.* Cambridge, MA: Productivity Press.

Peters, M. A. (2002). The University in the Knowledge Economy. In Simon Cooper, John Hinkson & Geoff Sharp (Eds.), *Scholars and Entrepreneurs: The Universities in Crisis*, pp. 137–152. Melbourne, Australia: Arena Publications.

Peters, M. A. (2003). 'The New Zealand Experiment: From Democratic Participation to Self-Management, and From Universal Welfare Entitlement to Private Investment'. In: Ka-ho Mok & Anthony R. Welch (Eds.) *Globalization and Educational Re-structuring in the Asia Pacific Region*, pp. 302–332. London, UK: Palgrave.

Peters, M. A. (2005). 'The Post-Historical University? Prospects for Alternative Globalisations'. In Heinz Sünker, Peter McLaren, Colin Lankshear (Eds.) *Critical Theory, Education and Social Futures: Cross Cultural Perspectives on the Foreseeable*. New York, NY: Peter Lang.

Peters, M. A. (2006). *'Performative', 'Performativity' and the Culture of Performance: Knowledge Management in the New Economy (Part 2)*, 18(2), 20–24, DOI: 10.1177/089202060401800205

Peters, M. & Marshall, J. (Eds.) (1996). *Individualism And Community: Education And Social Policy In The Postmodern Condition*. London, UK: The Falmers Press.

Peters, M. A. & Besley, T. A. C. (2006). *Building Knowledge Cultures: Education in the Age of Knowledge Capitalism*. New York, NY: Rowman & Littlefield.

Peters, M. A., Fitzsimons, P., & Marshall, J.D. (2000). Managerialism and Education Policy in a Global Context: Neoliberalism, Foucault and the Doctrine of Self-Management. In N. Burbules and C. Torres (Eds.), *Globalization and Education: Critical Perspectives*, pp. 109–132. New York and London: Routledge.

Peters, M. A., Paraskeva, J. & Besley, T. (2015). *The Global Financial Crisis and the Restructuring of Education*. New York, NY: Peter Lang.

Peters, M. A. & Tesar, M. (2016a). The Critical Ontology of Ourselves: Lessons from the Philosophy of the Subject. In M. A. Peters & M. Tesar, (Eds.), *Beyond the Philosophy of the Subject: An EPAT Post-Structuralist Reader*, pp. vii-xvii. New York, NY: Routledge.

Peters, M. A. & Tesar, M. (2016b). The Birth of Educational Research, Teacher Education and the Turn to Practice: From Practitioner Knowledge and Communities of Practice to Evidence-Based Policy and Practice. *In Search of Subjectivities: An EPAT Teacher Education Reader*, pp. 1–14 . New York, NY: Routledge.

Peters, M. A. & Tesar, M. (2016c). Bad Research, Bad Education: The Contested Evidence for Evidence-Based Research, Policy and Practice in Education. In J. Lynch, J. Rowlands, T. Gale & A. Skourdoumbis (Eds.), *Practice Theory: Diffractive readings in professional practice and education*, pp. 231–246. London, UK: Routledge.

Power, M. (1997). *The Audit Society; Rituals of Verification*. Oxford, UK: Oxford University Press.

Stewart, W. (2001). *Deng Xioaping. Leader in a Changing China*. Minnesota, MN: Lerner Publications Company.

Tesar, M. (2016). Policy and Philosophy in the Contemporary Educational Landscape. *Policy Futures in Education*, 14(3), 311–313. doi: 10.1177/1478210316640621

Thatcher, M. (1987). Interview for *Woman's Own* ("No Such Thing As Society"). Retrieved from http://www.margaretthatcher.org/document/106689

Chapter 2

Neo-Liberal Education Policy and the Ideology of Choice

John A. Codd

Reprinted by permission of Taylor & Francis Ltd, http://www.tandfonline.com, on behalf of © Philosophy of Education Society of Australasia.

Editors' Introduction

Codd's chapter argues that the ideology of choice became a major challenge to educational administrators and managers committed to equality of access and opportunity. In recent decades the issue of what is perceived as public choice in education has fast become one of the burning policy issues of the contemporary landscape. Following the recent educational reforms in several countries, this has been promoted on the basis that it will reduce centralized bureaucratic structures for the governance and provision of education and give human subjects more individual choice. As Codd argues, it cannot simply be assumed that the appeal of neo-liberal policies can be countered by 'consciousness raising' or by abstract appeals to social justice. The dominant ideology and its performance cannot adequately explain why some people decide to support educational policies that can be shown structurally to reduce their degrees of freedom and to increase their relative disadvantage. In Codd's chapter, such people are to be understood as rational actors situated in relation to the institutional structures of a modern capitalist welfare state. Thus, educational policies that promote choice at the cost of equity and social justice cannot be reversed until the political opportunities for such a change exist within the macro-social context. As he concludes, only by experiencing and monitoring the real social effects of these policies will people gradually work collectively to change them through the same democratic processes that have put them in place. In spite of opposition from many educators who are concerned about questions of equity and social justice, the proposal that schools should compete for students in an educational marketplace and that individuals should have greater freedom to choose the kind of education they will receive, is given serious consideration.

Introduction

The issue of "public choice" in education is fast becoming one of the burning policy issues of the 1990s. Recent educational reforms in a number of countries have been promoted on the basis that they will reduce centralised bureaucratic structures for the governance and provision of education and give people more individual choice. In spite of opposition from many educators who are concerned about questions of equity and social justice, the proposal that schools should compete for students in an educational marketplace and that individuals should have greater freedom to choose the kind of education they will receive, is being taken very seriously indeed. It is worth noting, for instance, that one of the most widely discussed books on education in the US popular press in recent years is a book that claims research support for the creation of educational markets (Chubb & Moe 1990). It is also no coincidence that the whole of a recent issue of the *International Journal of Educational Research* (Goldring 1991) is devoted to "parental involvement and public choice in education".

Consistent with these international trends, "choice" has also been a central plank in the educational reforms that have taken place in New Zealand since 1987 (Codd 1993). In the Picot Report, where these reforms were initially proposed, "choice" is declared to be one of the core values on which the new system is to be based. The report begins by describing "the present administrative structure" as one which is "over-centralised" and has "too many decision points" such that "almost everyone feels powerless to change things they see need changing" (Taskforce 1988, xi). Thus, the Report states that:

> Choice will involve providing a wider range of options both for consumers and for learning institutions . . . Only if people are free to choose, can a true cooperative partnership develop between the community and learning institutions.
>
> (Taskforce to Review Education Administration 1988, 4)

At the time, such statements could be read as expressing widely-held public perceptions and aspirations. They could also be read as expressions of "New Right" ideology. Those inclined to the latter interpretation (Codd 1990; Codd, Gordon & Harker 1990) were able to compare the text of the report to key passages that had appeared several months earlier in the New Zealand Treasury's *Brief to the Incoming Government*. The following passage is representative of the Treasury position:

> . . . government intervention is liable to reduce freedom of choice and thereby curtail the sphere of responsibility of its citizens and weaken the self-steering ability inherent in society to reach optimal solutions through the mass of individual actions pursuing free choice without any formal consensus.
>
> (Treasury 1987, 41)

This statement is a clear expression of the neo-liberal ideology that reforms public choice theory. It entails a deeply individualistic approach to social policy. All state intervention, in this view, is essentially bad, and all social goods are reduced to private goods that can be achieved only by individuals exercising rational choice within a free market (King 1987). "Society", or the "public", has no definable features and therefore no existence beyond the cumulative actions of individuals. Freedom to choose is no more than the absence of coercion or constraint by others.

However dubious this theory might be scientifically and philosophically, it is clear that many of the policies promoted under its banner have had a considerable democratic mandate. This poses a major challenge for social theorists and those who would seek to explain the current trends in social policy. Why have democratically-elected governments been able to dismantle welfare provisions in the name of increased individual freedom when the adverse effects on social justice appear to be so obvious? Can a theory of ideology account for the political ascendency of neo-liberal education policies? These are the questions that I seek to address in this paper.

I shall begin with some comments on the nature of ideology and suggest that totalistic irrationalist theories of ideology are unable to account adequately for the widespread acceptance of dubious neo-liberal beliefs. Drawing on recent work by the French social theorist, Raymond Boudon, I shall outline his restricted theory of ideology and show how it defines the limits of rational choice for socially situated individuals. In the final section, I shall draw on recent work of Claus Offe to examine the macro-social structures within which the political ascendancy of neo-liberalism has occurred. By combining individualist and structural modes of analysis, the theories of Boudon and Offe suggest why it may be rational for some individuals to adhere to false or dubious neo-liberal theories and to support anti–welfare-state policies that potentially could be contrary to their interests.

Towards a Restricted Theory of Ideology

For anyone familiar with the sociology of education of the past two decades, the recent onslaught of neo-liberal reform could be readily interpreted in terms of a "dominant ideology" thesis. Thus, the ideas of the "New Right" are dominant because these are the ideas of the ruling class. Any endorsement of these ideas through the electoral process is the result of rampant ideological hegemony which, in this view, accounts for the widespread support for "New Right" policies and the persuasive force of libertarian discourse with its illusory images of individual freedom, public choice and parental empowerment.

The commonly held neo-Marxist position on ideological hegemony can be described as totalistic and irrationalist. It is totalistic in the sense that it takes ideology to be a general and pervasive force that infuses all areas of social life— saturating the cultural, the political and the economic spheres of human existence. Aronowitz and Giroux present the position as follows:

> Hegemony in this instance signifies, first, a pedagogic and politically transformative process whereby the dominant class articulates the common elements embedded in the world views of allied groups. Second, hegemony refers to the dual use of force and ideology to reproduce societal relations

between dominant classes and subordinate groups . . . Hegemony in this account represents more than the exercise of coercion: it is a process of continuous creation and includes the constant structuring of consciousness as well as a battle for the control of consciousness.

(Aronowitz & Giroux 1985, 88)

Aronowitz and Giroux claim allegiance here to Gramsci but, as Roy Nash points out, their use of the term hegemony goes beyond the specific political meaning that Gramsci gave to this concept, and owes more to the influence of writers such as Raymond Williams for whom, as Nash points out:

. . . "hegemony" has come to signify the existence of a truly total system of thought, not merely secondary or superstructural, like ideology in its sense of false ideas, but an entire system of conceptualisation which is lived at such a depth, and which saturates society to such an extent, that it constitutes the substance and limit of common sense for most people under its sway.

(Nash 1989, 53)

This totalistic theory of ideological hegemony not only negates any teleological explanations of social action but it makes ideology an intrinsic part of every cultural practice. This produces both an over-generalised concept of ideology and a weakened, idealised concept of culture. Nash identifies the problem as follows:

If the notions of common sense are in themselves ideological, because they help sustain hegemonic relations, culturally embedded relations of class domination and subordination, and if those common sense notions are understood as cultural productions, which all sounds reasonable, then we have an argument that forces the identity of culture and ideology. But if culture is ideology then one of those concepts is redundant and it seems necessary to reject this conclusion.

(Nash 1989, 54–5)

A further problem with most theories of ideological hegemony lies in the presumption of irrationalism that they always seem to entail. Social actors unknowingly adhere to false ideas because they are trapped inside a total view which they must unconsciously accept because they cannot conceive of any criteria against which they could test its truth or falsehood. Social actors, in such theories, are presumed to be irrational because their actions are unconsciously determined by forces beyond their control. The main problem with irrationalist theories of this kind is that the concept of ideology becomes entirely normative and slides into a self-refuting relativism. If social analysis is to have scientific validity, it requires a theory of ideology in which ideological phenomena can be related to the criterion of true and false. Such a restricted rationalist theory of ideology is outlined in a recent book, *The Analysis of Ideology*, by the French social theorist Raymond Boudon (1989).

Boudon argues that the traditional definition of ideology, implicit in the writings of Marx, is based upon a criterion of truth and falsehood. Marx, according to Boudon, "defines ideologies as *false ideas* which social actors possess because of their 'material interaction' " (Boudon 1989, 18). Other more recent theorists of ideology, albeit not from within the Marxist tradition, whom Boudon considers as having accepted the true/false criterion, are Raymond Aron and Talcott Parsons. Some modern theories, however, according to Boudon, define ideology according to the criterion of *meaning*. Althusser is probably the most influential within the Marxist tradition, defining ideology as a "system of representations" to be distinguished from science. Other well-known non-Marxists define ideology as "symbolic action" (Geertz) or "belief system" (Shils).

Boudon finds these later definitions unsatisfactory because it is not clear what in fact they are signifying. But, more importantly, he favours the Marx–Aron–Parson's definition for the following two reasons.

1   The word 'ideology' achieved salience in the nineteenth century because it described a new social *reality,* that is, the more and more widespread trend to explain the bases of social order and political action by analysis of a scientific kind. Simultaneously, the pejorative nature of the word showed the limitations of this and the risk of distortion to which it was open.

2   Most ideologies, whether major or minor, "left-wing" or "right-wing", are characterised by the fact that they are based on doctrines conforming to the scientific approach. (Boudon 1989, 28)

Thus, Boudon defines ideologies as false or dubious scientific theories or doctrines based on theories which "have not been properly interpreted, and which are therefore given undeserved credibility" (Boudon 1989, 29).

Another important distinction in Boudon's analysis of ideology concerns the explanation of ideological phenomena. Such explanations are of two principal types: irrational and rational.

Marx's general theory of ideology is irrationalist and can be summarised, according to Boudon as follows:

People unknowingly adhere to false ideas because they are impelled by *unconscious* forces outside their control which make them slaves either to their own interests (if they belong to the ruling class) or to the interests of the ruling class (if they belong to the underclass).

(Boudon 1989, 41)

In some places, however, particularly in his analysis of specific ideological processes, Marx employs a rationalist theory of ideology. This occurs when people consciously adhere to useful beliefs, for example "when land owning aristocrats extol the monarchy because it sustains the system which gives them a social position to their liking" (Boudon 1989, 43).

Boudon calls this rational explanation of ideology Marx II to distinguish it from the more general irrationalist theory which he calls Marx I. Further examples of each type can be identified from outside the Marxist tradition.

On the one hand, Aron and Shils have both put forward theories of ideology based on irrational explanation. Ideology for these theorists is a product of fanaticism or the passions. On the other hand, theories based on rational explanation have been put forward by Mannheim and Geertz. For these theorists, adherence to ideological beliefs is manifested in decisions and actions that can be considered rational—that is, based on reasons that are intelligible and meaningful given the conditions and the context in which those decisions or actions occur.

Boudon does not deny that irrational explanations of ideology have a place, nor that modern definitions having no reference to the criterion of true and false could be useful for some kinds of analysis. What he is arguing, however, is that some analyses of social action require a rational true/false theory of ideology if they are to account for the fact that "in certain circumstances, social actors can for the best reasons subscribe to false ideas" (Boudon 1989, 67).

Socially Situated Rationality

What I want to suggest at this point is that Boudon's outline of a restricted theory of ideology provides a useful framework for the analysis of recent neoliberal education policies. It is particularly relevant to such policies because:

1   they have gained extensive adherence from large numbers of people who must be considered to be rational social agents; and
2   they are derived from theories of the market and society that are based, directly or indirectly, on scientific authority, and could, therefore, as theories, be shown (empirically and/or logically) to be dubious or false.

Later, I shall consider an explanation of why so many people have come to believe these theories but at this point Boudon's conception of socially situated rationality requires some further elaboration.

In his restricted theory of ideology, Boudon takes the socially situated rational individual as his basic unit of analysis. It is important to point out here that he does not mean that in order to be "rational" all actions of the individual should be deliberate or calculated. An action that is carried out "without thinking about it" may also be rational. Boudon gives the following example:

> . . . people have a positive attitude towards interest-free loans in a traditional society where the economy is based on reciprocity. They think it natural, because they see that everybody has this attitude; and they have probably never thought that there is in theory another possible system, charging interest on loans, which nobody they know has ever done. However, their positive attitude ought not to be attributed exclusively to the weight of tradition.

The explanation lies in the fact that it is a response which the subjects regard as well adapted to their social environment. Although it is not deliberate, it is meaningful and therefore rational.

(Boudon 1989, 53–4)

Within this broad notion of rationality, Boudon considers the conditions under which ideologies emerge. He also shows that science, while it is the source of true ideas, is capable of "confirming and propagating" false ideas. By science, he means the social sciences "since ideologies are systems of ideas which relate to society", and he takes the social sciences to include history and economics as well as anthropology, sociology and politics (Boudon 1989, 71).

Because individuals are socially situated, Boudon argues, the emergence of ideologies is partly due to what he calls *situation effects*. These tend:

. . . to make social actors perceive reality not as it is and as others can see it, but in a distorted or complete way. Moreover they will often have difficulty in realising that what they see is affected by the viewpoint from which they see it, even though this is not necessarily due to irrationality on their part. These situation effects are particularly important in that they often serve to explain why a social actor subscribes to a wrong or dubious notion.

(Boudon 1989, 71–2)

Situation effects can be further differentiated into *position* effects and *disposition* effects, both of which influence the acquisition of social knowledge by the individual. The former are due to the individual's position within the social order, whereas the latter are due to the socialisation process that the individual has undergone. These effects are analogous to those of perspective or viewpoint in social perception. Thus, social knowledge, like social perception, is not contemplative but active. Boudon summarises his argument as follows:

It is open to the sociologist to regard social actors as rational . . . At the same time however, there is a need to be aware of all the implications inherent in the fact that social actors are socially *situated,* in the sense that they have social roles, and belong to certain social backgrounds and certain societies, that they have access to certain resources (particularly cognitive), and that because of the socialisation process which they have undergone, they have *internalised* a certain number of skills and representations. For these reasons, they are subject to what I have called situation effects (position and disposition effects).

(Boudon 1989, 94)

Because individuals are socially situated, their social knowledge can never be entirely objective. Hence, whenever they choose from alternative courses of action, they cannot predict with certainty the consequences of their choice. This does not, however, render their decision any less rational than if they had been able to predict. Nor is their decision, because it is a rational choice, isolated or disconnected from the decisions of other social actors similarly situated. The aggregation of rational decisions can have social consequences that are unintended and may even be contrary to the interests of the individual social actors.

For example, in the area of neo-liberal education policy, the individual parent who is presented with an opportunity to *choose* the school that his or her children will attend, would be acting rationally by seizing that opportunity, even though the consequences if all others in similar social situations were to make similar choices, would be to severely reduce or eliminate the alternatives available to each individual (Jonathan 1989).

Thus, the rational choice of an individual, in terms of Boudon's theory, is always subject to situation effects and always made, therefore, on the basis of incomplete knowledge. In some cases, as Boudon points out:

> . . . one knows that one does not know the solution to a problem, but one has an idea of the possible solutions, though one is unable by demonstrative reason to choose between them.
>
> (Boudon 1989, 105)

In such situations, social actors are likely to choose "not the solution which seems most valid objectively, but that which for a variety of reasons seems to them the most desirable" (Boudon 1989, 105). Boudon illustrates this with the following example drawn from education policy.

Most postwar governments in France and similar countries have wanted to reduce educational inequalities. The problem was to decide what kind of curriculum structure would increase educational opportunity for children from disadvantaged backgrounds. Two totally different solutions have been proposed, each based on sound arguments. While some have proposed a common academic curriculum for all, others have proposed a "streamed" or differentiated curriculum from which the disadvantaged could choose options in keeping with their expectations. Neither solution, Boudon suggests, could be shown conclusively to produce less inequality of opportunity (in advance of the observable consequences) and each supporting argument could be matched by an equally plausible counter-argument. Thus, the decision to prefer one solution over the other depended upon situation effects, with "left-wingers" comprising the majority of the non-streams and "right-wingers" forming the majority of their opponents. The former were disposed to believe that any type of social differentiation was unacceptable, whereas the latter were disposed to believe that "equality cannot be bought whatever the price" (Boudon 1989, 107).

Another category of effects considered by Boudon to be essential to the analysis of ideological phenomena he calls *communication effects*. These occur because some actors acquire so much of their knowledge solely on the *authority* of the source of that knowledge. The authority resides in the communication of the knowledge rather than in its actual verification. Some theories, in other words, are what Boudon calls "black boxes". It seems rational, for example, "if one is not a physicist, to regard ideas in physics as black boxes which can be right or wrong not because one has reproduced the process allowing this evaluation to be made, but because people skilled in this area take them to be right or wrong" (Boudon 1989, 83).

Because of the range and complexity of knowledge in the modern world, relatively few theories can be understood by social actors as "white boxes", that is as "collections of totally clear statements". Thus, "the theory of relativity is really only clear to physicists, but that does not stop most people being prepared to accept that it is true" (Boudon 1989, 116).

Black box or communication effects are generally less problematic in the natural sciences than they are in the social sciences and it is in the latter that they have significance for Boudon's restricted theory of ideology. Thus, in the social sciences, a theory that may well be false or dubious could be propounded by experts who are properly presumed to be scientifically authoritative in their field. This theory may then become the basis for policy decisions, as the following example shows:

> . . . people whose jobs involve them in development policy will pay particular attention to theories of development put forward by economists. If they are not economists, however, these theories are likely to be black boxes as far as they are concerned. They will therefore be led to subscribe to a particular theory less because they have checked its truth for themselves than because it is propounded by a reputable economist.
>
> (Boudon 1989, 116)

The relevance of the above example to recent events in New Zealand is striking. Boudon's theory offers an answer to the perplexing question of why politicians with little knowledge of economics would make policy decisions that accorded with a particular economic theory. It helps us to understand the disturbing paradox in New Zealand's recent history where a Labour government adopted a raft of policies based upon neo-liberal monetarist economic and social theories. There could hardly be a more "reputable" group of economists than those who are employed by the New Zealand Treasury and there are large numbers of perfectly rational politicians, policymakers and ordinary citizens who regard their theories as black boxes. Thus, following Boudon's argument, we can begin to see how "belief in false ideas often comes from a readily understandable combination of communication effects and situation effects" (Boudon 1989, 117).

We do not need a dominant ideology thesis, therefore, to account for the widespread acceptance of neo-liberal or "New Right" theories. Nevertheless, these theories are ideological in a more restricted sense because:

1 they are accepted as black box theories by socially situated rational individuals;
2 they take the form of social scientific theories that are made up of explanatory claims; and
3 they can be shown (empirically or logically) to be dubious or false in their explanations or predictions.

It is important to note that only when all three criteria are met is it appropriate to describe theories as ideological (i.e. when socially situated, rational individuals accept them in the face of contrary evidence).

In the final section of the paper, I want to address the question of why neo-liberal theories are in a state of ascendancy at the present time in countries like New Zealand and the related question of why they are so influential in shaping current social policies.

The Macro-Social Context of Neo-Liberal Opportunities

The political ascendancy of neo-liberalism in most democratic welfare states over the past decade or so has been well documented (Levitas 1986; Barry 1987; King 1987). This movement has been shown to have three central elements:

1   libertarianism (i.e. the promotion of economic individualism and freedom of choice);
2   monetarism (i.e. the maintenance of free market forces within a rightly controlled money supply); and
3   privatisation (i.e. the advocacy of minimal government and reduced state provision).

In some welfare states, most notably Britain under the Thatcher government, neo-liberalism has been accompanied by an equally strong resurgence of neo-conservatism. The main features of this movement are: strong government; nationalism; social authoritarianism; managerialism; and hierarchical order. Although there are obvious contradictory tensions between these two movements, together they constitute a major force of opposition to traditional social democratic policies of welfarism and the expansion of citizenship rights.

The increasing prominence of both neo-liberalism and neo-conservatism, as Norman Barry points out, "has largely been generated by the crisis of inflation, high public spending, and slow growth that social democracies have experienced in the last ten years" (Barry 1987, 20). There is no doubt that welfare states all over the world have experienced similar structural crises. What is less clear, however, is why these crises have produced political opportunities for the resurgence of both neo-liberal and neo-conservative solutions. One theorist who perhaps goes further than most in providing a macro-social explanation for this re-orientation of political opportunities within the welfare state is Claus Offe.

The main thrust of Offe's project is to develop a theoretical analysis of the deep structural crises that have beset most capitalist welfare states over the past couple of decades (Offe 1984, 1985).

He argues convincingly that policies of state intervention, while being necessary to sustain capital accumulation, effectively weaken the viability of the market, generate chronic fiscal problems and force governments to adopt policies of crisis management. Such policies are frequently structural in nature, creating new forms of administrative control and disorganising previous avenues of political demand. Current educational reforms in New Zealand can be readily analysed in terms of this thesis (Codd 1990; Codd, Gordon & Harker 1990).

Offe theorises the liberal-democratic welfare state as comprising three inter-related institutional components or structural elements. These are:

1   the welfare state itself, with its state-provided services, programs and collective goods;
2   the market economy, with its guarantees of private property, free exchange and contractual rights; and
3   the system of political democracy, with its procedures for participation and representation.

Thus, according to Offe, the modern capitalist welfare state has a welfare component, a liberal component and a democratic component, each with its own tradition of political theory. Individual citizens can been seen to have a structural relationship to each of these institutional components. Firstly, they have a dependant welfare relationship to state-provided services and social security provisions. Secondly, they have an independent liberal relationship to the market economy. Thirdly, they have a participatory democratic relationship to the political system. What this means, according to Offe, is that citizens are:

> (i) the ultimate source of the collective political will, in the formation of which they are called upon to participate in a variety of institutional ways; they are also (ii) the "subjects" against whom this will can be enforced and whose civil rights and liberties impose, by constituting an autonomous sphere of "private" social, cultural, and economic action, limits upon the state's authority; and finally they are (iii) clients who depend upon state-provided services, programmes, and collective goods for securing their material, social and cultural means of survival and well-being in society.
>
> (Offe 1987, 501)

At a macro-social level, the three institutional components of the welfare state are also structurally inter-related, according to Offe. Their relationships to each other, however, are not necessarily harmonious. In fact, there are potential inherent tensions between each of the components and causal interactions that can be both supportive and antagonistic (Figure 2.1).

In his earlier work, Offe (1984) focuses mainly on the tensions and contradictions between the welfare state and the market economy. This has also been the main focus of neo-liberal theorists (Hayek, Friedman, Nozick) and some neo-Marxists (e.g. O'Connor 1984). Other theorists, as Offe points out (e.g. Wolfe 1977; Macpherson 1977; Levine 1981) have focused on the relationship between market liberalism and democracy. Thus, it is the third relationship (i.e. that between the welfare state and political democracy) that in Offe's view "is relatively the most neglected one in the theoretical literature" (Offe 1987, 503) and towards which he turns his attention in a recent paper (1987).

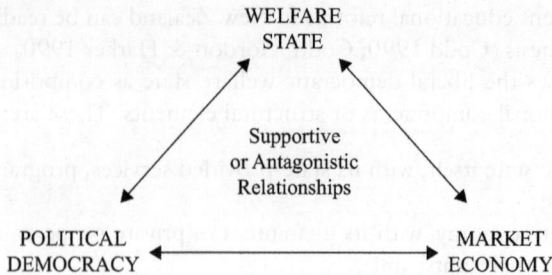

Figure 2.1 Structural Tensions Within the Welfare State

Offe's theoretical analysis of the welfare state is useful because it relates the political actions of individuals to macro-social structures and provides explanations that include both individualist and collectivist modes of analysis. His theoretical approach, therefore, has the same ontological base as Boudon's and provides macro-social explanations within which to locate Boudon's restricted theory of ideology and socially situated rationality. It is for this reason that Offe's analysis of the tensions between the democratic and welfare components of the state is particularly useful to an explanation of the social conditions within which neo-liberal policies have gained political support.

Offe begins his analysis of the relationship between the democratic and welfare components of the modern capitalist state by considering the plausible and, in his view, optimistic assumption that the relationship is necessarily a mutually supportive one. Underlying this assumption at the core of social democratic theory, Offe suggests, is:

> (i) a *model of rational collective action through democratic politics* and (ii) a model of self-stabilising and *self-reinforcing institutional dynamics*. The twin assumption is that rational actors in a democracy will join a pro–welfare-state majority and that, once the welfare state institutions are established, they become increasingly immune to challenges.
>
> (Offe 1987, 509)

Thus, the rational individual voter could be expected to support redistributive welfare policies for such reasons as: (1) to avoid collective social "evils" (e.g. crime, conflict, disease); (2) as an investment in a positive public good; (3) as an altruistic obligation to social justice.

While this makes sense in terms of social democratic theory, current social realities, Offe argues, present quite a different picture, such that:

> The mutually supportive relationship of mass democracy and welfare stateness . . . no longer amounts to a convincing hypothesis. To the contrary,

there are many indications . . . that lead us to expect that democratic mass politics will *not* work in the direction of a reliable defence (to say nothing about the further expansion) of the welfare state.

(Offe 1987, 511)

In support of this claim, Offe points to several trends in Western European democracies since the mid-1970s. In addition to the electoral defeats of many socialist parties, dramatic reductions in welfare budgets and a continuing decline of welfare services, there has been:

... the sometimes dramatic electoral defection of the core working class to liberal-conservative political forces, implying a strong sign of political support for anti-welfare-state cuts and legislation even among those who belong to the classes and social categories in whose name the ideals and ideologies of state-provided welfare have traditionally been advocated.

(Offe 1987, 513)

These phenomena cannot be explained, Offe argues, solely in terms of social structure without considering "the role of individual actors and their style of rational responses" (Offe 1987, 514). This necessitates a return to the level of empirical analysis, not to investigate the facts to which neo-liberal and neo-conservative propositions refer, but to investigate:

... the *actors* and their individual reasons for *accepting* these propositions as valid. In this perspective, the correspondence that would become the focus of critical attention is *not* the correspondence between facts and propositions. Neither would it be the correspondence between values and political projects. Rather it would be the correspondence between certain types of social actors and the parameters of choice given within their situation of action, on the one side, and their rational motivation to adopt certain interpretive patterns about the world, on the other.

(Offe 1987, 515)

While these empirical investigations remain to be carried out in different social contexts and in relation to different areas of social policy, there are major structural changes to be observed within modern societies that could be expected to influence the "interpretive patterns" of individuals. In particular, Offe considers what he calls "the destructuration of collectivities", which he defines as follows:

The disorganisation of broad, relatively stable, and encompassing commonalities of economic interest, associational affiliation, or cultural values and life-styles is in my view the key to an adequate understanding of the general weakening of solidaristic commitments. If it no longer "makes sense" to

> refer to a broad and sharply delineated category of fellow citizens as "our kind of people", the only remaining interpretive referent of action is the individual who refers to her- or himself in rational-calculative terms.
>
> (Offe 1987, 527)

Offe's argument is that the decline of political support for the welfare state:

> . . . can neither be fully explained by economic and fiscal crisis arguments, nor by political arguments emphasising the rise of neo-conservative elites and ideologies; nor can it be undone by moral appeals to the justice and legitimacy of existing welfare state arrangements.
>
> (Offe 1987, 528)

Rather, the tension between the democratic and welfare components of the state is due to a "structural disintegration process" through which individuals become "deeply distrustful of social policies as 'public goods' " (Offe 1987: 528).

Thus, the process of structural disintegration creates what Boudon calls "situation effects" such that social actors are disposed towards the interpretation of policies in terms of personal gains and losses or individual freedoms and constraints, rather than abstract principles of social justice. To understand why people support social policies that appear to be contrary to their interests we need empirical knowledge both of the rational choices they make in response to their perceived options and of the structural changes by which their collective interests have become disintegrated.

Offe summarises his argument as follows:

> As a combined effect of these structural changes, we may anticipate the rise of behavioural orientations of voters and citizens that give support to anti-welfare-state policies—not primarily for reasons of bad intentions, irrational drives, or a sudden shift to neo-conservative or market-liberal values and attitudes, but because of beliefs and preferences that are rationally formed in response to perceived social realities as well as to the actual experiences with the practice of existing welfare states.
>
> (Offe 1987, 535)

Countering the Ideology of Choice

At this point, the complementarity of Boudon's and Offe's theoretical positions, and their relevance to social policy analysis, becomes much clearer. To understand the full effects of neo-liberal policies, it is important to know how they are interpreted by rational social actors who respond to them from various social positions.

For those who have experienced the constraining effects of bureaucratic controls and regulations, policies promoting choice will have considerable rational appeal. Even when the theories on which such policies are based are demonstrated to be false, this does not necessarily reduce the extent of their political support. Because these theories are black boxes to many of the people who are called upon to assess them, the truth or falsehood of their propositions can only be known through direct experience of the consequences that follow from the practical solutions they generate.

In the UK, the 1988 *Education Reform Act* was defended by a strong ideology of choice. The major policies embraced by this Act were designed to increase competition between schools and encourage parental choice. In accordance with the 'free market' thrust of Thatcherism, and consistent with other moves towards privatisation, schools were given the right to 'opt out' of local authority control. The rationale proclaimed that choice would generate competition which consequently would raise educational standards. Although the empirical evidence does not support such a theory (Halpin *et al.*, 1991; Walford 1992) increasing numbers of schools continue to 'opt out' of local authority control (Bowe *et al.* 1992).

A similar situation has occurred in New Zealand following the abolition of regional education boards and the move to self-managing schools. To encourage parental choice, school zoning regulations have been abolished leading to differences between schools in their admission criteria. Competition between schools for both students and resources has increased markedly and predictably some schools are attracting more socially advantaged students.

School zoning policies were introduced in New Zealand in the 1950s to promote equality of educational opportunity, although they inevitably limited the freedom of some parents to choose (McCulloch 1991). When the Labour government restructured education, a school zoning policy was retained, although it could be seen to be anomalous within the overall neo-liberal rationale of the reforms. The present National government, however, has moved to eliminate this anomaly and the 1991 *Education Amendment Act* abolished school zoning regulations thereby allowing schools to compete freely for students and, supposedly, allowing parents more freedom to choose. It appears that many working-class parents supported this move. As individuals, they support a policy which they perceive as (1) removing bureaucratic interference in the sphere of their personal freedoms, and (2) providing an opportunity for them to make a real choice in relation to their children's education.

Because of its wide popular support, the ideology of choice presents a major challenge to educational administrators committed to equality of access and opportunity. They cannot simply assume that the appeal of neo-liberal policies can be countered by 'consciousness raising' or by abstract appeals to social justice. The dominant ideology thesis cannot adequately explain why some people decide to support educational policies that can be shown structurally to reduce their degrees of freedom and to increase their relative disadvantage. Such people are to be understood as rational actors situated in relation to the institutional structures of a modern capitalist welfare state.

Educational policies that promote choice at the cost of equity and social justice cannot be reversed until the political opportunities for such a change exist within the macro-social context. Only by experiencing and monitoring the real social effects of these policies will people gradually work collectively to change them through the same democratic processes that have put them in place.

References

Aronowitz, S. & Giroux, H.A. (1985), *Education Under Siege: The Conservative, Liberal and Radical Debate Over Schooling*. Massachusetts: Bergin and Garvey.

Barry, N.P. (1987), *The New Right*. London: Croom Helm.

Boudon, R. (1989), *The Analysis of Ideology*, trans. by M. Slater. Cambridge: Polity Press.

Bowe, R., Ball, S. & Gold, A. (1992), *Reforming Education and Changing Schools*. London: Routledge & Kegan Paul.

Chubb, J.E. & Moe, T.M. (1990), *Politics, Markets and America's Schools*. Washington, D.C.: The Brookings Institution.

Codd, J., Gordon, L. & Harker, R. (1990), "Education and the role of the State: Devolution and control post-Picot", in H. Lauder & C. Wylie (eds) *Towards Successful Schooling*. London: The Falmer Press, 15–32.

Codd, J.A. (1990), "Educational policy and the crisis of the New Zealand State", in S. Middleton, J. Codd & A. Jones (eds), *New Zealand Education Policy Today*. Wellington: Allen & Unwin, 191–205.

Codd, J.A. (1993), "Equity and choice: The paradox of New Zealand Educational Reform", *Curriculum Studies*, 1(1), 75–90.

Goldring, E.B. (ed.) (1991), *International Journal of Educational Research*, Special Issue on Parental Involvement and Public Choice in Education.

Halpin, D., Power, S. & Fitz, J. (1991), "Grant-maintained schools: Making a difference without being really different", *British Journal of Educational Studies*. 39(4), 409–24.

Jonathan, R. (1989), "Choice and control in education: Parental rights, individual liberties and social justice", *British Journal of Educational Studies*, 37(4), 321–38.

King, D.S. (1987), *The New Right: Politics, Markets and Citizenship*. London: Macmillan.

Levine, A. (1981), *Liberal Democracy: A Critique of its Theory*. New York: Columbia University Press.

Levitas, R. (ed.) (1986), *The Ideology of the New Right*. Cambridge: Polity Press.

Macpherson, C.B. (1977), *The Life and Times of Liberal Democracy*. Oxford: Oxford University Press.

McCulloch, G. (1991), "School zoning, equity and freedom: The case of New Zealand", *Journal of Education Policy*, 6(2), 155–168.

Nash, R. (1989), "Cultural choice: A reply to my critics", *New Zealand Sociology*, 4(1), 49–63.

O'Connor, J. (1984), *Accumulation Crisis*. Oxford: Blackwell.

Offe, C. (1984), *Contradictions of the Welfare State*. London: Hutchinson.

Offe, C. (1985), *Disorganised Capitalism*. Cambridge: Polity Press.

Offe, C. (1987), "Democracy against the welfare state? Structural foundations of neoconservative political opportunities", *Political Theory*, 15(4), 501–37.

Taskforce to Review Education Administration (1988), *Administering for Excellence* (Picot Report). Wellington: Government Printer.

Treasury, The New Zealand (1987), *Government Management*, Vol. 2. Wellington: Government Printer.

Walford, G. (1992), "Educational choice and equity in Great Britain", *Educational Policy*, 6(2), 123–38.

Wolfe, A. (1977), *The Limits of Legitimacy: Political Contradictions of Contemporary Capitalism*. London: Macmillan.

Chapter 3

Varieties of Neo-Liberalism
A Foucaultian Perspective[1]

J. D. Marshall

Reprinted by permission of Taylor & Francis Ltd, http://www.tandfonline.com, on behalf of © Philosophy of Education Society of Australasia.

Editors' Introduction

Marshall, in his chapter, analyses Michel Foucault's critique of neoliberalism and the neoliberal theorists, such as Hayek, who have influenced significantly recent changes of Western educational systems. Marshall's work uses Foucault to provide a genealogical argument to show that neo-liberal economic theory is not the inevitable outcome of the earlier economic theory. While Foucault saw liberalism as a collection of concepts and theories which were not always compatible and therefore provided a fertile critique for neoliberalism, Marshall considers his genealogical argument against Smith's version of neo-liberalism, to extend this argument in two directions. The first is a comparison of Adam Smith's and Adam Ferguson's versions of economic theory and the philosophical difference between their accounts of liberal concepts such as individualism. The second raises questions about whether Foucault's concept of governmentality is sufficient to explain how Smith's account of political economy became the basis for neoliberal thinking. Further, Mashall analyses how Smith's political economy, and of course its modern neoliberal equivalent, came to be 'accepted', and its critical implications for education. He argues for more attention to be paid to the performative aspects of language in education theory, philosophy and research.

> Never consent to be completely at ease with what seems evident to oneself.
> (Michel Foucault, 1979)

Introduction

In this paper I wish to consider Michel Foucault's critique of neo-liberalism. Neo-liberal theorists (for example, Hayek) often refer to Adam Smith and his hidden hand argument as a basis, if not the basis, of the recent neo-liberal economic and social theory which have impacted heavily upon recent 'reforms' of Western educational systems, particularly in New Zealand. Foucault provides a genealogical argument to show that neo-liberal economic theory is not the inevitable outcome of earlier economic theory suggested by the Scottish 'philosopher historians', especially Adam Smith. Even if Smith was a leader on many matters, his contemporaries—particularly Adam Ferguson, James Steuert and David Hume—held ideas which were different. As Foucault saw liberalism as a collection of concepts and theories which were not always compatible and, thereby, provided a fertile critique for neo-liberalism, I wish to consider his genealogical argument against Smith's version of neo-liberalism. It is my intention to extend this argument in two directions. First, Foucault's argument starts from a comparison of Adam Smith's and Adam Ferguson's versions of economic theory, and I will look more closely philosophically at their different accounts of liberal concepts such as individualism. Second, I wish to raise questions as to whether Foucault's concept of governmentality is sufficient to explain *how* it came about that Smith's account of political economy became the basis for neo-liberal thinking. My answer to this, as I explore some of the possibilities in the work of John Austin, will be negative.

First, I will make some analytical points about neo-liberal concepts. Second, I will look at Foucault's genealogical argument which is designed to show that at least two accounts of political economy were available in the late eighteenth century—those of Adam Smith and Adam Ferguson. Second, in relation to the emergence of Smith's account, I will consider the adequacy of analytic philosophical contestation of neo-liberalism. Whilst accepting Foucault's account of genealogy as providing *an* account of why political economy was to adopt and develop Smith rather than Ferguson, it needs to be part of a wider account of which it would be a necessary part. Here I look at the account offered by Meuret (1988). Finally, I explore Austin's (1962) account of performative language, arguing that Foucault and Meuret need to consider such aspects of language for their account to 'go through'.

Liberalism and Philosophy

Foucault was essentially a liberal who believed that liberalism provided a sufficiently fertile problematic for a sustained critique of minimalist neo-liberal individualism (Gordon, 1991, p. 8). However, unlike analytic philosophers, he is not interested in contesting the use of key liberal concepts by neo-liberals. It can be argued, first, that key liberal concepts are contestable and contested (for example, freedom and equality) and that, second, especially in education, neo-liberal theory is not as clear about the use of key concepts such as choice, freedom, quality, etc., as it might be.

Thus, in liberal theory individualism has been a contested concept—acknowledged by Hayek himself who distinguished between true liberalism (his version) and what he called collective individualism which he attributed to Rousseau, and which he believed led to socialism (Hayek, 1947, p. 4). Also, neo-liberal concepts in education are seldom defined. Thereby, in relation to *choice* it might be argued that choice presupposes autonomy, and therefore some notion of understanding about the ability to choose and the range of choices available. Choices must be made in a situation and if genuine choices are to be made then it would seem to be necessary to state some general conditions against which choice is to be made, as choice is not just an absolute notion (in contrast to the earlier Sartre). I can only choose between a range offered to me or from what it is in my power to obtain. Also, autonomy presupposes that the autonomous chooser is independent and has not been influenced, manipulated or determined to choose in certain general directions. It can be argued that if genuine autonomy is implied in the notions of choice by neo-liberals that in fact there is a limited and imposed sense of autonomy operating in this notion of the autonomous chooser (Marshall, 1996). Nor is freedom to be interpreted as merely freedom *from* constraints, that is in a negative sense, because there is also positive freedom, or freedom *to* (Berlin, 1969). But there are other key concepts. What is the difference between equality, equality of opportunity and equity? Quality requires some agreement upon what counts as quality and is not just determined by the consumers' market choices. And where does tolerance figure in neo-liberalism? What of those who do not wish to be conceived, perceived and theorised as utility maximisers? People may not be driven by egoistic desires to act ultimately in their own best interests as Adam Smith and market theory seems to presuppose. What of altruism, beneficence, martyrs, etc.? These traditional liberal concepts are therefore *contestable* and *contested,* and do not just possess unequivocally the meanings adopted by neo-liberalism. There is not space to develop such analytic forays further—if they were needed to make that point.

Nevertheless, the analytic critique has a limited force only. Given its conceptual concerns it does not manifestly impinge upon issues raised by these new neo-liberal theories in the important political areas of economics and public management. If the use of these liberal concepts and terms in these new theories provides some rhetorical thrust for these new approaches, or makes acceptance of neo-liberal ideas more palatable (we all want freedom, choice, etc.), the traditional liberal concepts may not be needed theoretically. New concepts can be used or traditional concepts redefined and used more rigorously to avoid such analytic criticisms. Indeed, this was a general move proposed by Hayek (1968) to both meet these criticisms and to advance neo-liberal economic theory. Thus the analytic critiques leave it open for these theories to coin new terms, as indeed they do—the self-managing school for example—and to tighten up their use of established and contested terms—for example, freedom. Therefore the purely analytic critique has limitations. Foucault of course does not take the analytic turn but, instead, examines the 'origins' of neo-liberal theories.

Foucault's Genealogical Argument

Foucault's genealogical argument is designed to show that there is not a steady line of descent from the times of Adam Smith to Hayek and the neo-liberals. There are two strands to this argument. First, there are substantive differences between

Smith's position and modern neo-liberalism which cannot just be described as a 'progression'. Second, there was no reason why Adam Smith's position should have won the day over, for example, against his contemporary, Adam Ferguson.

In similar fashion to the events of Damiens' execution in 1757 and the treatment of young offenders in Faucher's reformatory some 80 years later in *Discipline and Punish,* Foucault argues that there is not a continuous and progressive line of descent from the economic theories of Adam Smith to the present, for example, Hayek. It would be a mistake to see this line of 'descent' as a progression. We can see this by considering briefly some reasonably clear differences— there are of course others. First, Smith's individual in *The Wealth of Nations* (1969) is not the manipulable man of modern economic theory. Second, the hidden hand of the eighteenth-century philosophers, including Smith, is not the catallaxy of Hayek. Finally, for here, there has been the extension of what was an economic theory to cover all spheres of non-random human activity (see further, Gordon, 1991).

Smith's individual was driven by self interest, but was also conceived as autonomous (and possessed of sympathy as an ethical basis), choosing in the market 'rationally' in accordance with self interest. Smith's position on the individual was then reductionist to this metaphysical core of self interest, which was conceived as inviolable and not to be open to, or coerced by, the activities of governments. But that central metaphysical core has been invaded by the positing of a faculty of *choice* (Gordon, 1991, p. 43; Marshall, 1996) and thus open to the political invasion of the autonomy and self interests of such individuals by governments. Along with the positing of a faculty of choice (not that of personal autonomy— being able to decide for oneself) has come the notion that we can and must make *continuous* choices, that the modern life of the individual is an enterprise constituted by continuous choices. This is far from the *homo economicus* of Smith.

The hidden hand argument was advanced before Smith's version appeared (for example, Montesquieu, 1749). In Adam Ferguson's version the progress of society is a spontaneous process, not the result of any single plan or human scheme, but a product of a number of diverse purposes and plans which emerge from the fundamental *differences* between human beings. Progress did not depend therefore upon merely economic concerns and economic competition in a free market. It is precisely because men scheme and plan—they 'are sufficiently disposed to occupy themselves in forming projects and schemes'—that 'man will find an opponent in every person who is disposed to scheme himself' (Ferguson, 1966, p. 122), and that progress is the outcome of this *diversity.* He continues that men 'seldom are turned from their way, to follow the plan of any single projector'. Thus 'nations stumble upon establishments, which are indeed the result of human action, but not the execution of any human design' (ibid.). Smith's version of the human hand, however, depended upon *similarity,* upon the economic interests of individuals who were self-interested as part of their very nature.

Hayek developed the notion of catallaxy. It differs from the hidden hand in that whereas the hidden hand was used to explain the hidden effects of market exchanges, catallaxy is a technical concept used to *describe* 'the spontaneous ordering forces of the market'. It is not something then which can be ordered and controlled so as to develop and control the efficiency of the market (Hayek, 1968, p. 91). 'The ordered structure which the market produces is, however, not an organisation but a spontaneous order or cosmos . . .' (loc. cit.). A cosmos has no purpose and no regulating system outside of itself and is thus self-organising or self-regulating. Hayek believed that such a concept was necessary for the open society into which we were evolving. In that case, Smith's *The Wealth of Nations*, with all its suggestions for economic *order*, is otiose. Furthermore, neo-liberalism has been concerned to extend these economic theories beyond their original 'home' to all forms of non-random action, especially to management.

Thus there are fundamentally different ontological and metaphysical assumptions between Smith and Hayek. But can modern views of neo-liberalism be seen as a linear development of those earlier ideas? Foucault's answer would be 'no' because, in the interlude from Smith to Hayek, we can see the emergence and the exercise of *bio-power*, that form of power which operates on both individuals and populations. 'The disciplines of the body and the regulations of the population constituted the two poles around which the organization of power over life was deployed' (Foucault, 1980, p. 139). However, biopower, as a concept, needs to be replaced by something like *busnopower* (Marshall, 1996) which brings into play, in the guise of the entrepreneurial autonomous chooser, the interpenetration of truths by the ethics and standards of the commercial world and the workplace.

The Two Adams

Adam Ferguson in *An Essay on the History of Civil Society* (1966) starts from the premiss that the natural historian must study his 'object'—man—as 'he' is, and thus rejects rational reconstructions of the nature of man such as those found in Hobbes, Locke, Rousseau and Hume. There is no original condition: neither the noble savage, nor self preservationist, nor the isolated individual alienated from the other. And man is neither peace loving nor violent (Ferguson, 1966, p. 24). Nor have liberty, or justice, or rights anything to do with the object of study of the natural historian (Ferguson, 1966, pp. 34–35, 63–64, 156–157). Questions of origin therefore are irrelevant, Ferguson holds.

Ferguson also attacked Hume's 'psychology' which argued that the propensities of man had 'hidden' causes or drives (and thereby Adam Smith). These propensities are facts about man and we should not worry about their causes. Therefore, the fact that there is a propensity in man to take advantage of situations or of other human beings should not be based upon the *sentiment* of self interests. Furthermore, if we take the facts of human nature we find than man is found in groups, never by himself, and in a great variety of situations, all equally natural, and in all of which man appears very differently, if not in openly opposed conditions. Thus we agree and quarrel, we are selfish and unselfish, and social or unsocial. All of these varieties are important for Ferguson (especially that man is progressive). For Ferguson, then, it was unscientific to base society upon one alleged sentiment of man—especially self-interest—but one of his targets is a system of *ethics* based upon the 'selfish system'. If humans are sometimes selfish or primarily self-interested this is but one amongst many of the features of man, and one which is to be found in early society. It is not, therefore, the outcome of any hidden-hand effect upon society or the result of modern civilisation (Rousseau) or more modern relations of production (Engels and Marx).

Whilst Ferguson believed that man had progressed, such progress was not the outcome of planning because whatever man might plan or arraign with a leader could be seized upon and distorted, or even turned back upon the planner. If 'the rapacious were to seize his possessions, and the arrogant to lay claim to his service' (Ferguson, 1966, p. 122), then planning and subordination would come to nought, and thus what mankind planned in the way of removing inconvenience, or in gaining advantages, might backfire. Thus Ferguson is saying that the progress of society is a spontaneous process, not the result of any single plan or human scheme, but a product of a number of diverse purposes and plans which emerge from the fundamental *differences* between human beings. It is precisely because man schemes and plans—they 'are sufficiently disposed to occupy themselves in forming projects and schemes'—that 'man will find an opponent in every person who is disposed to scheme himself' (Ferguson, 1966, p. 122). He continues that men 'seldom are turned from their way, to follow the plan of any single projector'. Thus 'nations stumble upon establishments, which are indeed the result of human action, but not the execution of any human design' (ibid.).

According to Forbes (1966, p. xxiii) there are 'important differences between Ferguson's description of the progress of society and that of [Adam] Smith . . . [and] . . . they are the result of profoundly different philosophies'. The first major point would seem to be that man cannot be reduced to any single sentiment like self-interest as Smith seems to hold. Ferguson is quite adamant that we cannot reduce man as we find 'him' in his multifarious situations, all equally natural, to a single underlying origin or 'causal' drive (Ferguson, 1966, 25f.), for example, of self-interest in the pursuit of material goods and 'conveniences'. Not only is Ferguson opposed to such reductionism, because we must start as natural historians from man as we find 'him', but also because men 'are commonly most attached where conveniences are least frequent' and 'affection operates with the greatest force, where it meets with the greatest difficulties' (p. 19). On the other hand, he continues, it is:

> 'in a commercial state' . . . that man is sometimes found a detached and a solitary being: he has found an object which sets him in competition with his fellow-creatures, and he deals with them as he does with his cattle and soil, for the sake of the profits they bring. The mighty engine which we suppose to have formed society, only tends to set its members at variance, or to continue their intercourse after the bands of affection are broken.
>
> (p. 19)

Progress is not, therefore, to be found through the mighty engine of individuals pursuing their self-interest in the market (the 'mighty machine'). Affection and social well-being are not therefore the outcome of the hidden hand of the market, for that version of the hidden-hand theory acts contrary to affection, well-being and union, that is, community, according to Ferguson. But they can arise from a hidden hand emanating from human beings in all of their scheming and plans which, in turn, arise from a number of human instincts or propensities including self-interest, self-preservation, moral sentiment, a social instinct, principles of union and principles of dissension.

Adam Smith relied, first, upon the 'selfish propensities'. As he put it in a famous passage:

> It is not from the benevolence of the butcher, the brewer, or the baker, that we expect our dinner, but from their regard to their own self-interest. We address ourselves, not to their humanity but to their self-love, and never talk to them of our own necessities but of their advantages. Nobody but a beggar chooses to depend chiefly upon the benevolence of his fellow citizens.
>
> (Smith, 1969, p. 119)

Second, he concentrated on the economic aspect of human beings arguing that all that was necessary for his economic theory, morally and politically, was that the individual be restrained from harming others, in respect of their persons and their property (Skinner, 1969, p. 44). It is this premiss of self-interest, bolstered by the thesis of unintended outcomes, that constitutes the 'social' base of his economic analysis. Third, in his discussions of the division of labour it is clear that the individual is the economic unit (Smith, 1969, Book I, Chapter 1), and that it is economic interdependence between individuals that is crucial for the hidden hand to operate. The hidden hand does not arise from wider notions of interdependence as is to be found in Ferguson.

There are, therefore, crucial differences between the philosophies of Ferguson and Smith. At the very least these are that:

1   Smith is reductionist whereas Ferguson says that we must start from the propensities that we find;
2   Smith is reductionist to an underlying 'cause' of such propensities—namely self-interest—whereas Ferguson sees such origins and causes as invoking metaphysics;
3   Smith's basic ontological building block is the individual (an immanent *homo economicus*) whereas Ferguson sees in an ethical society the necessity of union (community in modern parlance);
4   Smith's hidden hand is one dimensional (the market) whereas Ferguson's hidden hand has many dimensions and facets; and,
5   moral notions are the outcome of the economic hidden hand for Smith, whereas for Ferguson, moral notions are part of his basic assumptions.

Foucault's genealogical argument juxtaposes Ferguson's account of political economy with modern neo-liberalism. The reasons why Smith's account may have prevailed are not simply a matter of power/knowledge for there are a number of new issues, for example, associated with security and welfare (Gordon, 1991). However, the choice of Smith's economic base over Ferguson's social base was neither inevitable nor necessary. It was a contingent matter, the effect of human discourses and practices, and therefore can be undone.

A New Representation of the Economy

Denis Meuret (1988) asks *how* we are to understand this question: 'why at the end of the eighteenth century Smithean political economy supplanted other representations of the economy, those of other schools of economists as well as those conveyed by different political thinkers' (p. 55). Meuret's answer is that Smith provided a new 'representation' of the economy, a new definition of the State's legitimacy concerning its role towards the economy and its political relationships with its populace or citizens so that governmentality was served—the best distribution of things, etc. Smith was able to provide a better representation of both the economy *and* the political in that what was advanced was both an image of reality and an ideal to which one might aspire. If governmentality was served, Meuret does not see it being served in quite the same way as Foucault.

He notes that Smith's 'political economy' is not a representation of actual economic life or an image of it, or an ideal to be aspired towards. Instead, the new language of political economy is seen by Meuret as a language which produced an effect, a language which had a *performative* aspect (Austin, 1962), though he does not use that philosophical concept. It was performative because its language aimed 'to produce as its effect what it describes as existing' (Meuret, 1988, p. 50). It does not describe the economy as it actually exists, but through its expression institutes what today we call the economy. The new economic language institutes and constitutes. But this language is neither an ideal language, nor a description of a utopia. Nor is it immersed in an ideology or, in the case of Smith's version of the political economy, reducible to a science (as Sraffa did to Ricardo, by formalising it—Meuret, 1988, p. 53). Rather it is 'a programme of truth', that is, 'an account with programmatic value more than a description of reality' (Meuret, 1988, p. 51).

To talk of it as a programme is to suggest that the account was constructed to make certain kinds of government possible? But what characteristics did this version of political economy have which made it able to fulfil the functions outlined by the account, and establish as *effects* the objects which it describes? The characteristics, if there are any, are not to be found in the particular account. They must be at a meta-level or suppressed as Kantian apriori or Foucauldean historical apriori principles (Hacking, 1981), for '[t]he particular discipline which constructs the political economy as its object cannot give us the basic presuppositions on which it itself is constructed' (Dumont, 1976, p. 34, quoted by Meuret, 1988, p. 54). How then did it succeed?

According to Meuret (1988) Smith's account of political economy succeeded in imposing itself 'because it offered through a redefinition of the economy and the state, new rules of the game to its players: the State, capitalism and the public' (p. 52). He treats this almost as a 'diplomatic' treaty, but it is not just political, because it was a compromise which each had to accept in order to be protected against the other two. It is a way of conceiving and perceiving the world so that people can live together politically *and* economically. Smith did not found political economy, but 'Smith founded a city, our own, in which this science is possible and necessary. Political economy is the story on which this city is founded, its "myth of origins" if you like . . .' (Meuret, 1988, p. 53). Through a new representation of the economy, Smith offered a new legitimation of the State, of its role in relation to commerce and capitalism, and of its role in its relations with its citizenry. At the time it was the best place to be accepted by the major players: the State, capitalism and citizens.

The State, then, is realigned by Smith in terms of governmentality. The State, instead of trying to organise the economy and to domesticate commerce in its own interest, or to form an alliance with commerce, is to be domesticated. It is redefined so as to prevent it being contaminated by commerce and to prevent it from entering too far into the affairs of citizens. Smith's solution is to abandon political conformity and to redefine the economy, particularly the internal economy, to present it as essentially the political and not merely concerned with commerce, and to present it as a *dynamic* and *individualistic* form of order. No longer is it the State that regulates on matters of order and disorder but *the public citizenry*. 'It is the public, as a collection of individuals, which restores [order] and also, as a set of social groups defending their interests against the interests of others, which produces deviations from it [namely, disorder]' (Meuret, 1988, p. 63). Smith's appeal here is clearly to man's desire to better his material condition which can be fulfilled by the free-market conditions outlined in *The Wealth of Nations*. Thus the criterion for judging the State from Smith's view of political economy becomes that of the improvement overall of the material conditions of society. If, for Smith, it was not the general progress of the 'being' of man, he did not however subscribe to the notion of the *minimal state* exemplified by modern neo-liberalism (Nozick, 1974).

But offering the account is not enough. This still does not answer *how* language had the effects that it had. To treat the emergence of modern neo-liberalism as based essentially upon a treaty (Meuret) is to treat the State as non-threatening to individuals because, in the notion of a treaty, the State's power is not drawn from itself but from the notion of a freely negotiated treaty or settlement. Furthermore, it seems to treat individual persons as autonomous. Foucault, rather differently, sees modern government as dependent upon its rationality of state but that this may need its *acceptance* as *truth* by the governed. However, if both Foucault and Meuret see the modern individual as *manipulable*, how has *language* had these effects?

Language as Performative

Neither Meuret in his article nor Foucault in general broach the necessary hard philosophical questions about language to answer their question. They do not in these sources consider philosophically the performative aspects of language. Foucault raises them only to leave them (Foucault, 1976). Thus whilst he sees that 'discourse is, with respect to the relation of forces, not merely a surface of inscription, but something that brings about effects' (1976, p. 124), he sees the study of discourse 'as ways of conquering, of producing events, of producing decisions, of producing battles, of producing victories' (1974, p. 539).

Foucault is sensitive then to Anglo-Saxon analytic philosophy and to the force or effects of language—that language is not merely used to describe. Whilst he was aware of the work of Wittgenstein on language and philosophy, and of John Searle (on speech acts—for example, Searle [1965]), he does not appear to turn explicitly to sources such as Austin (1962) where the performative use of language is extensively discussed. It may have been profitable for him to have done so.

In returning to Austin's (1962) notion of performative utterances I wish to consider the performative nature of statements made in educational institutions when, in characterising people in various ways we constitute them as people of a certain kind. Does Austin's (1962) work help us to understand the later work of those like Foucault who see the self as being constituted in certain ways? My argument (Marshall, 1999) is that it does, for we were offered conceptual tools some two decades ago for understanding how selves might be constituted as subjects of performativity.

Briefly, for here Austin's approach to performatives is to draw a distinction between constatives and performatives (1962, Chapter 1). Essentially, constatives are true or false. (The term differs from 'statement' or 'description' or 'fact', and is more like 'utterance'). In contrast to constatives, the category of the performative is used for utterances which do not describe, report or constate, that is, are neither true nor false. Here the utterance is a part of doing an action and not a mere saying of something. Thus 'I do' (uttered in a wedding ceremony), 'I name this ship the *Queen Elizabeth*' (said as smashing the bottle against the bow of a ship at launching) are seen as examples of the performative category (ibid., p. 5).

Furthermore, within the performative category Austin (op. cit.) draws distinctions between the locutionary, illocutionary and perlocutionary aspects of language. Briefly, these three correspond respectively to the utterance of a 'statement' which is to do something in the very utterance (provide a description, make a report, etc.), to doing something else in making that utterance ('I warned him that . . .'), and to bring about something different by making the utterance ('I do'). Some statements, such as descriptions, are either true or false and are locutionary acts—'roughly equivalent to uttering a certain sentence with a certain sense and reference, which again is roughly equivalent to "meaning" in the traditional sense' (ibid., p. 108). But other statements, whilst having a similar grammatical structure, actually involve an act of doing something and are illocutionary. In uttering the 'statement', 'I do', something else in addition to saying something occurs—it is part of the act of marriage. Similarly, in christening a ship by smashing a bottle of champagne on its bows and uttering' I name this ship *Queen Elizabeth*' I am not merely saying something but doing something. Other illocutionary acts are 'informing, ordering, warning, undertaking, i.e., utterances which have a certain (conventional) force' (ibid.). Finally, for the third class, perlocutionary, by saying something I may bring about or achieve something, 'such as convincing, persuading, deterring, surprising' (ibid.) that is, change a person by convincing, persuading, etc. I can of course get a person to do something else by saying, for example, 'Watch the cliff' because I may not only warn a person (illocutionary act) but 'get' them to change direction away from the edge—this is an indirect consequence of my illocutionary act of warning but it is not a perlocutionary act. Indeed, my warning may have been successful as an illocutionary act though the person concerned did not move back from the cliff because, for example, whilst warned, the person did not see the situation as sufficiently dangerous to move back. Austin concentrated on illocutionary acts to distinguish them, as far as possible, from the other two categories.

In addition, within performative verbs Austin (1970) identifies a class of cases where 'we deliver verdicts and make estimates and appraisals of various kinds' (p. 244). These are, he says, 'straightforward utterances with ordinary verbs in the first person present indicative active that couldn't possibly be true or false' (ibid., p. 235). From above, these are the sorts of statements used in the classification of people in Foucault's disciplinary institutions: 'I find you are guilty (failing, inadequate, etc.)' is a verdict: 'I grade you as A', is an appraisal; and, 'I estimate (think, hope) that you will be an "A" student' is an estimate. Now these are not mere descriptions or reports, and they are not true or false—as performatives are to be characterised by Austin, because they involve judgements, estimates and appraisals in fields which, in general, are constituted by rules and conventions. Austin talks of the conventional force of such statements because they are made by professionals in institutions which have certain purposes or functions. But importantly he does not develop the notion of the force of performatives.

Finally, according to Austin there must be an accepted conventional procedure which permits the situation in which certain words (such as 'I do') count as performing the act of marriage—this is to include the particular persons (that they are not already married, for example) and the circumstances (for example, that their 'partner' is not of the opposite sex, or it is not said in an appropriate approved place or site). Moreover, for the act to be 'proper' (or happy, or felicitous, in Austin's discussion), the participants should have the right intentions, feelings and attitudes towards the act and its consequences—otherwise, for example, the act of marriage is not consummated or becomes null and void because participants do not conduct themselves accordingly. This of course represents many ways in which the act of marriage, as a doing, can 'fail'—legally for various reasons, or because of bad faith on behalf of one or other of the participants.

In such a manner then Austin distinguishes broadly between 'statements' which are descriptive, or (mere?) reports, and statements in which, by uttering certain words, one does something else, over and above the mere utterance of words. Austin tries to identify performatives by the use of the first person 'I', the 'active' and the present tense; and sometimes by the addition of the term 'hereby'. Thus 'I do', 'I promise', 'I warn' seem to get into the net, and in their third person equivalent on signed notices and documents.

Conclusion

The conclusion is that, important as both of these genealogies of Foucault and Meuret are, their own central questions as to *how* such discourses and their internal utterances have effects upon people, remain in part unanswered. How Smith's political economy, and of course its modern neo-liberal equivalent, came to be 'accepted' still remains unclear without some philosophical analysis of language effects such as that advanced by John Austin. But there are two important implications here for education (at the least). First, as this paper has argued, a genealogical analysis of the state of neo-liberal theories in education suggests that their applications in modern educational theory are suspect in so far as they are based upon *homo economicus,* as they are not the natural or unequivocal outcome of the emergence of economic theory? *Homo economicus* was a contested and disputed notion. Second, more attention needs to be made to the *performative* aspects of language in education research and theory (for a discussion of this and Lyotard's notion of performativity see Marshall, 1999).

Note

1 An amended version of a paper read at the American Association for Research in Education Annual Conference, New Orleans, 24 April, 2000.

References

Austin, J.L. (1962) *How to do things with words* (Oxford, Oxford University Press).
Austin, J.L. (1970) *Philosophical Papers* (2nd Edn) (Oxford, Oxford University Press).
Berlin, I. (1969) *Four Essays on Liberty* (Oxford, Oxford University Press).
Dumont, L. (1976) *Homo Aequalis* (Paris, Gallimard).
Ferguson, A. (1966) *An Essay on the History of Civil Society* (Edinburgh, Edinburgh University Press, with an Introduction and Edited by Duncan Forbes. Original publication 1767).
Forbes, D. (1966) 'Introduction', Adam Smith 1966. *An Essay on the History of Civil Society* (Edinburgh, Edinburgh University Press), pp. xiii–xli.
Foucault, M. (1974) Pour 'Rhetoriser' La Philosophie, in: D. Defort & F. Ewald (1994) (Eds) *Dits et Écrits, 1954–1988,* Vol. 2 (Paris, Gallimard).
Foucault, M. (1976) Le Discours Ne Doit Pas Être Pris Comme, in: D. Defort & F. Ewald (1994) (Eds) *Dits et Écrits, 1954–1988,* Vol. 3 (Paris, Gallimard).

Foucault, M. (1979) Pour une morale de l'Incomfort, *Le Nouvel Observateur,* in: D. Defort & F. Ewald (1994) (Eds) *Dits et Écrits, 1954–1988,* Vol. 5 (Paris, Gallimard).

Foucault, M. (1980) *The History of Sexuality,* Vol. 1 (New York, Vantage).

Gordon, C. (1991) Governmental Rationality: An Introduction in: G. Burchell, C. Gordon & P. Miller (Eds) *The Foucault Effect: Studies in Governmentality* (Chicago, The University of Chicago Press).

Hacking, I. (1981) The Archaeology of Michel Foucault, *New York Review of Books,* 14 May, pp. 32–37.

Hayek, F.A. (1947) *Collectivist Economic Planning: critical studies on the possibility of socialism* (London, Routledge).

Hayek, F. (1968) *The Confusion of Language in Political Thought, with some suggestions for remedying it* (London, Institute of Economic Affairs).

Marshall, J.D. (1996) The Autonomous Chooser and 'Reforms' in Education, *Studies in Philosophy and Education,* 15(1), pp. 89–96.

Marshall, J.D. (1999) Performativity: Lyotard and Foucault through Searle and Austin, *Studies in Philosophy and Education,* 18(5), pp. 309–317.

Meuret, D. (1988) A Political Genealogy of Political Economy, in: M. Gane & T. Johnson (1993) (Eds) *Foucault's New Domains* (London & New York, Routledge).

Nozick, R. (1974) *Anarchy, State, Utopia* (Cambridge, MA, Harvard University Press).

Searle, J. (1965) What is a Speech Act?, in: M. Black (Ed.) *Philosophy in America* (London, George Allen and Unwin).

Skinner, A. (1969) Introduction, *The Wealth of Nations,* Bks I–III (Harmondsorth, Penguin).

Smith, A. (1969) *The Wealth of Nations,* Books I–III (Harmondsworth, Penguin).

Chapter 4

The Labouring Sleepwalker
Evocation and Expression as Modes of Qualitative Educational Research

Paul Smeyers

Reprinted by permission of Taylor & Francis Ltd, http://www.tandfonline.com, on behalf of © Philosophy of Education Society of Australasia.

Editors' Introduction

The question about the relationship between language and world, between a narrative and reality, leads thinkers to the concepts of 'expression' and 'evocation' which profoundly characterize human existence both ethically and aesthetically. Smeyers' chapter deals with the highly personal way in which an individual makes sense of the world in a way that avoids the pitfalls of so-called private language. For Wittgenstein following a rule can never mean just following another rule, though we do follow rules blindly. His idea of the 'form of life' elicits that 'what we do' refers to what we have learnt, to the way in which we have learnt it and to how we have grown to find it self-evident. But the reference to the 'bedrock', to what was originally learnt, is the only kind of situation for which it makes sense to ask whether the meaning of a concept is correctly stated. Dialogue, conversation, and exchange of ideas are the right ways to characterize all the other situations. The challenge of Wittgenstein's philosophy is therefore that of a balance of the individual and the community, of language and the world. His insistence on the third person (or the intersubjective level) is countered by the importance he gives to everyone's personal stance: persons must speak for themselves and do what they can do. Given the growing interest for the kind of educational research focused on the 'personal', Smeyers takes up the challenge to see how 'language' works, here and elsewhere. By making clear what it does for us, it will gradually become clear how this kind of research may itself have to be reinterpreted.

> I'll teach you differences.
>
> —King Lear; from the correspondence between
> Wittgenstein and Drury, in R. Rhees (ed.)
> *Recollections of Wittgenstein* (1984)

Introduction

Jim Marshall and I met first in 1990 at the second Conference of the International Network of Philosophers of Education (INPE) in London. Since then I have benefited enormously from the numerous discussions we had at the occasion of the projects we were both involved in or the conferences we attended. We share an interest in Wittgenstein and Nietzsche, in postmodern authors, in philosophy and philosophy of education, and in each other's company, and above all in long discussions in which Jim would point me to one two simple things which often throw a whole new light on what we are talking about. His philosophical craftsmanship and strength really lies in the intellectual honesty to search again and again for what is presupposed in this or that argument, and where it will lead us thus combining the very best of the Nietzschean and Wittgensteinian legacy with courage of Foucault.

He and I were always captivated by Wittgenstein's 'theory of meaning' and the possibilities generated for philosophy in general, and for philosophy of education in particular. But, we were also aware of the fact that there is more than one interpretation of his works. Indeed, they can be placed on a scale with at one end an emphasis on the importance of an actual (linguistic) community and, at the other end, a contrasting position of the possibility of giving personal (and maybe new) meaning to situations and phenomena. Both are dangerous: if the touchstone of meaning in the end is the community to which one belongs, there is a threat of conservatism and conformism—as the possible meaning is limited to the hitherto existing meaning; on the other hand if the touchstone is the individual, one has to delineate the boundaries of meaning so that not 'anything goes'. Jim has always been more receptive to the threat posed by the existing order, than I have been, which at least partly explains his interest in Foucault and in analyses of the neo-liberal society and an educational system that embraced that. Hence his penetrating critique of 'output' and 'performativity' that rules in New Zealand and elsewhere. Not only meaning and understanding, but *significance and relevance,* and therefore how power is distributed and dealt with in society, are at stake.

In this paper I chose to focus on the other arm of the opposition and will deal with the highly personal way an individual makes sense of the world in a way that avoids the pitfalls of the so-called private language. For Wittgenstein following a rule can never mean just following another rule, though we do follow rules blindly. His idea of the 'form of life' elicits that 'what we do' refers to what we have learnt, to the way in which we have learnt it and to how we have grown to find it self-evident. But the reference to the 'bedrock', to what was originally learnt, is however the only kind of situation for which it makes sense to ask whether the meaning of a concept is correctly stated. Dialogue, conversation, and exchange of ideas are the right ways to characterize all the other situations. The challenge of Wittgensteinian philosophy is therefore that of a balance of the individual and the community, of language and the world. His insistence on the third person (or the intersubjective level) is countered by the importance he gives to each individual's personal stance: persons must speak for themselves and do what they *can* do. Given the growing interest for the kind of educational research where the 'personal' is focused on, I will try to take up the challenge to see how here as elsewhere 'language' works. By making clear what it does for us, it will gradually become clear how this kind of research may itself have to be reinterpreted.

Disturbing the Unified Picture of Research

Within social sciences the qualitative approach enjoys a new *élan*. Witness to this are the many studies within sociology and psychology, as well as within the educational sciences. Particularly as regards research concerning schools and educational policy, it can be argued that for the major part of this kind of research within the U.S.A.—where, incidentally, one finds the largest concentration—the qualitative approach is the dominant paradigm. There are different methods used within this kind of research in educational contexts: participatory observation, narrative and biographical research and action research as well as clinical interviews, case studies and analysis of experiences. Setting aside the differences between these ways of investigating a particular reality, there are some presuppositions which are shared by all of them, in general: that it is not meaningful to speak of a world which is independent of or separated from the subject; that child rearing and education are primarily concerned with individuals and the way they make sense of the world; that knowledge of the particular rather than knowledge of the universal is to be aimed at. The legitimacy of these presuppositions can be made more explicit within an anthropological (Taylor) and an epistemological frame (Wittgenstein). But this point of departure also generates a number of problems: the degree of universality of the insights, the meaningfulness of this kind of enquiry, the differentiation between argumentation and evocation and what should be understood by the improvement of a particular practice. These problems emerge preeminently within narrative educational research where a narrative is central and is explicitly recognized as a 'story', problems which are furthermore similar to those one is confronted with in other kinds of qualitative research. Is the result something still to be called 'science' or is it no more than 'expression'? And is what one envisages with research a kind of evocation? Does one not presuppose without good reason that there is more coherence in someone's personal story than actually is the case?

This directs us to a first question, whether the enigmatic nature of narrative inquiries can be further elucidated by Wittgenstein and Taylor. By indicating the limits of our dwelling on reality (whether through empirical or philosophical research) and what occurs in novels and poems, the attention is focused on language, on expression and evocation themselves. What exactly is the role of each and every individual? How does she find a balance between what expression constructively contributes, and what is 'given', the passive element in all of this. Another question I want to ask concerns the manner in which contemporary literary theory reflects on the language of literature itself as a particular kind of expression and evocation of human existence. With this in mind, the debate within literary theory is scrutinized with a view to confronting the lines of force within the debate that concerns the nature of narrative (or qualitative) educational research. The question about the relationship between language and world, between a narrative and reality leads us to the concepts 'expression' and 'evocation' which profoundly characterize human existence both ethically and aesthetically. A further issue that comes up here concerns the vicissitudes of these concepts (and to what realisations they give occasion) within the educational literature. Finally one is confronted with the question of whether the resistance encountered in the realm of literature is analogous to the resistance of an educational practice. In other words, whether this practice too, and necessarily so, escapes the 'surview' research wants to offer. Ultimately this leads to an investigation of the consequences of the fact that qualitative research can be heterogeneous and produce different (kinds of) results presented in various ways, for the nature of educational research.

Evidently, what will be offered in this paper cannot be more than a number of sketches of landscapes which were made in the course of my own journeying of how I came to see the problems qualitative research confronts us with—to paraphrase Wittgenstein (cf. Wittgenstein, 1953, p. vii). It provides, one could say, a rationale of a 'new' way of looking at educational research. There too, 'A *picture* held us captive. And we could not get outside it, for it lay in our language and language seemed to repeat it to us inexorably.' (Wittgenstein, 1953, I, §115)

The Philosophical Framework for Qualitative Educational Research

The starting point of this research is the unity of 'language-and-the-world' as expressed by Wittgenstein in his later work through the concept of the *'form of life'*. At the basis of it one finds those fundamental presuppositions which support our speaking and acting on the epistemological, ethical, religious and metaphysical level. Language-games (which consist of particular expressions and activities) belong to a form of life. These translate as it were the context principle. Only within a language-game can one speak of justification, of evidence and proof, of errors, of good and bad reasoning, correct and wrong ways of measuring. This is the reason why we will always take the learning context into account in order to understand the meaning of a word. A radical separation between 'what is' (a state of affairs) and 'what is said about this' is not possible. Values and norms affect 'what is said by us' and refer to 'what is important for us'. Using the work of Charles Taylor (1985a and b; 1989; 1991) the Wittgensteinian third person perspective will be given shape at the level of the individual and from there the task of a social science will be elaborated.

For Charles Taylor:

> to be a full human agent, to be a person or self in the ordinary meaning, is to exist in a space defined by distinctions of worth. A self is a being for whom certain questions of category value have arisen, and received at least partial answers. Perhaps they have been given authoritatively by the culture

more than they have been elaborated in the deliberation of the person concerned, but they are his in the sense that they are incorporated into his self-understanding, in some degree and fashion.

(Taylor, 1985a, p. 3)

A 'naturalistic' interpretation is for him necessarily limited, as it has no eye for this interpretation of oneself and refuses, by the use of a neutral scientific language, to place the human being against the background of value distinctions. Thus an emotion such as 'shame' shows us that 'what we are ashamed of' is only conceivable within a form of life in which there is a striving for dignity, a life between others to whose respect one aspires. This is the reason why man cannot understand himself as an object between other objects: '*verstehen*' is his mode of being. In order to indicate the meaning which is present in our acting, Taylor uses the concept of 'practice': at this level there is a particular vision of the actor, a relationship towards others and society and there are furthermore implicit norms which have to be met. The task of social science is to bring clarity into these practices. A successful interpretation clarifies a meaning which is confused, fragmented, strange, puzzling, contradictory or present in a vague form and has to 'improve' that practice. But a theory of the human sciences 'only' rarely makes an actual practice explicit, in other words the understanding of those involved. A strong motive for theory construction but also for their adoption is the fact that our implicit understanding is in one way or another inadequate or mistaken. Theories enlarge, criticize and challenge our understanding. Of course, it can never just be a matter of applying these results (as in the case of the natural sciences). The practice we speak about has as its central element the understanding of those who are involved. Only in qualitative research is it possible to do justice to the subject as subject, and thus not to reduce it to an object.

The task of the social sciences as this is conceived by Taylor is analogous to Wittgenstein's understanding of the aim of philosophy. In its most general and positive form this aim is to offer an *Übersicht, surview* or *perspicuous representation*. This can only be achieved by a patient investigation of the way sentences and expression are 'applied' and of their rule-governed connections. Philosophy should not be involved with metaphysical propositions in order to express the essence of something; there are no new facts to be discovered, only new insights in old facts. Thus to recall the particular is THE method for every philosophical investigation: its result is also referred to as a new way of looking at things (cf. Wittgenstein, 1953, I, §401). Wittgenstein pointed out that giving reasons in philosophy can be compared with giving reasons in aesthetics. One may speak of a debate, but this does not lead to conclusions; rather, its function is to make those involved sensitive to the way something can be appreciated (cf. Moore, 1955). And where he describes his method he speaks of 'giving examples'. Such a philosophy may be written as a poetic composition (cf. Wittgenstein, 1980, p. 82). The descriptive method and the understanding Wittgenstein attributes to philosophy can also be applied to the human sciences. Besides a hypothesis which can explain a particular behaviour by indicating how different phenomena are explained by each other, one can make explicit the way one understands a particular practice. The difference lies in what one aspires to, what one is interested in. The perspicuous representation in the human sciences makes it possible to understand in the sense of 'seeing connections'. At other places he speaks of '*putting things side by side*'. What does this mean for the educational context?

What has been claimed concerning social science within this framework immediately applies to an empirical educational science. The theory will describe and challenge. It is the task of philosophy of education to make the grammar explicit: the presuppositions of the actual educational language and the contours of an educational question. Besides indicating demonstrable fallacies, mistaken arguments and inconceivable or unacceptable presuppositions, there is first of all the offering of an interpretation which can only evoke or speak to someone by making explicit the reasons which carry someone's *engagement*. But it will be clear that it is not all the same what is philosophically argued; to put this more precisely, it needs to be carried by the intersubjective level. Where it concerns empirical research within a Wittgensteinian framework, the determination of what is the case will assume precedence in order to reach an *Übersicht*. The focus of philosophy of education will be on the justification, of what is the case in a particular way but of which it is also accepted that it could have been different. Clearly, on both levels the focus is on the particular.

Thus far I have given an overview of the general framework. Discussions concerning this belong to the heart of every philosophical approach, but it is important to indicate that in the social sciences (and also within educational sciences—cf. among others Pring, 2000), these discussions have always claimed an important place (cf. Elster, 1989; 1999; Hempel, 1965; Hollis, 1994; Kincaid, 1996; Martin & McIntyre, 1994; Winch, 1958). Besides the indicated embeddedness within the Anglo-Saxon context, it needs to be underscored that the nature of research itself has also been a central concern within the continental tradition (such as within phenomenology or critical theory—see for an initial overview of the literature Levering, 2001; Masschelein, 2001; Carr & Kemnis, 1986).

Evidently, the positions concerning philosophical or empirical research within the tradition of Wittgenstein and Taylor also confront us with a number of problems. For the time being I accept that though they cannot be separated, they can at least be distinguished. Among the most important problems are the degree to which results can be generalized and, combined with this; the nature of research itself, the possibility of distinguishing evocation and argumentation, and last but not least what is to be understood by an improvement of a particular practice. These problems can be illustrated by qualitative educational research. By way of example I have chosen narrative analysis.

A Paradigmatic Example: Possibilities and Pressing Problems for Narrative Analysis in Educational Research

According to Polkinghorne (1995, pp. 5–7) narrative research distinguishes itself from other kinds of qualitative research by the use of diachronic data. Contrary to synchronic data this is material that is characterized by a particular evolution in time or a developmental perspective. There is a starting point in the past and a progress in time which leads to the actual state. Polkinghorne (1995) uses '*narrative inquiry*' as the broad term in which he distinguishes between an '*analysis of narratives*' and '*narrative analysis*'. In the '*analysis of narratives*' the researcher assembles stories and then looks for common themes within them. This is a paradigmatic approach because it aims to allocate the assembled cases to different categories. In order to achieve this one looks for characteristics which are common to the different cases, thus making abstraction from the particular. The degree to which one uses existing theories may be different. The aim is not only to discover and describe classes of cases, but also to indicate relations between them. Thus the reality becomes easier to survey, though this is at the cost of what makes some things unique, or by ignoring context data. In '*narrative analysis*', on the contrary, one wants to understand a particular case not by allocating it to a broader category, but by highlighting its particularity. One does not make abstraction of its uniqueness, but tries precisely to show it as a particular story. The data used here are not exclusively story-like. Information can be gathered from various sources (transcriptions of interviews, diaries, policy documents, reports of observations, notes of fieldwork, etc.). In the process of writing the report the researcher relates the events and activities to each other by presenting them as contributing to the development of a plot, i.e. the narrative structure which indicates how the different events form part of a certain outcome. During the process of writing, the researcher appeals to his expertise in the discipline. The resulting story does not only have to correspond with the data, but at the same time it has to reveal a particular kind or order and meaningfulness which as such was not clear before. This result should therefore not be seen as a report of what actually happened from an objective point of view, but instead as the result of consecutive constructions. It is thus evident that at least in principle more than one story can be written and that almost every researcher might write a different one. Thus justice is done to the multifariousness of reality, but at the same time this raises problems about the nature of research, in its most radical form phrased as whether this is really still research.

In the present context, theoretical justification (both for the use of narrative materials and for what one does with them) is often sought by referring to the writing of Paul Ricoeur. According to this author personal identity has to be understood after the model of a story. Only thus can it be guaranteed that someone remains identical. According to Ricoeur our lives are a quest for a narrative identity to be acquired by 'applying' models which are passed on to us by the culture we share. But the subject cannot autonomously give shape to her identity; the intersubjective context takes precedence. Not only does it start by means of language—which is foremost the language of the others—but the individual is also already part of the stories told (about her) by the others, which sets limits to the composition of one's narrative identity. Therefore, to tell a story becomes according to Ricoeur (1991a, p. 30) a secondary process which is grafted on our being entrapped in stories. Ricoeur tries to show through his dealing with the so-called threefold mimesis that there is a necessary connection between the activity of telling a story and the temporal character of human experience. In Mimesis 1, acting is understood from our acquaintance with the conceptual network and symbolic mediation and presupposes an acknowledgement of temporal structures; here what is at stake is a kind of implicit understanding we have of human activities and their temporal character. Mimesis 2 is understood as '*mise en intrigue*' which mediates between separate events and history as a whole and which brings together divergent elements such as actors, aims, means etc. and takes care that concord conquers discord, in other words, that unexpected things are integrated in the plot. What is involved here is the process of emplotment ('*mise en intrigue*'), the stage in which the events are brought together in the composition of the story. Finally, and of the utmost relevance too for the further use of Ricoeur within the context of educational research, there is Mimesis 3: through the intersection of the world of the text and the listener the story gains the power to open the horizon of possible experience; the process of composition of the configuration does not occur within the text but within the mind of the reader. New evaluations of reality are possible through the emancipation from the ordinary. The meaning of a story is generated by the intersection of the world of the text and the world of the listener or reader. Through this a reconfiguration of life by the story becomes a possibility. Through stories in which there is necessarily a plot (cf. Mimesis 2, a subcategory of 'texts') and thus not through immediate intuition, it is for Ricoeur at least partially possible to understand human existence (including the way one understands oneself). The result is not a substantial but a narrative identity.

But again we are confronted with a crucial problem which concerns the ambiguous nature of reality. I will not deal here with Ricoeur's wrestling with the problem of reference (for instance the metaphorical in history and fiction) called '*refiguration*' in his later work; it is remarkable however that he does not want to take sides in the dichotomy between fiction and 'what is real' and because of that he cannot offer a satisfactory solution for the problem of reference. Ricoeur's enticing analysis moreover conceals an important presupposition, namely the extent to which the self can appear as transparent to herself. To put this more simply and immediately within the context of research: telling a story about oneself urges one to force the elements in the contours of a plot, compelling them in spite of everything into a whole. That our acting is intelligible, that it can be spoken of as a unity, seems to contradict, however, the fact that we sometimes do things which just don't make sense. Indeed, things sometimes appeal to us, we are moved, fascinated, do things against our better judgement, and for this there seems to be hardly any place within such a paradigm of relative transparency. Yet it seems that the kind of research we are envisaging exactly presupposes that there is such a place within a unity, that it can and even must be there. This is more important than may appear at first sight, for if our actions (perhaps our most important activities) have to be characterized in this rather passive manner, then this puts severe constraints on the possibility of using stories in order to understand what people do. Again we are confronted with the radical question of to what extent there is more than ever-renewed expression, more than just making explicit the meaning of something, and this immediately challenges the legitimacy of any research in the human sciences.

These fundamental questions are also raised where empirical educational researchers discuss the nature of *analysis of narratives* or *narrative analysis*. Thus Waite (1994) claims that choosing narrative research may be an easy way out because one simply registers the stories of those involved and reports them, accepting that they can offer an interpretation of their own world (p. 14). Connelly and Clandinin, two important writers in this field, are not at ease either. They admonish that however liberating and emancipatory '*narrative inquiry*' may seem, it ought to contribute to the functioning of a particular practice and cannot just lead to a confirmation of the status quo (1992). For Goodson (1995) too, working with stories is only a starting point. Stories must be seen and judged as social constructions which enable us to localize and question the social context in which they find their place. Through such socio-philosophical analysis the focus is shifted which raises new questions. D. C. Phillips claims that in narrative research epistemology has been blown away and replaced by politics (1993, p. 4). And though he recognizes the sometimes justifiable political ambitions, this in his eyes is not an argument to dictate that a story must be accepted as credible or that it as such deserves a central place in educational research. Stories have to be epistemologically respectable. This can be seen as a different interest. Thus Connelly and Clandinin hope that narrative research will contribute to the relationship between theory and practice and that the institutional anchoring will change what they call the professional knowledge contexts. From this perspective it is understandable that they propose '*an engaging plot*' as a criterion. It is indeed imaginable that a good, moving story has a strong evocative power and because of that urges more easily to change than a sound but dull research report. But Phillips (1993) rejects criteria such as '*adequacy*', '*plausibility*' and '*an engaging plot*' because they are according to him scientifically and epistemologically irrelevant. This becomes more concrete where the consequences are discussed of the narrative approach concerning the relationship between theory and practice in the field of teacher training. A radicalisation of the idea of the personal story character of teaching may lead to a rejection of every generalization connected with education. All generalizations are then marked as distortions of 'real' stories of teachers and as collaborations with the ruling class which tries to subject the teachers. Carter (1993) warns that to over-emphasise what something means for a particular teacher may imply that these stories turn out to be relevant only for the person who wrote them, and moreover that an idolization of the 'voice of the teacher' gives these stories a kind of authenticity which is simply not justified. She shares the opinion of Elbaz (1991) who claims that teachers are not privileged authors who somehow enjoy direct access to the truth and who are the only ones who control the possibility of telling the whole story. The recognizability which naturally explains the attraction of narrative research and its possible impact on educational practice is thus confronted with some fundamental questions.

To sum up, the paradigmatic thinker searches for what is common and by doing that indisputably slights the particular. The narrative solution, on the contrary, does justice to the uniqueness of every subject. Narrative educational research, however, leads to new questions such as whether what is offered is more than just the construction of the researcher, or whether the rejection of the positivist paradigm also entails abandoning all the generally accepted criteria for scientific research. Narrative educational research gives occasion to questions which are analogous to those brought to the forefront by the framework of Wittgenstein and Taylor. Wittgenstein points at the groundlessness of that in which we are embedded through the language-games belonging to a form of life, but keeps an important place for the individual in all of this. But he is reticent about what the latter precisely implies. Where he speaks about the role of the human sciences, he 'only' refers to 'description' or to *a new way of looking at things*. He confronts us with *philosophy leaves everything as it is*, but the human being who might become different. Research too in some sense leaves everything as it is. It can offer clarity where there is vagueness, but, as Charles Taylor claims, it can also challenge us to see things differently. It can inspire us through Mimesis 3 to *a new way of looking at things* (another Wittgensteinian phrase which he sometimes uses to character-ize philosophy). But is this really more than taking notice of what is happening in order to understand what is going on? And if its aim is not to have control, why is it worthwhile at all? Is its result more than just a commentary on reality which is governed by its own rules and dynamism? Taylor's notion of a 'practice' incor-porates the idea of 'better', but he does not expand on what exactly this means. That the particular as it is embedded in the intersubjective plays an important role, goes without saying, but how exactly this has to be understood remains obscure. And if we accept that reality and truth is something that happens in which new things appear and others disappear and more generally if we accept *post-foundationalism,* is a theoretical reflection then more than just *Spielerei* and at the same time different from and more than *common sense*? Can something more be said than that it has to meet the requirement that it be interesting? This confronts us with the question whether and how a theoretical reflection, if it is indeed a kind of dwelling on reality, is fundamentally different from what is offered in novels and poems? These radical questions force us furthermore to think about the nature of expression and evocation. Can some further foothold be found elsewhere, and how should we address the problems at stake there?

The Limits of our Language and the Value of Narrative

In educational research what is at stake is the understanding of a particular reality brought to the fore by language: this presupposes that this reality can be understood and moreover that its intelligibility can at least partially be made explicit. But is that really the case? The focus on language is without doubt the primordial interest of twentieth century philosophy, though the mentioned presuppositions are not accepted by everyone. In the *Tractatus* Wittgenstein tried to indicate the boundary between what can be said and what can only be shown and he held the position that the limits of my language are the limits of my world (Wittgenstein, 1922, §5.6) and that the subject does not belong to the world but forms its limit (ibid., §5.632). He accepts the idea that the world consists of states of affairs which exist independently of each other. He holds the so-called *picture theory of language*: we make images of facts and the relationship between a fact and an image is one of similarity. A revelation of its form will give us the logical structure: 'Everything that can be thought at all can be thought clearly. Everything that can be put into words can be put clearly (Wittgenstein, 1922, §4.116). According to him every object must have a sign, but only objects may have it. If we want to speak about values and meaning this has to be sought outside of the world. Thus it follows in section 7 that, 'What we cannot speak about we must pass over in silence'. Though the presuppositions of the calculus model of language of the *Tractatus* will be rejected later, Wittgenstein remains faithful to his basic assumptions: that the real problems about our life do not belong to the world, that a solution for these must be sought outside of the facts (of the world), a solution which is labelled 'the mystical'. It concerns a particular way of seeing the world which indicates that what he has in mind is something that has to do with overcoming oneself, a personal struggle which everyone must engage in to find quietness and peace in the world. It is about working on oneself. By doing philosophy Wittgenstein tried himself to deal with his demons: 'Working in philosophy . . . is really more a working on oneself. On one's own interpretation. On one's way of seeing things. (And what one expects of them)' (1980, p. 16e—a remark from 1931).

   Language as a possible way of signifying (by expression and evocation) myself and the other, is, as already touched upon, not only an instrument of rational inquiry. It also figures in attempts to express human existence in its non-reducible plurality—the beautiful as a sanctuary of what is not yet tied, not yet given a particular shape. Words may comfort us, may appeal to us, or make us angry, can apologize, can express regret or remorse, may insult or support; one can thank someone (at the occasion of a farewell for instance) with beautiful words and one can thank others for such beautiful words. One can express oneself by what one says, by the particular manner of saying something. Words are given and at the same time we use them—everyone gives meaning to them. 'We talk, we utter words, and only *later* get a picture of their life' (Wittgenstein, 1953,

II, p. 209e) and Wittgenstein speaks about the '*feeling of meaning*'. The core of the conception of language of Wittgenstein's later work is that any attempt to say something is always partial, that it is always one-sided. No way of speaking, no doctrine whatsoever can control cultural practices and thus liberate us from the restlessness and incertitudes of the human existence, of the search for meaning in our life. He points to the fact that what we do can never be completely transparent, that it is always characterized to some extent by arbitrariness. Thus it becomes clear that in what we say we bear witness to what we long for, but also to what we are not certain of, how we try to express ourselves, try to be coherent. In an analogous way Cavell argues that we should not try to escape from the existential conditions we find ourselves in in order to look for false certainties, but urges us to be born continuously and thus to be mortal. In his *In Quest of the Ordinary: Lines of Skepticism and Romanticism* (1988) he maintains that, among other things, words in philosophy may create a distance. They allow us to start over and over again and thus generate an alliance with others who are also focused on this. Words may help us escape, but at the same time they create a home. Thus philosophy is engaged in a certain revision of the way one sees particular things and the philosopher may identify herself as someone who '*reviews her vision*', or else '*revises her reviews*', in a reflection of what one is conscious of.

The conceptualisation of social (and political) problems demands an ever-renewed rethinking of reality with similar instruments. To think again can only mean to think from a different point of view what one is trying to understand (perhaps change?). From the previous philosophical framework it will be clear that we can never be pleased with the investigation of what is already in existence. What is at stake shifts to what is at stake for someone (again for the other and for myself), where the other is recognized in her personal struggle as an emotional being—unstructured justice. Rigid approaches to social (and political) problems will have to be complemented by a more flexible ethical sensibility. Here it is no longer possible to ignore the recognition of emotions as an essential component of a comprehensive social rationality (Nussbaum, 1997): the message is to feel again. To see the other is to look for the way in which the other expresses herself, gives shape to herself in the struggle with herself. But to touch the other is also to confront the other with one's own struggle by means of the evocative instruments which are at my disposal. That we inevitably violate the other is clear enough. After all, the understanding of the other is at the same time a negation and a constitutive affirmation. We understand the other as an intentional object which we crave to understand. We want to read the story of the other, too often without recognizing the illegibility of her story. This does not necessarily imply that we would not be able or do not have to understand her. The reading of the story of the other is however at the same time a reading which is interfered with by my own story. What remains for us is to surrender to the intersection of this reading with its reader, and to what this does to us. As mentioned above, this insight has already been elaborated by Ricoeur, but the problems it gives occasion to have only partially been answered by him. It remains unclear how the other can confront us completely with her otherness.

A foothold may be found by investigating how the subject is part of the inter-subjective level. Wittgenstein's *Investigations* show the value of our freedom, of our autonomy, not as the exercise of an arbitrary choice, but as the result of the way in which nature as well as artistic products and moral responsibilities are taken seriously and even seen as necessary. He mocks those who are seduced by the promise to be able to control the cultural and who think they are able to rep-resent our thoughts and concepts as necessary. To write is for him to surrender to certain readings (words seen as 'what is given to us') and philosophy as the result of a 'play' of reading and writing on the basis of one's own authority. Or we are able to rethink a thought that comes our way, to possess it and to judge it, or to let it go; it does not belong to us. This kind of philosophy expresses one's own life or is futile. Cavell quotes Emerson: 'The simplest words—we do not know what they mean except when we love and aspire'. To understand their meaning we have to be in a certain mood (of the heart). We find ourselves and in the answer to the way we see ourselves we find a place to begin. We have to live this antagonism: hope and despair (Emerson's *odious facts*) and thus he quotes Wittgenstein approvingly: 'It is in language that an expectation and its fulfilment make contact' (Wittgenstein, 1953, I, §445). Cavell refers to the consolations of the word; to *this* meaning for the other; as a song; as sharing in the case of food and drink, to have in some sense the 'same' experience. Here, to write becomes a means to fight the struggle with oneself (with one's own language), and poetry a means to make a bridge. In the words of Cavell:

> that what we are is written all over us, or branded; but here especially the other way round, that our language contains our character, that we brand the world, as for example with the concept of Fate; and then listen again to such an idea as that one's character is one's fate. Now it says openly that language is our fate. It means hence that not exactly prediction, but diction, is what puts us in bonds, that with each word we utter we emit stipulations, agreements we do no know and do not want to know we have entered, agreements we were always in, that were in effect before our participation in them. Our relation to our language—to the fact that we are subject to expression and comprehension, victims of meaning—is accordingly a key to our sense of our distance from our lives, of our sense of the alien, of ourselves as alien to ourselves, thus alienated.
>
> (Cavell, 1988, pp. 39–40)

This feeling of desolation presupposes an expression of the struggle with one-self, presupposes expression as a kind of surrendering. The written word, the poem is a weapon in this struggle. It requires no other material presence; it does not want to explain; it only suggests seeing things in a particular way. It seems a 'means' to be at home for a moment, for the lonely individual, for the subject-with-the-others.

The continuance of Wittgenstein's legacy in the work of Cavell is accompanied by a remarkable intensification of the attention on literature. This forms the foothold for an investigation in which contemporary literary theory reflects on the notion of literary language as a special kind of expression or evocation of human existence. Most pertinent in the present context is the gradually growing research concerning the relationship of literature and ethics.* One of the most prominent advocates for the recognition of literary fiction as a privileged medium for moral education in a broad sense is Martha Nussbaum. Her insights in this context are, however, not welcomed unreservedly. From a philosophical perspective she encounters a kind of criticism which bears many resemblances with what one finds concerning narrative educational research (namely the reproach that a clear and justified argumentation is given up too quickly in favour of a rather too vague, evocative 'expression' of moral problems in particular stories). But questions are also raised on the part of literary theory concerning Nussbaum's instumentalisation of literary imagination for moral aims. Such questions are a part of an already long standing renewed interest in the relationship between ethics and literature where particular attention is paid to the role of narrative (cf. Geoffrey Galt Harpham (1992) and Adam Zachary Newton (1995); also the work of Robert Eaglestone, Jill Robbins, Derek Attridge and Rei Terada; see also the recent special issue on 'Objectivity in ethics, politics and aesthetics' of the leading journal *New Literary History,* 32:4; from a more philosophical point of view the work of Richard Eldridge and for an empirical examination of Nussbaum's narrativism from the perspective of literary studies, see Hakemulder). Here the question is also raised whether the case of literature may not in fact involve something else. Perhaps literariness has to be conceived as a kind of resistance to understanding, a resistance to a 'perspicuous representation' (and thus it may perhaps not fulfil the role attributed to it by authors such as Nussbaum, i.e. to evoke sympathy). Thus attention can be given to the work of literary authors such as T.S. Eliot, Banville and Swift. Here the focus is the liberation of literature from reality, its distance and proximity, the progressing emancipation of literature and language, intensified by the impossibility to entertain an unambiguous verifiable communication with the world, finally what this says about the individual and her kind of existence.

The debate within literary theory may be investigated in order to confront its lines of force with the debate concerning the nature of educational research. This line of inquiry has not yet been pursued and is not only innovative, but extremely relevant for qualitative educational research. Incidentally, it is especially remarkable that this path has as yet not been taken given the fact that the interpretation of a literary critic of a novel or poem is to a large extent analogous to the interpretation of a particular educational practice. Granted, a careful distinction needs to be made between literary stories as instruments within a broadly understood educational context and stories as documents resulting from or about a more strictly specified educational situation. This distinction, however, does not diminish in any sense the pertinence of a critical investigation into the functioning of literary stories for the criticism of narrative educational research. This kind of research finds itself, whether it likes it or not, in a postmodern condition where stories resist the latent omnipresence of a meta-narrative in which the particular is neutralized. The research within literary theory into narrative ethics is precisely an exploration of never-ending narrative resistance within the medium of narrative intensity *par excellence*—which could be called a perverse but important and necessary detour.

Education and Self-Expression and Their Relation to Educational Research

The question about the relationship between language and world, between a narrative and reality leads us to the concepts 'expression' and 'evocation' which profoundly characterize human existence both ethically and aesthetically. Thus one is confronted with the vicissitudes of these concepts (and to what realisations they give occasion to) within the educational literature. It should be possible on the basis of the outlined analysis to give these concepts a different place. A study could be made of the way 'expression' has been used in educational contexts and to what realisations this has led. Not only has the possible role of the aesthetic been contemplated in the context of bringing up children or of education (cf. among others Reid, Steiner), but also attention has been given to the experience of the child in the progressive and child-centred movement. There it has been explored what is required to enable children to express themselves, in other words what this demands of the organisation of the educational situation (cf. Rogers, Freire, Gordon and others). Subsequently, it could be investigated how this looks from the perspective of the later Wittgenstein (cf. Schulte for a psychological and Tilghman for an aesthetical angle) and integrated with the results of the previous analysis of the concepts of 'expression' and 'evocation'. And it can be worked out whether the resistance against understanding encountered in the realm of literature is akin to what is expressed by Lyotard's concept of 'event', which leads to the question whether there is an analogous resistance in an educational practice, whether it too eventually and necessarily escapes the 'surview' research wants to offer.

At first sight this resembles what is at stake where education is involved in thinking about plurality. There the starting-point is that it can no longer be held that the subject is autonomous first, after which it engages in relationships with others. The relationship with the other is, contrarily, constitutive of her own autonomy and thus takes precedence. What is questioned here is how a different relationship with others/otherness is possible if others have to be understood as (other) singularities; how the contact with others, with what is unfamiliar, can be learned, and how one can acquire the 'skill' to tolerate, endure and reshape difference, plurality, complexity and contingency; finally, how the experience of the limits of comprehensibility can be seen as an enrichment and not as a threat.

Thinking about the nature of a story may be a way to express this. On the one hand a story can be conceived as what joins people together, on the other hand as what can only 'show'. And if that is so, does education ultimately have to be conceived as an initiation into what is 'groundless'? And in that case can an educator and a student of this area do more than give expression to her story, and appeal to the *educandus* by what she holds to be constructive? If educational research can be heterogeneous and produce different (kinds of) results and moreover can be presented in various ways, if different stories can be told, will this eventually lead to the classical insight that in essence education is a matter of instilling a good disposition? Finally one is confronted with the question whether consequently educational research has to be conceived as another way to express this 'showing', as a mode of the will to join in this kind of speaking and doing: a conception which can be related to Taylor's stance concerning social sciences and enable us to characterize in a new way the nature of educational research.

Many educational researchers have been lying awake thinking about the world in order to find information that is 'useful'. Their dedication cannot be doubted. The dream of the labourer, to interpret 'what is the case' and by this knowledge to grasp 'what is predictable, what can be influenced' is, however, based upon a kind of thinking which is in need of reconsideration. '*The story* before bedtime' may offer a way out for the 'labouring sleepwalker'. Once it has been recognized that not everything can be understood, the human being can only be touched by the transcendent. One cannot *not* initiate the child. One cannot but initiate the child into one's own story. Woven into a growing network of stories, everyone articulates what she is (expression), everyone touches the other and is touched by her (evocation). That which touches is the other, with whom I am joined in an intersubjective manner, who expresses herself by what evocation is capable of. The one who says 'I' is only thanks to the other joined in what we are touched by, what cannot be said anymore, but only shown, that what is for us. And the story of the researcher—it may touch us as any other story, may invite us to tell a new, perhaps (partly) different tale, in which the thread is taken up again, the existence articulated and challenged.

Acknowledgement

*I am indebted to Ortwin De Graef of the Faculty of Arts, KULeuven for discussions I had with him concerning the relevance of literary theory for qualitative research in general and for numerous suggestions of particular works.

References

Attridge, D. (1999) Innovation, Literature, Ethics: Relating to the Other, *PMLA*, 114:1, pp. 20–31.
Bridges, D. & McNamee, M. (eds) (2001) The Ethics of Educational Research [Special issue], *Journal of Philosophy of Education*, 35:3.

Carr, W. & Kemnis, S. (1986) *Becoming Critical. Education, knowledge and action research* (London, The Falmer Press).

Carter, K. (1993) The Place of Story in the Study of Teaching and Teacher Education, *Educational Researcher*, 22, pp. 5–12, 18.

Cavell, S. (1988) *In Quest of the Ordinary* (Chicago, University of Chicago Press).

Cavell, S. (1990) *Conditions Handsome and Unhandsome* (Chicago, University of Chicago Press).

Cavell, S. (1994) *A Pitch of Philosophy* (Cambridge, MA, Harvard University Press).

Cavell, S. (1995) *Philosophical Passages: Wittgenstein, Emerson, Austin, Derrida* (Oxford, Blackwell).

Connelly, F. M. & Clandinin, D. J. (1992) *Asking Questions About Telling Teaching Stories.* Paper presented at the Annual Meeting of the American Educational Research Association.

Connelly, F. M. & Clandinin, D. J. (1997) Narrative Inquiry, in: J. P. Keeves (ed.), *Educational Research, Methodology, and Measurement: An international handbook* (Oxford, Pergamon) (pp. 81–86).

Eaglestone, R. (1997) *Ethical Criticism: Reading after Levinas* (Edinburgh, Edinburgh University Press).

Elbaz, F. (1991) Research on Teacher's Knowledge: The evolution of a discourse, *Journal of Curriculum Studies*, 23, pp. 1–19.

Eldridge, R. (1997) *Leading a Human Life. Wittgenstein, intentionality, and romanticism* (Chicago, University of Chicago Press).

Elster, J. (1989) *Nuts and Bolts for the Social Sciences* (Cambridge, Cambridge University Press).

Elster, J. (1999) *Alchemies of the Mind. Rationality and the emotions* (Cambridge, Cambridge University Press).

Freire, P. (1972) *Pedagogy of the Oppressed* (Harmondsworth, Penguin).

Goodson, I. F. (1995) The Story So Far: Personal knowledge and the political, *International Journal of Qualitative Studies in Education*, 8:1, pp. 89–98.

Gordon, T. (1975) *Parent Effectiveness Training: The tested new way to raise responsible children* (New York, Wyden).

Hakemulder, J. (2000) *The Moral Laboratory: Experiments examining the effects of reading literature on social perception and moral self-concept* (Amsterdam, John Benjamins).

Harpham, G. (1992) *Getting it Right: Language, literature and ethics* (Chicago, University of Chicago Press).

Hempel, C. (1965) *Aspects of Scientific Explanation* (New York, Free Press).

Hollis, M. (1994) *Philosophy of Social Science* (Cambridge, Cambridge University Press).

Kincaid, H. (1996) *Philosophical Foundations of the Social Sciences. Analyzing controversies in social research* (Cambridge, Cambridge University Press).

Levering, B. (2001) Van Fenomenologie naar Hemeneutiek, in: P. Smeyers en B. Levering (eds), *Grondslagen van de Wetenschappelijke Pedagogiek. Modern en postmodern* (Amsterdam, Boom) pp. 73–92.

Lyotard, J.-F. (1998) A propos du Différend. Entretien avec Jean-François Lyotard, *Les Cahiers de Philosophie*, 5.

Lyotard, J.-F. (1988) *The Inhuman: Reflections on time* (G. Bennington and R. Bowlby, trans.) (Cambridge, Polity).

Lyotard, J.-F. (1991) *Lectures d' Enfance* (Paris, Galilée).

Martin, M., & McIntyre, L. (eds) (1994) *Readings in the Philosophy of Social Science* (Cambridge, MA, MIT Press).

Masschelein, J. (2001) Kritische Theorie en Kritische Pedagogiek, in: P. Smeyers en B. Levering (eds), *Grondslagen van de Wetenschappelijke Pedagogiek. Modern en postmodern* (Amsterdam, Boom), pp. 93–111.

Moore, G. E. (1955) Wittgenstein's Lectures on Ethics, *Mind*, 64, pp. 1–27.

Newton, A. Z. (1995) *Narrative Ethics* (Cambridge, Harvard University Press).

Nussbaum, M. (1997) *Cultivating Humanity. A classical defense of reform in liberal education* (Cambridge, Harvard University Press).

Phillips, D. C. (1993) Gone with the Wind? Evidence, rigor and warrants in educational research, in: J. Tooley (ed.), *Papers of the Annual Conference of the Philosophy of Education Society of Great Britain* (Oxford, PESGB), pp. 4–11.

Phillips, D. C. (1997) Telling the Truth about Stories, *Teacher and Teacher Education*, 13, pp. 101–109.

Pring, R. (2000) The 'False Dualism' of Educational Research, *Journal of Philosophy of Education*, 34, pp. 247–260.

Polkinghorne, D. (1995) Narrative Configuration in Qualitative Analysis, *International Journal of Qualitative Studies in Education*, 8:1, pp. 5–23.

Ricoeur, P. (1991a) Life in Quest of Narrative, in: D. Wood (ed.), *On Paul Ricoeur. Narrative and interpretation* (London, Routledge), pp. 20–33.

Ricoeur, P. (1991b) Narrative Identity, in: D. Wood (ed.), *On Paul Ricoeur. Narrative and interpretation* (London, Routledge), pp. 188–199.

Robbins, J. (1999) *Altered Reading: Levinas and literature* (Chicago, University of Chicago Press).

Rogers, C. (1969) *Freedom to Learn. A view of what education might become* (Columbus, OH, Merrill).

Rhees R. (ed.) (1984) *Recollections of Wittgenstein* (Oxford, Oxford University Press).

Schulte, J. (1993) *Experience and Expression. Wittgenstein's philosophy of psychology* (Oxford, Clarendon Press).

Taylor, C. (1985a) *Philosophical Papers. Vol. 1. Human agency and language* (Cambridge, Cambridge University Press).

Taylor, C. (1985b) *Philosophical Papers: Vol. 2. Philosophy and the human sciences* (Cambridge, Cambridge University Press).

Taylor, C. (1989) *Sources of the Self. The making of the modern identity* (Cambridge MA, Harvard University Press).

Taylor, C. (1991) *The Ethics of Authenticity* (Cambridge MA, Harvard University Press).

Terada, R. (2001) *Feeling in Theory: Emotion after the 'Death of the Subject'* (Cambridge MA, Harvard University Press).

Tilghman, B. R. (1991) *Wittgenstein, Ethics and Aesthetics: The view from eternity* (Basingstoke, Macmillan).

Waite, D. (1994) Ethnography's Demise: What's next for narrative? Paper presented at the Annual Meeting of the American Educational Research Association, New Orleans.

Wittgenstein, L. (1922) *Tractatus Logico-Philosophicus* (D. Pears & B. F. McGuinness, trans.) (London, Routledge).

Wittgenstein, L. (1953) *Philosophical Investigations/Philosophische Untersuchungen* (G. E. M. Anscombe, trans.) (Oxford, Basil Blackwell).

Wittgenstein, L. (1979) Remarks on Frazer's Golden Bough, in: C. Luckhardt (ed.), *Wittgenstein: Sources and perspectives* (Hassocks, Sussex, The Harvester Press), pp. 61–81.

Wittgenstein, L. (1980) *Culture and Value/Vermischte Bemerkungen* (G. H. von Wright, ed.; P. Winch, trans.) (Oxford, Basil Blackwell).

Winch, P. (1958) *The Idea of a Social Science* (London, Routledge and Kegan Paul).

Chapter 5

The Learning Society, the Unfinished Cosmopolitan, and Governing Education, Public Health and Crime Prevention at the Beginning of the Twenty-First Century

Thomas S. Popkewitz, Ulf Olsson and Kenneth Petersson

Editors' Introduction

Popkewitz, Olsson and Petersson in this chapter indicate how society is governed in the name of a cosmopolitan ideal that, despite its universal pretensions, embodies particular inclusions and exclusions. These occur through inscribing distinctions and differentiations between the characteristics of those who embody a cosmopolitan reason that brings social progress and personal fulfilment and those who do not embody the cosmopolitan principles of civility and normalcy. Mapping the circulation of the notion of the 'learning society' in arenas of health, criminal justice and school reforms, examine the mode of life of the citizen of this society, the learner, as an 'unfinished cosmopolitanism' and also directs attention to its 'other(s)'—those that are outside. Their discussion attempts to put the normative and utopian claim about this unfinished cosmopolitanism to rest. It is not only about empowerment and the future: there are internments and enclosures that continually need diagnoses that historicize the 'commonsense.' The Learning Society is a governing practice and an effect of power. Its pedagogical individuality circulates to order, differentiate and divide who is and who is not the 'reasonable' cosmopolitan. By focusing on the broader concept of the unfinished cosmopolitan, the authors' intent is to historically explore how it is possible that the Learning Society, the individual as a lifelong learner and, more broadly, the policy sciences 'think' about change and choice, and human interests. The notion of governmentality provides a strategy to historicize this present.

Introduction

While there are probably earlier references to the learning society, but browsing educational journals from 1982 there appeared an article, titled 'Japan: The learning society' (Schiller & Walberg, 1982). It was written at a time when the US feared that the Japanese society was moving economically ahead and that fear gave expression to the need to reform its educational systems. The American educators argued that schooling permeates the whole of Japanese society and that it was a prime instrument in the country's miracle of the 1970s and 1980s. The Learning Society that Japan typified was, according to the authors, related to 'post-industrial, global society in which information is more than ever the primary source of economic development and cultural influence'. And as a prophecy of the benefits of the Learning Society and the need for American educational reforms, the authors forecast the future that Tokyo will become the world's central city.

As such prophecies go, Japan had its cultural and economic difficulties since then. But the idea of a learning society is a persistent cultural theme that is not merely instrumental in relation to economic growth and national exceptionalism. It embodies a cultural thesis about a cosmopolitan mode of life that mutates through modern schooling. An idea of a learning society is embedded in Dewey's pragmatism. Pragmatism embodies a mode of living through the use of reason as a continual process of problem solving in which the individual is linked to the collective good of the society (the community). That optimistic future is mutated in the new millennium talk about the learning society and other phrases such as the global society and the information society, used to mobilize school reforms in the making of a new world order. A European Union planner in a recent speech reiterated this optimism in a range of policies from the 1980s that emphasized the future of European spaces as occupied by lifelong learners and the learning society.[1]

Our interest in cosmopolitanism is not one that traces a philosophical discourse from Diogenes or Kant to the present. Cosmopolitanism is an historical 'tool' to consider the transmogrifications of European Enlightenment images of a universal reason, rationality and progress as a mode of living inscribed in the Learning Society.[2] The learner of this new society is a cosmopolitan guided by compassion for continual change and innovation. It is a consuming project of life that regulates the present in the name of the future action. For some, the learning society is composed of a continual process of individual choice that promises the Philosopher's Stone. Maeroff (2003), for example, offers online learning as enabling a learning society where all children and adults are cosmopolitan in outlook through a continual process of learning made possible through the computer and Internet. The new technologies, he argues, provide a new era that relates the free-market neoliberalism approaches and equity in schooling through online learning. It interjects 'more choice into the system, advocates reason, the richer the offerings and the greater the benefits to consumers (students and their families)' (Maeroff, 2003, p. 4). From a different ideological perspective, Hargreaves (2003) speaks against the overly stressed materialism and marketization of neoliberal reforms. In its place is a knowledge society that 'is really a learning society . . . [that] process(es) information and knowledge in ways that maximize learning, stimulate ingenuity and invention and develop the capacity to initiate and cope with change' (Hargreaves, 2003, p. xviii). Schooling, he continues, is an institution that prepares the child for the future. Also concerned with equity and justice, the child of the Learning Society has 'a cosmopolitan identity which shows tolerance of race and gender differences, genuine curiosity toward and willingness to learn from other cultures, and responsibility toward excluded groups within and beyond one's society' (Hargreaves, 2003, p. xix).

What can we make of these prophecies of the Learning Society as a moral life organized through continuous innovation with no finishing point? In the following, the prophecy of the Learning Society is treated as a technology that orders, interns and encloses the possibilities of one's life. Our framing of the problem, discussed in the first section, is through the notion of cosmopolitanism. Cosmopolitanism is a cultural thesis about modes of living. The Enlightenment's cosmopolitan was an urbane individual who possesses agency. That agency entails the use of reason and rationality to promote universal values of progress and humanity. Cosmopolitanism, we argue, is a continual theme of pedagogy inscribed in the Learning Society. That inscription entails principles about who 'we' are, should be, and who is not that 'we'—the anthropological 'Other' who stands outside reason and its civilizing manners of conduct.

Cosmopolitanism functions as an interpretive lens to explore the political objects of social administration of the child and family. We are interested in the rules and standards of conduct in producing the self-governing actors who are simultaneously responsible for the social progress and for the personal fulfilment of one's life. Today's cosmopolitan, as in the turn of the 20th century, is spoken about as the global citizen freed from provincialism and tradition, and ruled by universal principles of human rights rather than social or theological certainties. The contemporary form of this mode of living is expressed as the *topoi* of 'the knowledge' and 'communication society' and the child who is a lifelong learner who continually re-creates one's self through being a problem solver. Cosmopolitanism, then, provides a way to examine the systems of reason that regulates, differentiates and divides the acts and participation of the child in the name of universal human principles such as the Learning Society.

Working through Foucault's (1991) notion of governmentality[3] the first section explores cosmopolitanism as an intellectual tool. It considers the changing pedagogical practices to enact a change in the conditions of people as enacting changes in who those people are and should be. The second section focuses on the Learning Society, with Swedish and US schooling, and Swedish health promotion, and crime prevention as our sites of investigation. We discuss the learner of the Learning Society as fabricating[4] the unfinished cosmopolitanism. That individuality is talked about as a lifelong learner. It is an individuality that plans one's biography as continuously solving problems, making choices and collaborating in 'communities of learners' in a process of continuous innovation. The only thing about the future that is not open to choice is choice itself. We talk about the unfinished cosmopolitan rather than use the contemporary phrase of lifelong learner to historicize the present and its cultural thesis about a mode of living. The third section concerns the problem of the notion of design in making the unfinished cosmopolitan: design is what one does with problem solving to order one's mode of living, and design is what research does to calculate and administer the future of who is to design one's life. These first two sections explore the cosmopolitanism in policy and research as the characteristics and capabilities of the unfinished cosmopolitanism cultural practices assembled and connected to form the principles governing who the child and citizen are and should be.

The fourth section links the universal claims of inclusion with exclusions. Embodied in the design of the unfinished cosmopolitan is a duality. The unfinished cosmopolitan inscribes fear of what is not cosmopolitan and 'civilized'—the disadvantaged and at-risk child, the sickly individual, and the criminal. Our analysis moves across different sites with broad strokes and we realize that nuances and differences are left unexamined, limitations we believe are warranted at this point in the diagnosis of the present.

Governmentality and Cosmopolitanism

If we examine the two above references about online learning and the knowledge society, cosmopolitanism is a theme within the Learning Society that moves along different ideological positions. It also travels in a range of literatures about transcendental values of a global citizen, reason, and action untangled from provincialism, tradition, and social or theological certainties (also see, e.g. Beck, 2000; Castells, 2000).[5] But the narratives and images of the individuality that brings forth the future of progress are not merely there by the grace of contemporary wisdom. It is a mutation that moves in uneven flows and different configurations from the European Enlightenment and the Reformation to the present.[6] The investigation of the learner of the Learning Society requires historicizing the mutations as narratives of cosmopolitanism and its production of the 'Others' travels to the present.

The images and narratives of the Enlightenment's cosmopolite are neither as straightforward nor as universal in values as they might seem. The ideal(s) of the cosmopolitan was not only an altruistic quality or about pure thought that was superimposed on the historical individual. The seeming universalism of cosmopolitanism embodies a particular historical scaffolding of rules and standards about who the citizen is or should be, and who does not embody that reason and 'reasonableness'. The values and norms of the Enlightenment's cosmopolitan have a mixed history. European cosmopolitan values have been used in battles against European colonialists. It has also been used in committing violence of colonialism in justifying the superiority of the West. The ironies, internments, and enclosures are evident as the northern European Reformation and the Enlightenment that were to rise above the nation in securing progress. Its universalism was in fact inscribed in the construction of the nation, for example, in the American and French Revolutions. Further and central to this study, cosmopolitanism was and is about exclusions, in its inclusions that disqualified some as not embodying the capabilities of the 'reason' of the cosmopolitan.

At this point, we can summarize briefly our use of cosmopolitanism as an intellectual tool to diagnose the mode of life embodied in the Learning Society in US schooling, and Swedish health and the social policing of crime.

First, the notion of Learning Society makes it possible 'to think' and act through a range of historical inscriptions that travel in the present about a cosmopolitan way of living. That is, cosmopolitanism is not one thing or a constant that moves untouched within the vagaries of history. Whether one approaches cosmopolitanism from the social or individual side of the Learning Society, there is an Enlightenment attitude toward 'reason' and rationality, to use Foucault's (1984) discussion. But cosmopolitanism is formed through an assemblage in which reason is related to notions of agency and progress, stability and consensus as governing principles of action and reflection. Today's cosmopolitan is the agential individual who is talked about as empowered, having a voice, and self-responsible in producing innovation in the processes of change. That notion of agency and the universality of reason in the processes of change is not one that merely appears in the present but is an historical construction of 'the self'.

Second, there is a sacredness that inscribes agency in cosmopolitanism in the theories of pedagogy and the social and educational sciences; yet it is rarely explored that this agency is a particular register that intersects with the formation of the modern state and the art of governing. Meyer (1986) argues, for example, that there was a progressive discovery of human personality in the eighteenth and nineteenth centuries; that each person carries a whole system of motives and perceptions that reflect different biological and social forces through which the individual self is integrated. Theories of the agential individual constituted persons as moral subjects of their own actions. Theories of action and actors/agency were central to the international spread of mass education in the construction of the modern nation in the late nineteenth and early nineteenth centuries (Meyer, Boli, Thomas & Ramirez, 1997).

Third, cosmopolitan reason is the cornerstone of agency, but also the limit and object of government.[7] From Kant through Dewey and into current notions of emancipation and empowerment, the calculation of cosmopolitan reason and the 'reasonable person' is a *sine qua non* of the joining of individual enablement and public capabilities. Cosmopolitanism recovered Stoic ideas in French intellectual circles of the Enlightenment to join the natural (nature) and human realms of reason (Toulmin, 1990, pp. 68–69). The reason of the Enlightenment was to correct visual perceptions and the errors of the senses. Kant's (1784/1970) 'What is the Enlightenment?' offers the enlightened leader as a guardian, who teaches the duty of all citizens to think for themselves. But the guardian in Kant's text embodies the dual attempt to order the world through reason and to administer through reason. Augustus Comte's positivism epitomized the double time of reason as bringing order and harmony as well as change, captured in his famous phrase about the new secular religion of positivism, 'Order and Progress'. The cosmopolitanism of Comte embodied science as 'the Religion of Humanity, and all true Positivists sought to unite science and religion' (Nisbet, 1979, pp. 172–173). Reason, then, is not something that is merely there to recuperate in decision making or problem solving; rather reason comprises historically produced systems of rules and standards that order reflection and participation. The notion of cosmopolitan reason is something calculated and administrable, for governing reflection and action in the name of social progress and personal fulfilment.

Fourth, while the Enlightenment philosophers talked about reason and rationality (science) as values that enable the individual to transcend the local and the provincial, the rules and standards of cosmopolitan reason assume a particular type of expertise in ordering daily life. Science becomes experimental and empirical and thus no longer merely the provenance of philosophers. And science is not merely a professional activity to gain knowledge and control of the external physical world. The human sciences emerge as particular technologies that give attention to the internal qualities of the mind and social interaction. The expertise of human sciences were to constitute cosmopolitan freedom and liberty. John Dewey, an American philosopher and progressive educator, is one icon in bringing notions of a cosmopolitan individual into a populist form related to everyday activities. Dewey thought of the scientific method as the most potent force shaping the modern world in images related to Enlightenment ideals of cosmopolitanism. He wanted to humanize the creative power of science in the name of universal values and 'thereby to gain control of the future' (Rockefeller, 1991, p. 3). The cosmopolitanism of the new sciences of pedagogy and childhood organized life through values that were thought of as universal, and which promised progress through individual and community actions.

This brief discussion about the scaffolding of different cultural practices that give focus to cosmopolitanism, is a strategy to think historically about the Learning Society and its learners. Current reforms about the lifelong learner and the Learning Society make 'sense' in this historical context of narratives and images of cosmopolitanism. They function as technologies of administering the principles of self-reflection, action, and participation. Agency, progress, and reason are part of this grid, as is the taming of change in the name of progress and self-fulfilment. The inscriptions of the Learning Society, as Wagner (1994) writes more generally about modernity, 'cannot simply be written in terms of increasing autonomy and democracy, but rather in terms of changing notions of the substantive foundations of a self-realization and of shifting emphasis between individualized enablements and public/collective capabilities' (Wagner, 1994, p. xiv).

'The Learning Society as the Future Here and Now—What Are We Waiting For!'[8]

This and the next section focus on three overlapping cultural practices in policy and research that connect in the cosmopolitanism of the Learning Society—the inscription of the future as a regulating principle of the present, design as a practice of planning biography, and community as a space to link collective norms and values to individuality. Whereas one can think of the child and adult of the late 19th century as a subject who embodied the collective social narratives of the nation, today's individuality is a 'lifelong learner' who is flexible, continuously active, and works collaboratively for the future in a decentralized world.

The future functions as a governing practice. This future is not something decreed by Fate and out of sight of our own activities. Nor is this a future of strange, unexpected spaces that must be defended against. It is a future mobilized to design people in the present. As one Swedish politician recently said, 'We have to mobilize people to be citizens of the new Society'.[9] This future of a new society is of the here and now. The US educational policy reform document *No Child Left Behind* (Bush, 2001),[10] as well, makes the future in the governing of the present. The goal is a future inclusive society through school reform that is 'to build the mind and character of every child, from every background' (Bush, 2001).

In different contexts and with different logics, the same story seems to be told. The story is that we are now, more or less, obliged to live with constant change in society. Modern schooling, for example, continually links the individual to narratives of social or economic progress and the revitalization of democracy that will bring personal betterment. In a statement resonating across American school subject reforms, the National Council of Teachers of Mathematics (2000) model for curriculum reform argues that the student needs to be prepared for a future where change is 'a ubiquitous feature of contemporary life, so learning with understanding is essential to enable students to use what they learn to solve the new kinds of problems they will inevitably face in the future' (pp. 20–21). The 'ubiquitous' uncertainty of the future that mathematics education tames has less to do with learning the norms of inquiry in mathematics than with the inscription of particular norms for planning one's future of continuous innovation and choice through, as we argue in the next section, a self-improvement process of problem solving.[11]

In a similar way, the Swedish Public Health policy is not simply about health. First and foremost the narrative about health is about Society, the Citizen, and the Future. The Swedish Governmental Commission, Health on Equivalent Conditions—National Targets for Health (SOU, 2000: 91) proposes national targets for public health in Sweden that seems to carry the same language. State health reforms are concerned with present changes in society in order to secure the future. According to the Commission, the Swedish model of the welfare state and public health development is 'exposed to huge outer and inner tensions' and 'different kinds of threats' (p. 55). Increasing differences in health and social conditions threatens the basic trust in society and the possibility of founding a society on solidarity between different population groups.

A pedagogical paradigm of a Learning Society is inscribed as a public health strategy and the public health paradigm. According to the Commission, it is 'important for a society that the citizens look upon learning and personal development as a life-long process' (SOU, 2000: 91, p. 423). Being a lifelong learner is significant for the health of the population and the future conduct of the individual subjects not only within formal educational settings, but also in people's everyday life and in society as a whole. Schooling is seen 'as a fundamental and gigantic public health investment' and a key element to bring about changes needed to make health a possibility for all (p. 385). The State Committee strives to make visible, problematize and reorganize the activities in schools with this view of pedagogy as an organizing principle for the future health of the public.

Present Swedish crime prevention, as well, is ordered as a pedagogical problem of the future of a Learning Society rather than being about the punishment of wrongdoing. Crime prevention is about learning to be law-abiding, problem solving, communicative and responsible than about punishment for wrongdoing. The offender must be instructed and educated to gain a better insight into the consequences of crime. And the victim is invited to listen, to understand, and to learn the whole story of the offender's crime activity. The Public Health Committee emphasizes that the mentalities and the knowledge of health issues needed are something that the subject has to capture over and over again; it's a life-long project (SOU, 2000: 91).

The narratives of the unfinished cosmopolitan in the Learning Society embody new relations between individuality (the lifelong learner) and the social. The fabrication of the child as a problem solver no longer bases responsibility in the range of social practices directed toward a single public sphere. The new individuality traverses diverse and plural communities to constitute the common good. The struggle is now in the autonomous learners who are continuously involved in self-improvement and ready for the uncertainties through working actively in communities of learning (see, e.g., The National Council for Teachers of Mathematics, 2000). Reason is no longer for the perfection of the nation as the collective embodiment of the social good. Change, contingency and uncertainty in daily life are tamed through the rules and standards that place the problem-solving child in diverse communities where the common good is formed.

Education is once again a project for national mobilization, but with a hugely different meaning than in earlier times. Education as once before, forms the ethical substance of the individual in all social activities. But the pedagogical principles of learning are spread now to the entire social body. 'Working with education' is not limited to learning and training of pupils in the classroom or to a specific place or time; rather school and education have to be expanded and connected to all aspects of society in an everlasting way. The subject must be prepared to learn during the whole life and be connected to learning in a wider sense (see Dalin, 1994, p. 11).

The notions of life-long learning and a Learning Society operate in different political and institutional areas are no longer enclosed in the previously conceived spaces of the educational.

The life-long learning destroys the boundaries between political sectors. Education policy, employment policy, the policy of industry and commerce, regional development policy and social policy have a common responsibility for life-long and life-wide learning (The Swedish National Agency for Education, 2000, p. 10f).

The governmental reason of the 21st century takes the pedagogical task of learning as a boundary-crossing route to unite the increasing and unforeseeable multiplicity, fragmentation and diversity within subject-oriented democratic education. The pedagogical reason is expected to both widen and strengthen the solidarity of society (see Petersson, Olsson, Hultqvist & Popkewitz, 2004). The governmentality orders and controls the future in the present by qualifying and preparing the individual citizen with dispositions for new cosmopolitan commitments. This is evident in the writing of a prominent Scandinavian educator in an authoritative professional journal. The Learning Society is viewed as a sign of the future and part of a visionary world.

> We are entering a knowledge society since the speed of the changing process is increasing and since the new society demands new, increasing and greater qualifications of each of us. Education will no longer be something linked to a certain range but will be a necessity and a self-evident part of everyday life to all ranges, social classes and occupational groups. We are already there. We know that 'life-long education' has become a reality.
>
> (Dalin, 1994, p. 143)

The citizens' work toward a never-ending future as an educational subject. It does not seem farfetched to argue that society has turned into a school (see Hultqvist & Petersson, 2000). Thus, Dewey's notion of 'School as Society' has been reshaped into 'Society as School'.

The Unfinished Cosmopolitan: Designing the Problem Solving Lifelong Learner and Community

One might say that most of the above is only policy about The Learning Society of the future, so let's get to what is happening on the ground. The divisions of text/context and the ideal/real create binaries that misrecognize how knowledge fabricates, that is, both construes and constructs, and thus functions 'materially.' The unfinished cosmopolitan inhabitants of the Learning Society are an assemblage of practices that order a cultural thesis about a mode of life. The taming of change is one part of the assemblage. In this section, we discuss (a) the notion of designed spaces and the designed individuality, (b) the making of the characteristics of the problem solver in search of a life of choice and innovation, and (c) 'community' as a place of belonging and home in the problem solving of the future. We call these 'cultural practices' as they overlap in ordering a mode of living of the unfinished cosmopolitan as an unfinished lifelong learner.

The Learning Society as a Design Problem

Today's pedagogical reforms and research talk about children and teachers designing their own learning, and research as a particular design problem to produce the agency of the individual who lives a life of continual innovation. The notion of design embodies a turn in 21st century narratives of democracy, empowerment and human agency for teachers, children and researchers.

The design for the future is a word that previously spoke in terms of what God gave to human affairs. The social and pedagogical interventions of 19th century America and Sweden were to complete the latent design of God within each child, the family and the citizen in their ways of living.[12] The Swedish educator Rudenschöld placed the notion of design in the Ståndscirkulation, the outer technological side of an evolutionary process that would inaugurate Christian values and life forms on earth (Hultqvist, 2004). The evolutionary process embodied Sweden as an exception from other nations through its heritage of the virtues of modesty or freedom from vanity and the Lutheran ethic of individualism and self-improvement.

The idea of design in making the citizen was also a part of an American Exceptionalism. The Exceptionalism was an epic of the nation told as a unique human experiment of a society that provides an exemplar of the highest ideals of human values and progress. The early founders of American sociology sought to guarantee the future of the republic's exceptionalism through deliberately designing the social order and the individual. The notion of design embodied elements of a social gospel that contained secularized elements of Puritan notions of salvation. Urban design and the design of the inner characteristics and capabilities of the child were to produce the 'reason' and 'reasonable' citizen of the future. The new psychologies, for example, envisioned the empirical building blocks of selfhood as of deliberate design rather than of something related to a static, metaphysical soul (Sklansky, 2002, pp. 148–9). William James' notion of a pragmatic psychology placed a premium on habit formation as the main means of acting in accord with one's designs (p. 146). Design's reach into the interior of the individual was spoken of as bringing the great panacea of equality.

Today design is to fabricate the individuality of life in the Learning Society. At one level, it is spoken about as part of democracy and its cosmopolitanism. Design in the online learning spoken about earlier is to make an individual whose life is of infinite choices. Design is also a research project of the learning sciences directed at the continuous intervention in the classroom. Design Research treats the classroom as a continuous open system for continuously inventing feedback loops. Feedback loops are to bring together reform goals, the ongoing development of the system, dispositions of participants, and professional expertise. Biography is the project of design. That biography is of an unfinished cosmopolitan in which deliberate, intentional acts lead an individual from one sphere of life to another as if life were a planning workshop that had a value in and of itself. Action is a continual flow toward a future that occurs through designing not only what will be done but also planning who that person will be.

The learning, problem-solving design of pedagogies is morphologically related to new principles of restorative criminal justice. The tools of this reasoning are communication and interaction between parties involved in crime and it focuses on what should be done (the future), not on what has been done.

> Restorative justice places both victim and offender in active problem-solving roles that focus upon the restoration of material and psychological losses to individuals and the community following the damage that results from criminal behaviour. Whenever possible, dialogue and negotiation serve as central elements of restorative justice. (This is true primarily of property crimes, although also of a growing number of more violent offences.) Problem solving for the future is seen as more important than establishing blame for past behaviour. Public safety is a primary concern, yet severe punishment of the offender is less important than providing opportunities to: empower victims in their search for closure and healing; impress upon the offender the human impact of their behaviour; and promote restitution of the victim.
>
> (Umbreit, 1994, p. 2)

The unfinished cosmopolitan in these different social spheres is oriented to the future through unfinished processes that are viewed as expressing universal human attributes of reason, science and progress. The unfinished cosmopolitan problem-solves to chase desire and works in a global world in which there is no finishing line. The child, for example, is someone who can choose to refuse allegiance to any one of the infinite choices on display, except the choice of choosing. The ordering, designing, and taming of the undefined future is a technology that connects the scope and aspirations of public powers with the personal and subjective capacities of individuals through mediating the 'interactions between intervention and setting' (The Design-Based Research Collective, 2003, p. 5).

Community as 'the Home' of the Unfinished Cosmopolitan

The autonomy of the problem solver is given a home and sense of belonging by connecting learning psychologies with communication and interactional practices embodied in the notion of 'community'. The problem solver learns by participating in a classroom community, 'a community of discourse', 'a community of learners', and 'a community of mathematicians'. Earlier 20th century notions of the classroom spoke of it as a place for socialization in which the child was to internalize universal, collective norms of identity that are pre-established. Today's reforms involve the continual forming of identity mediated through the communication systems of the classroom community (see, e.g. Cobb, 1994). The classroom community is thought of as a 'participation structure' in which communication theories are concerned with the ongoing processes that create fluid identities. Community inscribes cultural spaces in which problem solving and the Learning Society function as a performative quality of 'community'.

The evocation of community is intended to revive the ideals of a democracy by producing greater representation of those directly involved in schooling, public health and victim-offender mediation. Community evokes a concept of restorative justice and the reformation of democracy through the governing patterns of community. Community embodies a salvation theme about involvement and empowerment, in which problem solving produces responsible citizenship. The communication networks are a way of providing harmony; that is, we make peace by speaking to each other and we become reconciled with each other by telling the 'truth' about ourselves. This new way of doing justice is very much about interaction, at the same moment as it is an ambition to personalize and humanize the judicial process in order to facilitate 'the empowerment of both parties to resolve the conflict at a community level' (Umbreit, 1994, p. 17).

Community is a discursive site to connect the intimate relations and inner capabilities of the child and family with cosmopolitan images and narratives of collective belonging and 'home'. The 'Community Sociology', developed at the University of Chicago during the early decades of the 20th century, sought to reshape the urban culture of immigrant families through social psychologies of the child and family, of, for example, Charles Horton Cooley, George Herbert Mead and John Dewey. Cooley saw the family and the neighbourhood as providing the proper socialization through which the child could lose the innate greed, lust and pride of power that was innate to the infant, and thus become fit for civilization. The communication systems of the family would, according to Cooley, establish the family on Christian principles that stressed a moral imperative in life and self-sacrifice for the good of the group. These Christian principles were viewed as the embodiment of a cosmopolitan citizen in a democratic society. Theories of the family and social interactions were a social education in which school and local communities related to a cosmopolitan image in which the individual submitted to a 'wider outlook, a higher and clearer idealism, and so be prepared to create that free, righteous and joyful system of life to which they aspire' (Cooley cited in Reuben, 1996, p. 156).

Contemporary crime prevention, misconduct and wrong behaviour re-inscribe notions of community as governing practices but in a different assembly of practices than at the turn of the 20th century. Crime is corrected and prevented informally at the local level (The National Council for Crime Prevention, 1999: 12, p. 11). In this context 'The State' is no longer imagined as the victim, rather 'restorative justice theory postulates that criminal behaviour is first a conflict between individuals' (Umbreit, 1994, p. 2). One of the aims of the restorative mediation is to have the offender confess shame and ask the victim's forgiveness. The victim is invited to listen, and to understand, the whole story of the offender's crime activity, and the story has to be told in front of the mediator/confessor. But crime prevention as a project of restorative justice is also part of the curriculum of the Swedish high school. State curriculum projects function to link the student with the broader purpose 'to provide a basis for pupils to continue in community involvement both as citizens and professionals (. . .) to nurture pupils in democratic participation' and 'to provide knowledge and therewith the power to realize positive changes both on the individual and social level' (p. 4). This course in crime prevention is a course to improve the feeling of agency or empowerment, a course that is well suited to The High School's 'obligation to nurture civic awareness' (The National Council, 2002, p. 1).

There is a paradox involved here. On the one hand, it seems that educational thought is spreading and tends to take charge of even more spaces in the name of the future and the enlightened cosmopolitan. The prevention of criminality, the bodily and mental health of a person, and the citizen of the future are all in the hands of pedagogy. But the learning society of this unfinished cosmopolitan has enclosures and internments. 'The theory of restorative justice contributes to the will of empowering the local community and the local influence of the individual by moving the legal system to a lower level—one is of the opinion that misconduct and wrong behaviour should be corrected in a more informal way by social control on the local level' (The National Council for Crime Prevention, 1999: 12, p. 11).

Paradox involved in the Learning Society moves between broader tendencies of a society as a school and the tendencies to narrow the same to a question of individual commission (often expressed, for example, in terms as life-long and life-wide learning, self-regulation, and empowerment) seems to be the governmental condition in the early 21st century. The governing of the society, the nation and the future seems to make this detour through the individual (educable) subject.

But there is more to the paradox. The future citizens are both more and less active participants. Problem solving and collaboration give flexibility in learning how to appreciate the majesty of that already-given reality. Science curricula across different nations followed a similar pattern (McEneaney, 2003). The curriculum provides students with greater opportunities for participation. But this participation occurs with more and more of the world represented by the iconic images of the expertise of science. Thus, while there is greater participation of the student in the curriculum, that participation occurs in narrower areas as the expertise of science is given increasing authority.

Turn of the 20th and 21st century reforms no longer seem guided by externally validated social morals and obligations as earlier. The freedom of the empowered who lives in multiple communities is to secure change, contingency and uncertainty in daily life. The contingency is tamed through the rules and standards of 'reason' that place the problem-solving child and participation in spaces increasingly classified through the iconic expertise of science and its consecrated knowledge of the world.

The Lifelong Learners and Those Who Are Not Learning

The redemptive hopes and desires of the unfinished cosmopolitan are a double narrative that expresses the fears of the individual who will prevent and destroy that future and its notions of the civilized. The affirmations are simultaneously narratives of moral disintegration and apprehension about those who will bring down the walls of civilization. The dangers are, for example, of the child not adequately prepared to live in the global world while still maintaining a collective national identity. The fears, however, do not appear as such. They are often expressed in terms of inclusion and questions of equity, to reach out to those at risk of falling behind or not catching up—immigrants, ethnic, and racial groups who have not succeeded and who are marginalized. Fears about the psychological decay and social psychological conditions that produced the decay are part of the policy and research about the 'sanctity' of the traditional family and its norms of the home and childhood. These fears are rarely talked explicitly through categories of race, gender or class but are established through categories of difference in policy and research such as the single parent, and the teenage mother, or the at-risk child.

In the Swedish context, the fear of the crime prevention is the prisoner who does not become a member of the Learning Society. The redemption of the criminal is to embrace the cosmopolitan mode of living as 'a lifelong learner'. The fear of the criminal seems less in what crime was committed, than in reclaiming one's self through the redemptive treks of lifelong learning. This requires a correctional system that deals with the intimate social and psychological relations of the criminal being reclaimed. Programs are composed of 'offering the prisoners possibilities to life-long learning as close as possible to their own settings and with the possibilities of online learning support wherever it is possible' (Sjöberg & Roitto, 2001, p. 10).

Most crime prevention investments do not target the criminal but young prospective offenders. The logic is clear: the child and the youth have to be rescued before they enter the gateways to the prison, since the prison does not provide the rescuing 'skills' in the same effective way as it provides skills for a further criminal career. The potential criminal limits the possibility of learning to become a proper citizen. The potential criminal, the criminals, and the recidivists share common psychological and social family backgrounds in terms of low education, drug abuse, unemployment and so forth. The same characteristics appear when it comes to the question of identifying those who are able to learn or not in the context of restorative justice. The offender and the at-risk offenders are offered a chance to be rescued and included and integrated into the community, and to be educated into a civic manner, but if he/she does not accept the offer, the other side of the coin is obvious: that is exclusion.

The anxiety of Public Health is about citizens only grasping a partial understanding of what life-long learning is and refusing to learn that health is not only about health. The anxiety is not directed to the sick but towards where the autonomous subject egotistically does not take responsibility for his community by quitting smoking or drinking. Each are seen as unhealthy moral dispositions that overlap with a physical degeneration that has an impact on others as well as one's self. The healthy citizen feels and acts with responsibility for their immediate and broader community as a personal obligation for the future and the society as a whole.

On a more general level we can say that the anxieties of both crime prevention and the health field are twofold. On the one hand, to paraphrase Rose (1993), it is about the fear of governing too much, which is not, in the name of liberal way of ruling, the proper way of designing, empowering and ordering the autonomous cosmopolitan modes of living. On the other hand it is also about the fear of governing too little, which is the fear of not making a success of preparing and ordering all individuals and groups (not yet included) into the society in the name of learning, agency and community-participating. These double-edged styles of governing do not always operate in opposition to each other, but rather in a cross-fertilizing manner.

The fears of social disintegration, the loss of civilization, and moral degeneration are not only about the probability of rescue and redemption. The individual who is not the unfinished cosmopolitan is distinct human kinds that demand programs to govern the processes of exclusion in the move to create an inclusive society. This is one way to read educational research and reform proposals that speak of redressing the inequities of education as the need for *all* children to learn, for all children to be lifelong learners with No Child Left Behind, the title of US legislation in 2001. The phrases 'that all children learn' and 'that no child is left behind' express concerns and general commitments for redressing situations of poverty and discrimination. But the general hope and commitments also embody the fears of the society. Special theories and programs are constructed to make the excluded into unfinished cosmopolitans (see Popkewitz, 1998). The social practices about exclusion embody recognition of cultural and social distinctions about deviance and difference. The clarion call for reform is not only a call to meet future economic progress but is also a call about the threats of moral and cultural disorganization.

A continuum of values is evoked through phrases about programs to ensure that all children learn. The phrase 'all children' provides determinate categories and distinctions about a particular 'child' who does not fit into the maps of 'all children'. It is the child, but also the future adult, who does not choose, chases desire, and becomes a lifelong learner. The children who are included in the distinctions given to the category of 'all children' have particular characteristics. The characteristics of children who are not included in the distinctions given to the category of the child is one 'who live[s] in poverty, students who are not native speakers of English, students with disabilities, females, and many nonwhite students [who] have traditionally been far more likely than their counterparts in other demographic groups to be victims of low expectations' (National Council of Teachers of Mathematics, 2000, p. 13).

This Other child is to be rescued through finer and finer distinctions that order and classify the wayward child; the child is one who has not yet the 'problem-solving skills' and is not a flexible learner. The child who does not 'fit' in the map of the 'all children' is the child who lacks self-esteem, who has a poor self-concept, and scarcity of skills, and does not embrace 'problem solving', collaboration, and a life of continuous innovation and choice that mark the autonomous, unfinished cosmopolitan.

The fears of moral disintegration and social instability projected into psychological qualities of learning, problem solving and self-esteem overlapped with social narratives about the moral disintegration of the community, family and environment. The latter are single parents and teenage mothers, and 'recidivists'. The determinate categories of this human kind relate to other distinctions that function as both symbols of deviance and targets of rescue, such as low income, lack of books in the home, unemployment, drug abuse (see, e.g. Popkewitz, 1998; Lindblad & Popkewitz, 2004).

The inscriptions come together as an assemblage of characteristics to produce a determinate classification that performs in criminal prevention, schooling, and health education, with some variation on a theme of the categories in the two countries about who is left behind. This latter human kind, in comparison to the lifelong learner, has qualities and characteristics of the child who needs remediation. Difference is discursively made into characteristics of deviance! While programs are to rescue that particular human kind through better management and self-management, the human kind is one that is in perpetual preparation but never achieves the norms of 'the average'.

The Art of Governance in the Name of Cosmopolitan Learning Society

Knowledge, we have argued, is not epiphenomenal but is itself part of the productive qualities of the world. This concern with the making of 'reason' and 'the reasonable person' in the Learning Society today stands as an embodiment of the cosmopolitan who is civilized and progressive. We have sought to diagnose cosmopolitanism as a cultural thesis in generating principles governing who the individual is and should be in the Learning Society. Our focus on cosmopolitanism is to historicize its present as a phenomenon transmogrified into the present from the northern European Enlightenment. Its narratives are about individuals whose lives are ordered through principles of rationality, progress and of a universal reason.

What is 'new' in the present is the particular amalgamation of cultural practices that fabricate 'the social' and individuality. Our relating 'society' and 'learner' in the Learning Society focuses on the cultural practices that generate principles about who 'we' are, should be, and who is not that 'we'. This context of governing we spoke about in the designing of the unfinished cosmopolitanism as embodying an individuality of never-ending changes where choice and lifelong learning are the only things that are certain. This autonomous cosmopolitan subject has a double responsibility. There is responsibility for one's own life-style and for creating an environment, supportive for learning and for the security and health of everybody, including one's self. But those images and narratives of the social and the individual are also divisions that place some as outside its cultural mapping: uncivilized, barbaric and outside the pale of humanness.

The qualities of the unfinished cosmopolitan circulating in Sweden and the US produce a pedagogical world where the governing principles of the child are morphologically related to multiple arenas of social life. Dispositions for a personal commitment to the unfinished cosmopolitan in family life and participation in volunteer organizations are significant parts of the new ordering of hope and fear in Public Health policy, new pedagogies of the school, and crime prevention. While Swedish reformations of Criminal Justice and Public Health and US schooling are bearers of their own specific traditions and terms of opportunity, they have morphological relations in the ordering of the objects of reflection and action.

One might say, as do many of the authors of the texts examined here who embrace the idea of a Learning Society, that this new individuality brings to fruition the realization of the goals of the Enlightenment. Our discussion should put this normative and utopian claim about this unfinished cosmopolitanism to rest. It is not only about empowerment and the future. There are internments and enclosures that continually need diagnoses that historicize the 'commonsense.' The Learning Society is a governing practice and an effect of power. Its pedagogical individuality circulates to order, differentiate and divide who is and who is not the 'reasonable' cosmopolitan.

Our focusing on the Learning Society and the lifelong learner within a broader historical context of cosmopolitanism is to focus on the changing enablements, enclosures, and internments of the present. This historicity in contemporary analyses of policy and the problem of changes provides an alternative to policy studies that view the changes in individuality as part of a global example of neo-liberalism. The difficulty of such neoliberal arguments is that they take a contemporaneous framework of national and international policy about privatization and marketization as the categories of analysis, thus reinserting and conserving the existing framework of reasoning as its foundation of critiques. It is as though the lifelong learning or the unfinished cosmopolitan miraculously appears with the Chicago economists in the 1950s, and brought into the political projects of Reagan, Thatcher and world agencies such as the World Bank. By focusing on the broader concept of the unfinished cosmopolitan, our intent is to historically explore how it is possible that the Learning Society, the individual as a lifelong learner, and more broadly the policy sciences 'think' about change and choice, and human interests. The notion of governmentality provides a strategy to historicize this present.

Notes

1 These different policies are interesting in themselves, as education is an official prerogative of the nation and not of the European Union, but concerns about European identity are placed within labour policy. See the discussion in Nóvoa and Lawn, 2002.
2 Recent scholarship has pointed to the different notions of the Enlightenment, differentiating it in the fields of cultural and political practices in Britain, France, and the United States, for example. It is this historical differentiation that Foucault (1984) made indirectly when he talks about the *attitude* of the Enlightenment versus the doctrine of modernity.
3 Foucault and political reason is discussed in, for example, Barry, Osborne & Rose, 1996; Hultqvist & Dahlberg, 2001; Popkewitz, 1991, 1998; Popkewitz & Brennan, 1998; and Popkewitz, Franklin & Pereyra, 2001.
4 We use 'fabricate' to focus on a double quality of 'thought' that construes and constructs.
5 The power of the normative images of the cosmopolitan can be seen in the Soviets' incorporation of the slogans of the French Revolution of equality, liberty, and fraternity as a step towards the fulfilment of a communist society.
6 It is embodied in the work of Adam Smith, Karl Marx, the Fabians, Durkheim, among others. This is not to say that an image of the individual as a cosmopolitan miraculously appears in the Enlightenment or that there were not multiple cosmopolitanisms (see, e.g. Breckenridge *et al.*, 2002). Rather, the long 19th century is a point of entrance. The national projects, the secularization, individualization, and imposition of science in the ordering of reason make this a convenient starting point in our discussion.
7 Our argument about agency here and later is its inscription in social and educational practices as a governing mechanism. Our discussion is historical and not normative about its goodness or badness.
8 The title is borrowed from Lena Fejan Ljunghill's article in *Pedagogiska Magasinet* (The Journal of Education), published by the Union of Teachers, no. 1, 1996, p. 6.
9 Ibid., p. 7.
10 The same trend is evident in the reforms of Swedish teacher education.
11 Mathematics education as a governing practice is more fully discussed in Popkewitz, 2004.
12 There are differences in this notion of design in the Counter-Reformation, Counter-Enlightenment, although one can also point to a particular globalization occurring in relation to discourses of Learning Societies and the lifelong learner. We can only point here to some general diagnostics while recognizing there are different patterns and assemblies as well as counter discourses. In a different context, we have talked about this through exploring the multiple modernities constructed in the 20th century (Popkewitz, 2005). Also see Simola, Johannesson & Lindblad, 2002; Nóvoa & Lawn, 2002 and Tuschling & Engemann (in this issue) for discussions of lifelong learning in Europe. Thus, while our documentation is related to Sweden and the US, we do not think that we are examining only local phenomenon.

References

Barry, A., Osborne, T. & Rose, N. (1996) *Foucault and Political Reason. Liberalism, neo-liberalism and rationalities of government* (Chicago, IL, The University of Chicago Press).

Beck, U. (2000) The Cosmopolitan Perspective: Sociology of the second age of modernity, *British Journal of Sociology*, 51:1, pp. 79–105.

Breckenridge, C., Pollock, S., Bhabha, H. & Chakrabarty, D. (eds) (2002) *Cosmopolitanism* (Durham, NC, Duke University Press).

Bush, G. W. (2001) *No Child Left Behind* (Washington, DC, Department of Education, US Government Printing Office).

Castells, M. (2000) Materials for an Exploratory Theory of the Network Society, *British Journal of Sociology*, 51:1, pp. 5–24.

Cobb, P. (1994) Where is the Mind? Constructivist and sociocultural perspectives on mathematical development, *Educational Researcher*, 23:7, pp. 13–20.

Dalin, P. (1994) *Utbildning för ett nytt århundrade. Bok 1*. (Stockholm, Liber).

Foucault, M. (1991) Governmentality, in: G. Burchell, C. Gordon and P. Miller (eds), *The Foucault Effect: Studies in governmentality*, (Chicago, IL, University of Chicago Press).

Foucault, M. (1984) What is Enlightenment? in: Paul Rabinow (ed.). *The Foucault Reader* (New York, Pantheon Books) pp. 32–50.

Hargreaves, A. (2003) *Teaching in the Knowledge Society, Education in the age of insecurity* (Maidenhead, Open University Press).

Hultqvist, K. & Dahlberg, G. (eds) (2001) *The Changing Child in a Changing World: Current ways of thinking and practicing childhood* (New York, Routledge Falmer).

Hultqvist, K. & Petersson, K. (2000) Iscensättningen av samhället som skola. I Pedagogik en: Jens Bjerg (ed.), *Grundbok*, (Stockholm, Liber).

Hultqvist, K. (2004) The Travelling State, the Nation and the Subject of Education, in: B. Baker & K. Heyning (eds), *The Uses of Foucault in the Study of Education*, (New York, Peter Lang).

Kant, E. (1784/1970) Idea for a Universal History with a Cosmopolitan Purpose, in: *Kant's Political Writing*, H. Reiss (ed.) H. B. Nisbet (trans.) (Cambridge, Cambridge University Press).

Ljunghill, L. F. (1996) The Future is Here and Now—What Are We Waiting For! *Pedagogiska magasinet*, 1:1, pp. 6–7 (Stockholm, Lärarförbundet).

Lindblad, S. & Popkewitz, T. (eds) (2004) *Educational Restructuring (International Perspectives on Traveling Policies)* (Greenwich, CT, Information Age Publishing).

Maeroff, G. (2003) *A Classroom of One: How online learning is changing our schools and colleges* (New York, Palgrave Macmillan).

McEneaney, E. (2003). Elements of a Contemporary Primary School Science, in: G. S. Drori, J. W. Meyer, F. O. Ramirez & E. Schofer (eds), *Science in the Modern World Polity: Institutionalization and globalization* (Stanford, CA, Stanford University Press) pp. 136–154.

Meyer, J. W. (1986). Myths of Socialization and of Personality, in: M. S. Thomas, C. Heller and David E. Wellbery (eds), *Reconstructing Individualism: Autonomy, individuality, and the self in Western thought* (Stanford, CA, Stanford University Press) pp. 208–221.

Meyer, J., J. Boli, G. Thomas, and F. Ramirez (1997) World Society and the Nation-State, *American Journal of Sociology*, 103: 1, pp. 144–181.

Nóvoa, A. & Lawn, M. (2002) *Fabricating Europe: The formation of an education space* (Dordrecht, Kluwer Academic Publishers).

Petersson, K., Olsson, U. Hultqvist, K. & Popkewitz, T. (2004) *Reframing Educational Thought, Subjects and Technologies of the Future in the Early 2000's*. Paper given at The European Conference on Educational Research, Crete.

Popkewitz, T. (1991) *A Political Sociology of Educational Reform: Power/knowledge in teaching, teacher education, and research* (New York, Teachers College Press).

Popkewitz, T. (1998) *Struggling for the Soul: The politics of education and the construction of the teacher,* (New York, Teachers College Press).

Popkewitz, T. (2004) The Alchemy of the Mathematics Curriculum: Inscriptions and the fabrication of the child, *American Educational Research Journal,* 41:4, pp. 3–34.

Popkewitz, T. (2005). *Inventing the Modern Self and John Dewey: Modernities and the traveling of pragmatism in education* (New York, PalgraveMacmillan).

Popkewitz, T. & Brennan, M. (eds) (1998) *Foucault's Challenge: Discourse, knowledge, and power in education* (New York, Teachers College Press).

Popkewitz, T., Franklin, B. & Pereyra, M. (eds) (2001) *Cultural History and Critical Studies of Education: Critical essays on knowledge and schooling* (New York, Routledge).

Reuben, J. (1996) *The Making of the Modern University: Intellectual transformations and the marginalization of morality* (Chicago, IL, The University of Chicago Press).

Rockefeller, S. (1991) *John Dewey: Religious faith and democratic humanism* (New York, Columbia University Press).

Rose, N. (1993) Government, Authority and Expertise in Advanced Liberalism, *Economy and Society,* 22:3, pp. 283–99.

Schiller, D. P. & Walberg, H. (1982) Japan: The learning society, *Educational Leadership,* 39:6, pp. 411–414.

Simola, H., Johannesson, I. A. & Lindblad, S. (eds) (2002) Changing Education Governance in Nordic Welfare States: Finland, Iceland and Sweden as cases of an international restructuring movement, *Special Issue of Scandinavian Journal of Educational Research,* 46:3.

Sjöberg, H & Roitto, M. (2001) *Kriminalvårdens klientutbildning—kartläggning, problembeskrivning och förslag till åtgärder,* (Norrköping, Sweden, Kriminalvården, Kriminalvårdsstyrelsens Förlag).

Sklansky, J. (2002) *The Soul's Economy: Market society and selfhood in American thought, 1820–1920,* (Chapel Hill, NC, University of North Carolina Press).

SOU 2000:91. *Health on Equivalent Conditions—National Targets for Health,* (Stockholm, Social-departementet).

The Design-Based Research Collective (2003) Designed-Based Research: An emerging paradigm for educational inquiry, *Educational Researcher,* 32:2, pp. 5–8.

The National Council of Crime Prevention (1999) '*The Hjällbo Estate Security Group*', (The local Council of Crime Prevention in Hjällbo): http://www.bra.se/extra/publication/.

The National Council of Crime Prevention (2002) '*Via Wargen—a course in crime prevention in a High School*', (The Local Council of Crime Prevention in Östersund): http://www.bra.se/extra/publication/.

The National Council of Teachers of Mathematics (2000) *Principles and Standards for School Mathematics* (Reston, VA, NCTM).

The Swedish National Agency for Education (2000) *The Life-Long and Life-Wide Learning* (Stockholm).

Umbreit, M. S. (1994) *Victim Meets Offender. The impact of restorative justice and mediation* (New York, Willow Tree Press).

Wagner, P. (1994) *The Sociology of Modernity* (New York, Routledge).

Chapter 6

What Were You Thinking? A Deleuzian/Guattarian Analysis of Communication in the Mathematics Classroom

Elizabeth de Freitas

Reprinted by permission of Taylor & Francis Ltd, http://www.tandfonline.com, on behalf of © Philosophy of Education Society of Australasia.

Editors' Introduction

The primary aim of De Freitas' chapter is to bring the work of Deleuze and Guattari to bear on the question of communication in the classroom. She focuses on the mathematics classroom, where agency and subjectivity are highly regulated by the rituals of the discipline, and where neoliberal psychological frameworks continue to dominate theories of teaching and learning. Moreover, the nature of communication in mathematics classrooms remains highly elusive and problematic, due in part to the distinct relationship the discipline has with verbal language and thought. Her chapter first discusses current attempts to better address the embodied nature of communication in mathematics classrooms, and argues that these remain overly logo-centric and language-centric in their conception of thinking. In De Freitas' argument, Deleuze and Guattari's perspectives on thought as a radical disruptive event can be used effectively to critique current pedagogical practices that privilege a narrow conception of communication in the classroom. She examines a set of exemplary classroom videos used in mathematics teacher education to argue that the current approach fails to honour the highly creative and disruptive nature of thinking. This critique of mathematical thinking, as it is conceptualized in current educational practice, might allow us to break free from the confines of royal or state mathematics, and create lines of flight where a more adventurous mathematics might emerge. Mathematics is thus perceived as out of the technical procedural tyranny of school mathematics, and to inspire a resistance to the containment of such cultural capital. Deleuze and Guattari demand that we imagine another mathematics, in contrast to the 'severe mathematics' of the state, a 'schizophrenic mathematics, uncontrollable and mad'.

Introduction

Although many mathematics classrooms remain sites where little to no dialogue occurs, during the last twenty years the educational reform movement in the

U.S. has advocated for increased emphasis on student communication. Policy and curricular changes reflect this new emphasis, and mathematics teachers are now meant to engage students in 'whole-class conversations' where participation and expression are highly valued:

> Mathematical communication is a way of sharing ideas and clarifying understanding. Through communication, ideas become objects of reflection, refinement, discussion, and amendment. When students are challenged to communicate the results of their thinking to others, orally or in writing, they learn to be clear, convincing, and precise in their use of mathematical language.
> (National Council of Teachers of Mathematics, NCTM, 2000)

The communication standard is one of the more problematic process standards mandated by the NCTM because of its tacit assumptions about the relationship between thinking and communicating. State curricular guidelines and state-sanctioned textbooks demand that communication be a central activity in the mathematics classroom, without adequate interrogation of the very concept of communication. Teachers often take up the concept of communication as though it were merely a matter of student speaking or writing, without recognizing the embodied and deeply material nature of all interaction.[1] Although there is a burgeoning research literature on the multi-modal nature of mathematics classroom discourse,[2] some of it exploring issues of embodiment and materiality,[3] one finds for the most part that teachers address the communication standard by asking students to *verbally share their thinking*. This 'think aloud' strategy is also prevalent in reading instruction where it is sometimes referred to as 'languaging' (Swain, 2006).

The primary aim of this article is to bring the work of Deleuze (1993, 1994) and Deleuze and Guattari (1987, 1994) to bear on the question of communication in the classroom. I focus on the mathematics classroom, where agency and subjectivity are highly regulated by the rituals of the discipline, and where neoliberal psychological frameworks continue to dominate theories of teaching and learning. Moreover, the nature of communication in mathematics classrooms remains highly elusive and problematic due in part to the distinctive relationship the discipline has with verbal language and thought.[4] I first discuss current attempts to better address the embodied nature of communication in mathematics classrooms, and argue that these remain overly logocentric and language-centric in their conception of thinking. I then show how the work of Deleuze and Guattari on thinking as a *radical disruptive event* can be used effectively to critique current pedagogical practices that privilege a narrow conception of communication in the classroom. I examine a set of exemplary classroom videos used in mathematics teacher education to argue that the current approach fails to honor the highly creative and disruptive nature of thinking.

Communication in the Mathematics Classroom

Stockero and Van Zoest (2011) note that mathematics educators ask students to share their thinking for a variety of reasons, including such diverse aims as enhancing student problem solving skills (Fello & Paquette, 2009), broadening student views on what constitutes mathematical activity (Hodge, 2009), and offering opportunities for teachers to study student thinking (Kastberg, Norton & Klerlein, 2009). Similarly, Bochicchio et al. (2009) suggest five essential components of successful whole-class conversation, the second being 'publicizing' student thinking:

> The teacher must support students in sharing their ideas so that other students have the opportunity to hear and comprehend those ideas and subsequently think about and respond to them. Without this step, discussion is not possible. The teachers' actions can include asking students to go to the board and share their work or thinking as well as having a student's idea restated by the student, other students or the teacher.
>
> (p. 608)

Although Stockero & van Zoest (2011) suggest that teachers need to move beyond a 'replication' model where students are simply asked to *share* their thoughts in order to enhance engagement and participation, they continue to support the notion that 'explanation' can capture student thinking, and they fail to problematize the relationship between thinking and the verbal processes of 'making thinking public'. Van Zoest et al. (2010) define thinking as students' 'ideas about approaching problems, what led them to their solutions, their justifications for solutions, and their reflections on mathematical activity, as well as their solution methods and answers to problems' (p. 50). Such a definition confines thinking to a matter of signification (justification, reflection, method, solution). Similarly, drawing on Vygotsky (1986) and his assertion that 'thought is not merely expressed in words; it comes into existence through them' (p. 218), Shreyar et al. (2009) define mathematical thinking as 'a reflective activity of making sense of indeterminate problematic situations by organizing (mathematizing) them with semiotic mediation tools (models)' (p. 1). Although this research has contributed significantly to the study of classroom discourse, it often imposes an overly rationalistic linguistic or semiotic model on creative and potentially disruptive acts of thinking. Conceptions of thinking and its relation to language remain dualistic and simplistic in much of the research on mathematics education, often reducing the concept of thought to a form of inner speech. Sfard (2008), drawing on Bhaktin, Vygotsky and Wittgenstein, proposes that we overthrow this tradition by recognizing how thinking is an inherently public activity, an always already collectively performed patterned activity, 'an individualized version of *interpersonal communication*' (Sfard, 2008, p. 81). For Sfard, communicating is a *patterned collaborative activity* which comes before individual thinking. This approach helps us revise our interpretation of classroom discourse by pointing to the externality of thinking. Sfard's work tackles the well-entrenched beliefs of those who would defend an ontology of private cognitive acts. The challenge for such an approach, however, is to move beyond the language-centric assumptions about thinking (and communication) that one often finds in Vygotsky-inspired work. Sfard announces that 'thinking encompasses more than inner speech' and addresses 'all forms of communication' (p. 100), but she tends to rely on language-centric examples. For instance, when Sfard states: 'I expect little disagreement regarding the claim that self-communication (for example, in the form of "inner speech") can be considered as a case of thinking' (2008, p. 82), and then proceeds to argue that all thinking can be considered an instance of self-communication, I am concerned that there is no room in this approach for thinking as a radical asignifying creative act. One wonders what is lost if thinking remains chained to, and contained within, a regime of signification that cannot fathom (nor abide) the disruptive and rupturing nature of thought outside of communication?

Hwang and Roth (2011) have drawn extensively on phenomenology to theorize the role of the body in learning math and science, arguing that Vygotsky's 'logocentric approach' conflated or reduced thought to language (p. 25). According to these authors, the typical classroom task of recounting or explaining one's thinking—on demand and supposedly after the fact of thinking—fails to capture the complex embodied nature of communication: 'There is not first thought, which is then emptied out into the public. Speakers find out about their thinking as much as listeners. This more holistic theory of conceptions considers different, irreducible modes of communication as a whole' (p. 29). According to this approach, 'the living body constitutes the mediating hub in communication; my body is my expression rather than merely a tool for expressing what is in my mind' (p. 29). In an effort to further center the body as the locus of learning, they broaden their conception of communication to include all sensory modalities—gesture, intonation, appearance, etc. And although, in arguing that 'thought is dynamically related to the whole unit of communication rather than to words alone,'(p. 28), they rescue thinking from a purely linguistic frame, they continue to confine thinking to models of communication, albeit more broadly conceived.

Language and Assemblage

Deleuze and Guattari (1987, 1994) challenge us to think the radical nature of thought outside a communication model. Instead of a logic of communication and its requisite binaries of sender/receiver or signal/noise or content/message, they offer a logic of intensities, a logic of ontogenetic 'assemblages engaging in irreversible durations' (Brunner & Rhoades, 2010). According to this logic, interaction is a creative practice of material experimentation within rhizomatic ecologies (Guattari, 2008). In a rhizomatic assemblage, there is no center nor root, but a proliferation of entry and exit points, a dispersal of lines (traits) that erupt outward and often loop back. This is a topo-philosophy in which regimes of signification impart more and more signifier, saturating the acentric network, while disruptive lines of flight spur new potentialities. This radically material ontology of interaction demands that we think the 'thisness' or 'haecceity' of becoming, so that we might study classrooms in terms of fluidity, affect and the exteriority of thought.

Deleuze & Guattari (1987) push back at the totalizing eye of linguistics and other discourse frameworks that reduce activity to language. A rhizomatic assemblage is ontologically heterogeneous, incorporating and developing in and through diverse entities, so that language becomes just one trait (or line) in the assemblage. Perhaps more importantly, lines (traits) in the rhizomatic assemblage are not all ultimately linked to linguistic features. The rhizomatic assemblage is composed of diverse realities, most of which are not bound to language. In other words, there are ways of expression that do not pay lip service to an image of thought (or becoming) that is entirely dominated by linguistic or discourse models: 'semiotic chains of every nature are connected to very diverse modes of coding (biological, political, economic, etc.) that bring into play not only different regimes of signs but also states of things of differing status' (Deleuze & Guattari, 1987, p. 7).

This approach aims to decenter language from the analysis: 'A semiotic chain is like a tuber agglomerating very diverse acts, not only linguistic, but also perceptive, mimetic, gestural, and cognitive . . .' (Deleuze & Guattari, 1987, p. 7) They criticize Chomskian linguistics for not being sufficiently abstract in that it fails to connect 'a language to the semantic and pragmatic contents of statements, to collective assemblages of enunciation, to a whole micropolitics of the social field' (Deleuze & Guattari, 1987, p. 7). Linguistics, like psychoanalysis, is too keen to reduce difference and repetition to marks of an underlying sameness. It's not that we aren't to study language as part of the system of affect, but just that arborial models—unlike rhizomatic ones—are always imposing images of language on the assemblage that make language the transcendental coding, 'A method of the rhizome type, on the contrary, can analyze language only by decentering it onto other dimensions and other registers' (Deleuze & Guattari, 1987, p. 8).

Not only is language decentered, but language itself is reconceived outside of a communication model. Language is neither informational nor communicational. Language is itself a 'collective assemblage of enunciation' which forms one of many regimes of signification whereby bodies are inscribed with power. In the context of the classroom, language is less about information and more about imposing 'semiotic coordinates' on the child. The bodies in the classroom are 'emitting, receiving, and transmitting' the 'order-word' that constitutes language as obedience (p. 77). Language is not a code nor is speech the communication of information. Language is a material act or effectuation: To 'order, question, promise, or affirm is not to inform someone about a command, doubt, engagement, or assertion but to effectuate these specific, immanent, and necessarily implicit acts' (p. 77). One can no longer imagine a clean distinction between speech and language (parole and langue), since there is no pre-existing syntax or primary signification. Nor can one imagine language as the translation of prior thinking into verbal expression. For Deleuze and Guattari, the only possible definition of language is 'the set of all order-words, implicit presuppositions, or speech acts current in a language at a given moment' (p. 79). It is not the case, however, that order-words are equal to language, but that they constitute its very possibility. Language-use is performative in that it 'presupposes a conventional context of eligibility', prescribing or in the least confining the possible manner of response (Massumi, 2002, p. 9). While communication relies on the mirror-like function of language, order-words realize the molding function of language.

The interesting tension is thus between the 'indisciplines at work in language' and the order-word as discipline. It is precisely the sites of indiscipline where an asignifying thought bores a hole in the surface of language and disrupts the order word. If we speak in indirect discourse, that is to say, if the 'collective assemblage of enunciation' speaks through us, then speech acts are multifarious and emit 'all the voices present within a single voice' (p. 80). But these same acts must, on occasion, function as points of disruption and nodes of emergence whereby the collective assemblage of enunciation is broken or torn, and the site marks the emergence of something outside of language—if only momentarily, a line of flight tears off from the rhizome and zigzags away, creating a new territory. Direct discourse (speech on one's own behalf) 'is a detached fragment of a mass and is born of the dismemberment of the collective assemblage' (p. 84). Accordingly, 'There is no individual enunciation. There is not even a subject of enunciation' (p. 79), but there are sites or events of asignifying disruption where thinking punches its way through the surface of language.

The communication model has long been suspect because of the way it privileges the existence, intention and rationality of an interior life that is both subject of and subject to the transmission of information between private and public spheres (Massumi, 2002). Deleuze and Guattari (1987) appeal instead to the concept of *expressionism*. Expression is never simply a matter of representing, describing, corresponding or complying, but neither is expression the causal construction of content or thought. Instead the linear causal link between content and expression is disrupted or inflected by chance. Expression's potential is linked to accident, event, singularity, change. The singular is not an instance or a member of a set, but an occurrence that envelops a potential collective. It is a disruptive event which nonetheless acts as a magnet in structuring the behavior of others around it. Deleuze's concept of singularity comes directly from the mathematics of discontinuous curves—mathematical singularities mark ruptures in a curve, sudden shifts in direction, and the flight of the infinite (Deleuze, [1968]1994; Smith, 2005). They break through the ontological rules that structure the relationship between language and content. Thus the singular act of expression is not an act confined to language, despite it being spoken in some sense by a collective. As Massumi (2002) suggests, one can accept that the subject is 'in a sense spoken by extra-linguistic forces of expression' without reducing the expressing individual to an instantiation of a system (p. 7). In the gap between thought and language, or content and expression, lies 'the immanence of their mutual deterritorialization' (Massumi, 2002, p. 9). It is in these gaps or breaks that the classroom as assemblage (a mix of machinic and ennunciative operatives) reassembles itself, and the points of suture or 'expression-content articulations' migrate and re-couple, the one form passing over to the other (Massumi, 2002, p. 10). Expression and the act of expressing are meant to capture the absolute materiality of the thinking-speaking relationship. There are thus intermediate entities between thought and language, asignifying particles of expression. These particles are atypical and stammering, constituting the 'cutting edge of the deterritorialization of language' (Deleuze & Guattari, 1987, p. 99 cited in Massumi, 2002, p. 15).

Analysis of the Video

The videos discussed in this article are from a teacher education resource entitled *Connecting Mathematical Ideas: Middle school video cases to support teaching and learning* (Boaler & Humphreys, 2005). The video resource, which is based on a Noyce-funded video study of middle school mathematics teaching, is used extensively in mathematics teacher education. The videos document a series of grade 7 algebra lessons in California. The classroom was videotaped everyday for a full year. Every few weeks the teacher, researcher and research assistants together watched and discussed videos that were collaboratively selected. The resource consists of a series of edited videos documenting Cathy Humphreys teaching. The accompanying book includes Humphreys' reflections as well as commentary by Jo Boaler, the principal investigator of the project. Boaler has written significantly about reform mathematics during the last ten or more years, and is a well-established scholar in math education. The book's foreword is written by Deborah Loewenberg Ball, who has authored or co-authored over 150 publications, acted on various national advisory boards, and has lectured and made numerous major presentations around the world.

Boaler and Humphreys' goal in offering the case study 'was to provide a landscape of teaching and learning interactions that others could use to explore their own thoughts and questions about teaching' (Boaler & Humphreys, 2005, p. 3). I offer this Deleuzian/Guattarian analysis as one such exploration, inspired by the compelling nature of these videos as teaching instruments, while at the same time deeply concerned by the misguided notions about classroom communication that are exhibited therein. The authors claim that they selected videos that focused on 'particularly interesting, unexpected, and sometimes difficult moments that occurred during ordinary lessons' (p. 10). But what disturbs me about these videos is the sense that there is almost nothing 'unexpected and sometimes difficult', and that they capture instead an all-too-sedate and state-sanctioned performance whereby the radical nature of thought is twisted into submission.[5]

I have chosen to analyze these popular videos because they function as pivotal texts in the production of legitimate classroom practice. To what extent the original researchers have edited or processed the original video data is of less relevance than that these video-texts are sanctioned and circulated as teacher education resources. Of the various classroom videos in the resource, I have chosen to discuss the first because (1) the focus on algebra allows me to show how algebra itself—as a regime of signification—functions in the delineation of thought from language, and (2) the whole-class discussion is typical of many classrooms where communication is central, whereas the later videos reveal a more nuanced approach to interaction. My analysis of the video borrows strategies found in intercultural sociolinguistics, which examines the shape and form of interaction in relation to both governing power relations and unconscious cues and framing.

What strikes one immediately when watching the videos is the considerable emphasis on oral communication and whole-class conversation. Although the camera records some of the student contributions during small group work, the focus is primarily on the whole-class segments. Students' hands shoot up, as many want to share. As the authors state in the introduction, 'Student thinking and sense making are at the heart of each case, as we see students wrestle with new ideas and conceptions of themselves, of mathematics, and ultimately, of their world' (Boaler & Humphreys, 2005, p. 4). The teacher adeptly calls on students, 're-voices' their responses and asks other students to re-voice as well, while she simultaneously documents on the white board their various procedures. Students are invited to go up to the overhead projector and use the diagram as they explain. From the perspective of the reform mathematics education movement, the focus on communication and multiple representations is sound pedagogy. Indeed, the teacher does an impressive job of moving the students towards generalizing their procedures so that they might begin to think 'algebraically' about finding the answer to a more general question. But it is precisely this emphasis on the verbalizing of thought that seems problematic in its implementation, despite my well knowing that 'thinking aloud' is considered good practice in mathematics classrooms.

The classroom video exemplifies the *verbally share your thinking* approach to communication. The class begins with the teacher placing a diagram of a 6×6 square border (picture frame) on the overhead projector (Figure 6.1), and asks the students to determine how many unit squares are in the border. Students are first asked to 'mentally' determine the number of unit tiles.

The teacher asks them to do so 'without talking, without writing, and without counting one by one' and then asks them to verbalize their methods. During the ten minute whole class conversation episode, the words 'thinking' or 'think' are used 21 times (15 times by the teacher). On all but two of those occasions 'I was thinking' declares a verbal representation or reportage of cognition.[6] After listening to the video numerous times, and counting and mapping the way this utterance occurs, one begins to hear the compulsive inscription performed by the discursive move 'what were you thinking?' repeated again and again as the teacher

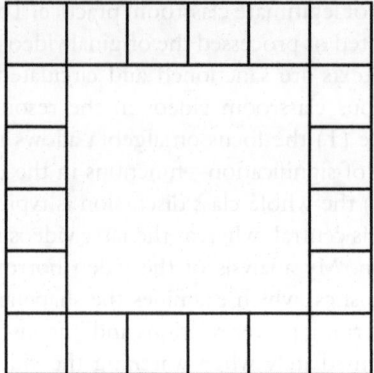

Figure 6.1

moves from student to student. One begins to notice the oppressive function of 'what were you thinking' as it repetitively reinstates a regime of signification and disallows disruptive thought. As Lecercle (2002) suggests, 'the speaker is in constant danger of being burked by language: a wet blanket of signification smothers any attempt at expression' (p. 6). In this video, the repeated refrain 'what were you thinking?' actually *betrays* thought because language can never reproduce the radical event-structure of thinking. The refrain 'what were you thinking' actually functions as a wet blanket, smothering the students' capacity to think otherwise, while enforcing the use of language as denotation/manifestation/signification.[7]

Just as 'I was thinking' fails to represent the thought to which it refers, it is the 'aura of signification' (Lecercle, 2002, p. 249) which is substantiated and validated through the repeated act of asking students to verbalize their thinking. Serres (2008) suggests that 'words fill our flesh and anaesthetize it' and that speaking in particular is like a 'discursive breastplate', a shield to numb our encounters (p. 59). This ceaseless talking and listening leaves no space for the senses. There is no place to think in this diluvian din of order-words. If thinking is in the flesh, then this constant turn to verbalize our thinking seems to work against embodied conceptions of learning. In the transcript excerpt below (see Table 6.1), and elsewhere in the video, Sharmeen submits to language so obediently and masterfully that she is often called on to manage the more stuttering students. Colin, on the other hand, speaks in terms of doing instead of thinking, and the teacher invites him to use the diagram and the pointer, and thereby opens up a space for expression and the body to re-enter the interaction. Might this significant break with the sitting-speaking subject—instead a subject that moves across the room and interacts with the diagram—be exactly the kind of event when links between expression and content are broken and re-assembled? Colin's language becomes completely indexical as he touches and interacts with the diagram. And yet the task itself is in essence trapped within the denotation/manifestation/signification circle since it is merely an exercise in naming.[8]

Table 6.1

1	Teacher	Did anyone think it was maybe thirty-eight first? A few people, OK. And, so, when you talked it over in your group, those of you [who] thought forty, what were you thinking? All right, Stephanie, what were you thinking?
2	Stephanie	Uh, I was thinking that one side is ten and then there's four sides and times ten by four is forty.
3	Teacher	OK. How many were thinking just like Stephanie? All right, what about the thirty-eight people, what were you thinking? Uh, Mindy?
4	Mindy	I was thinking about the top two are ten and so ten plus ten equals twenty, and then the other two to get were nine each, so that really makes eighteen, and twenty plus eighteen . . .
5	Teacher	OK. All right. So now let's just see some different methods—you know how we like to gather different methods. Let's see some different methods for getting the thirty-six. So, let's see, let's have Sharmeen. Sharmeen, what's your method?
6	Sharmeen	Well, Krysta started out with forty from ten times forty [four] and then I subtracted four from that because there would be four squares overlapping, and so that got thirty-six.
7	Teacher	Raise your hand if you understand how Sharmeen did it. And the four was for . . .?
8	Sharmeen	The squares that overlap.
9	Teacher	OK. And this four was for?
10	Sharmeen	The four sides.
11	Teacher	And this ten was for?
12	Sharmeen	The ten squares on each side.
13	Teacher	OK. Another way to do it? Colin?
14	Colin	All right, how I did it was, I just put one side was obviously gonna be ten, so it's ten, and then I did like the bottom one and that was gonna . . .
15	Teacher	Could you go up and show us? I think that might help us.
16	Colin	Can I use like a pointer-thinger (unintelligible)?
17	Teacher	The pointer's in the top drawer if you want to use it . . . top . . . right in the center . . . there it is.
18	Colin	All right I found it. Anyway, so I, like, I know this side is ten so I just did like ten and then this one, this one's the overlapping one, so then this would be nine, then this one would be nine, too, because this one's overlapping. And then for this, one it's be eight because these two, this one is being used by this one and this one is being used by that one.

This aura of signification[9] finds further substantiation in the actual focus of the lesson—the development of 'algebraic thinking'. The lesson aims to enculturate the students into habits of generalization and skills at generating algebraic rules. During the episode when students share their thoughts, each 'different method' described by each student is recorded by the teacher on the whiteboard as a different numeric expression. A major goal of the lesson, however, is to help the students grasp that all these differences are reduced to sameness through the power of algebra. The one correct answer—confirmed at the outset of the lesson—drives the diversity towards a unified and singular utterance. Ultimately, the differences in student thinking are deemed superficial, as the algebraic letter is enlisted to erase any divergences.

The teacher's well intended attempts to subject this fluid affect and perception to the *algebraic letter* and the regime of language (as communication) functions quite literally as a confining axiomatics[10] that imposes the state sanctioned forms of legitimate formulation—that being algebra and its power to obliterate difference. Algebra has a long history of erasing the body and the diagram from mathematics (Netz & Noel, 2007), and it functions here in the classroom to serve the state's algebraic image of mathematics. Algebra will only liberate these students when, or rather if, the *letter* is somehow breached from the whiteboard and made material and mobile in such a way that the students are able to leverage it as affect. But instead the regime of algebra is never dethroned, and grade 7 marks the beginning of its rule. In the excerpt below (Table 6.2), the teacher, after noting

Table 6.2

37	Teacher	OK. That whole thing about when, why you might need another letter. Kimberly, you were thinking that you need another letter, right? Why were you thinking that? Because that's a really important thing; when do you need another letter and when don't you? Why did you think you did?
38	Kimberly	Because we have, um, four letters and I was thinking, cause she read her, um, her thing there and I said it was kind of complicated so I was thinking that (*inaudible*) . . .
39	Teacher	OK. What do you think now?
40	Kimberly	We don't need it anymore.
41	Teacher	You're sure? You're convinced? OK. Um, Travis, were you going to add anything to that? OK. Yeah, Pam.
42	Pam	Well, the reason I was thinking we needed another letter is because in the beginning we needed two different numbers. So, maybe you needed two different letters.
43	Teacher	Oh. Oh, that's . . . yeah, right, right.
44	Pam	It kind of, like, if you were talking about what's the same and what's different. So in the algebraic formula it's, the things that are the same and different are not the same and different on the numbers.
45	Teacher	Right.
46	Pam	So, I think that when you asked what was the same and what was different, it kind of confused me.
47	Teacher	I'm glad it confused you in that way because it brought out a really important thing that we're going to be grappling with in some other problems. Because sometimes you are going to need a different letter, and sometimes you're not. Why don't you need another letter in this case? I mean, like, if you can do it without another letter, you want to keep it simpler. Why can we, why can we? Sarah. Yeah, this Sarah. Sarah Stanley.

that some students had wrongly introduced a second letter in their attempts to generalize the problem to any size of picture frame, asks the class to discuss when more than one letter is needed in an algebraic expression or equation.

Precisely when Kimberly's 'so I was thinking' becomes inaudible, she is swiftly disencumbered of that mistaken belief by the teacher's adept use of grammar in 'OK. What do you think now?' This stammering moment might have been the event or singularity that breached the wet blanket of language and opened up the interaction with new lines of flight, but Kimberly loops back into the regime of the letter with her dutiful response, 'we don't need it anymore'. Pam, who is an eager speaker in class, announces that it is exactly in the transition from numbers and their concrete specificity to letters and their aura of signification that confusion emerges. She points out that it is the very concepts of same and different that differ from one domain to the other. Indeed, Pam points out how language itself fails to adequately bridge the relation between number and letter, and the teacher, although too quickly packaging this confusion into something palatable, recognizes the significance of this insight.

Conclusion

Although the contribution of Deleuze and Guattari to contemporary theories of subjectivity is undeniable, and one can trace the impact of their work across the social sciences, there remains a need to further explore the potential of this work within education (Semetsky, 2006). In particular, we need to study how the concepts of the assemblage, the rhizome and the fold might be leveraged so as to shed light on classroom interaction (Goodley, 2007; Gough, 2004, 2005, 2007). By looking closely at video and transcript data, this article attempts to show how these key concepts can be used as analytic tools for critiquing current practices regarding communication in the classroom. According to Bogue's (1989/2001) reading of Deleuze, there is, within language, an anonymous nomadic 'aleatory point' which manifests itself as nonsense or paradox, a site that 'possesses no particular meaning but is opposed to the absence of meaning.' (Deleuze, 1990, p. 89, in Bogue, 1989/2001, p. 76). This point traverses the surface of words and things and is generative of life. The aleatory point is a mobile element or empty slot: 'it lacks its own identity, it lacks its own resemblance, it lacks its own equilibrium, it lacks its own origin' (Deleuze, 1969/1990, p. 55). Thought discovers its 'higher power' in an aleatory point, a Nietzschean inspired break with rational thought (Bogue, 1989/2001). Thinking is 'no longer a ratio reinforcing a reactive, sensory-motor forces, but an unbounded creativity from which active affections flow' (Hughes, 2011, p. 91). Or, in other words, as Deleuze states, 'To think is to create' (1994, p. 192).

> Thought strikes like lightning, with sheering ontogenetic force. It is *felt*. The highest operation of thought is not to choose, but to harbor and convey that force, repotentialized. The thinking is not contained in the designations,

manifestations, and significations of language, as owned by a subject. These are only partial expressions of it: pale reflections of its flash. The thinking is all along the line. It is the process: its own event.

(Massumi, 2002, p. 28)

Deleuze and Guattari (1987, p. 376) point to the dangerous 'private thinker' whose thinking is oppositional (citing Kierkegaard and Nietzsche). They bemoan the term 'private thinker' because of the way it conjures an interiority that they are trying to subvert, arguing that it is these sorts of thinkers and acts of thinking that actually 'place thought in an immediate relation with the outside' (p. 377). Such thinking is not to oppose one image against another, but to depose image reproduction altogether. Making thought exterior is a method of undoing the subjection of thought to the true model or ideal form, it is a nomadic strategy for crushing the machine that regulates the distribution of copies. The form of 'exteriority' has no space for model and copy, no striated space for the point-by-point adherence to method, but occupies instead the smooth space of ambulant differentials. Deleuze and Guattari refer to the 19th century writer Heinrich von Kleist (2004) who describes thought as a proceeding or process and not a controlling conceptual regulator of speech and affect. For Kleist, thought is pure intensity, a swirling of inarticulate sounds and unanticipated conflations, and not that which controls language in some legalistic state sanctioned way (Deleuze & Guattari, 1987, p. 378). Thus we are as a foreigner in our own language. It is precisely through this decoupling of thought and language that the exteriority of thought is given life. Only then can thought participate in becoming-minor, in becoming event, problem, haecceity. As Massumi (2002) suggests, the event or singularity of thought must fall through the 'propositional mesh' of language and *express* 'the field conditions that gave rise to it and the collective potential its occurrence envelops' (p. 24). The individual student lives this expression as an intensity across his or her body, impacted by and impacting on the micro-perceptions and tiny molecular articulations that hum and twist in all interaction: 'The body has become an expressive event: a voluble singularity' (Massumi, 2002, p. 27).

I have focused on mathematics because it seems to enact so perfectly the severe harnessing of thought that Deleuze and Guattari bemoan, and because 'think aloud' strategies are highly touted as a way of making mathematics more public and social. A mathematics classroom where radical disruptive thinking is evident seems almost unimaginable. And yet surely the mathematics classroom, for this reason if no other, is precisely the place to interrogate the nature of thought and its relation to language. My aim is to think mathematics differently, to interrogate its mannerisms as a material-cultural enterprise, and to articulate a new philosophical framework for conceptualizing the learning of mathematics. My hope is that a critique of mathematical thinking, as it is conceptualized in current educational practice, might allow us to break free from the confines of royal or state mathematics, and create lines of flight where a more adventurous mathematics might emerge. We need to think mathematics out of the technical procedural tyranny of school mathematics, and inspire a resistance to the containment of such cultural capital. Deleuze and Guattari demand that we imagine another mathematics, in contrast to the 'severe mathematics' of the state, a 'schizophrenic mathematics, uncontrollable and mad'.

Notes

1 See for instance Lynn, 2010 or Whitin & Whitin, 2002.
2 See O'Halloran, 2007.
3 See Radford, 2009.
4 Although there isn't room here to address this complex relationship in full, it is worth noting that the standard philosophical treatments of mathematics (formalism, logicism, intuitionism, naturalism) are at heart concerned with the ontological status of mathematical entities and the epistemological issue of how one comes to know these entities and to what extent mathematical statements capture, represent or exhaust these entities.
5 It is important to mention that the critique I offer in no way intends to play into the recently reheated debate between 'student centered' versus 'teacher centered' instruction, triggered in part by the 2008 National Mathematics Advisory Report which reiterated this unfortunate binary. I fully support Boaler's critique of the report, and I agree with her when she says that 'Researchers in mathematics have worked to understand and analyse the different aspects of effective teaching, and few have concerned themselves with trying to show that one extreme approach is better than another (Boaler, 2008, p. 589). In addition, it's important to say that I use these videos in my own work with pre-service mathematics teachers, and that the videos are of great value to the profession. I offer this critique as a way of opening the conversation up about communication in classrooms.
6 On the other two occasions 'think' is used modally to indicate the degree to which a student believes in what they are saying.
7 In the *Logic of Sense*, Deleuze (1969/1990) describes the confining circle of denotation/manifestation/signification as that which fails to address the event (sense) of the boundary between language and content.
8 Another reading of Colin's contribution is that he is more confident and speaks without the use of a modal 'I think' to hedge his assertions (rather than an 'I think' that reports on thinking).
9 I follow Lecercle (2002) in the use of this term to underscore the ways in which we grant signification infallible referential power.
10 Deleuze points to a nomadic mathematics that troubles and threatens axiomatic mathematics. Although algebraic methods might be leveraged in either tradition, they operate all too often as a confining and legislative discourse in school mathematics. Of interest here is the tension between Deleuze and the work of Alain Badiou, who pursues a more axiomatic and set theoretic approach to mathematics.

References

Boaler, J. (2008) When Politics Took the Place of Inquiry: A Response to the National Mathematics Advisory Panel's review of instructional practices, *Educational Researcher*, December, pp. 588–594.

Boaler, J. & Humphreys, C. (2005) *Connecting Mathematical Ideas: Middle school video cases to support teaching and learning* (Portsmouth, NH, Heinemann).

Bochicchio, D., Cole, S., Ostein, D., Rodriguez, V., Staples, M., Susia, P. & Truxan, M. (2009) Shared Language, *Mathematics Teacher,* 102:8, pp. 606–613.

Bogue, R. [1989] (2001) *Deleuze & Guattari.* Taylor and Francis elibrary. Retrieved from http://www.scribd.com/doc/58238982/Deleuze-and-Guattari-Ronald-Bogue.

Brunner, C. & Rhoades, T. (2010) Transversal Fields of Experience, *Inflexions,* 4 (December). Retrieved from http://www.senselab.ca/inflexions/volume_4/n4_introhtml.html.

Deleuze, G. [1988] (1993) *The Fold: Leibniz and the Baroque* (Minneapolis, MN, Regents of University of Minnesota Press).

Deleuze, G. [1969] (1990) *The Logic of Sense,* M. Lester, trans. (New York, Columbia University Press).

Deleuze, G. [1968] (1994) *Difference and Repetition,* Paul Patton, trans. (New York, Columbia University Press).

Deleuze, G. & Guattari, F. [1980] (1987) *A Thousand Plateaus: Capitalism and schizophrenia,* B. Massumi, trans. (Minneapolis, MN, University of Minnesota Press).

Deleuze, G. & Guattari, F. [1991] (1994) *What is Philosophy?* (Trans. H. Tomlinson & G. Burchell) (New York, Columbia University Press.

Fello, S. E. & Paquette, K. R. (2009) Talking and Writing in the Classroom, *Mathematics Teaching in the Middle School,* 14:7, pp. 410–414.

Goodley, D. A. (2007) Becoming Rhizomatic Parents: Deleuze, Guattari and disabled babies, *Disability and Society,* 22:2, pp. 145–160.

Gough, N. (2004) RhizomANTically Becoming Cyborg: Performing posthuman pedagogies, *Educational Philosophy and Theory,* 36, pp. 253–265.

Gough, N. (2005) Geophilosophy and Methodology: Science education research in a rhizomatic space, in: *Methodologies for Researching Mathematics, Science and Technological Education and Societies in Transition* (UNESCO—SAARSTE)

Gough, N. (2007) Changing Planes: Rhizosemiotic play in transnational curriculum inquiry, *Studies in the Philosophy of Education,* 26, pp. 279–294.

Guattari, F. [1989] (2008) *The Three Ecologies,* I. Pindar & P. Sutton, trans. (New York, Continuum).

Hodge, L. L. (2009) Learning from Students' Thinking, *Mathematics Teacher,* 102:8, pp. 586–91.

Hughes, J. (2011) Believing in the World: Towards an ethics of form, in: L. Guillaume & J. Hughes (eds), *Deleuze and the Body* (Edinburgh, Edinburgh University Press), pp. 73–95.

Hwang, S. & Roth, M. (2011) *Scientific and Mathematical Bodies* (Rotterdam, Sense Publishers).

Kastberg, S. E., Norton, A. III & Klerlein, J. T. (2009) Trusting Students, *Mathematics Teaching in the Middle School,* 14:7, pp. 423–429.

Kleist, H. von (2004) *Selected Writings,* D. Constantine, trans. (Indianapolis, IN, Hackett).

Lecercle, J-J. (2002) *Deleuze and Language* (Basingstoke, Palgrave Macmillan).

Lynn, R. (2010) Communication Speaks, *Mathematics Teaching in the Middle Grades,* 17:1, pp. 22–26.

Massumi, B. (ed.) (2002) *A Shock to Thought: Expression after Deleuze and Guattari* (New York, Routledge).

National Council of Teachers of Mathematics [NCTM] (2000) *Executive Summary: Principles and Standards for School Mathematics: Standards for Pre-K-12 Mathematics*. Available at: http://www.nctm.org/uploadedfiles/math_standards/12752_exec_pssm.pdf

Netz, R. & Noel, W. (2007) *The Archimedes Codex: How a medieval prayer book is revealing the true genius of antiquity's greatest scientist* (Cambridge, MA, Da Capo Press.)

O'Halloran, K. L. (2007) *A Multimodal Approach to Classroom Discourse* (London, Equinox).

Radford, L. (2009) Why Do Gestures Matter? Sensuous cognition and the palpability of mathematical meanings, *Educational Studies in Mathematics*, 70:3, pp. 111–126.

Serres, M. (2008) *The Five Senses: A philosophy of mingled bodies*, M. Sankey & P. Cowley, trans. (London, Continuum).

Semetsky, I. (2006) *Deleuze, Education, and Becoming* (Rotterdam, Sense Publishers).

Sfard, A. (2008) *Thinking as Communicating: Human development, the growth of discourses, and mathematizing* (New York, Cambridge University Press).

Shreyar, S., Zolkower, B. & Perez, S. (2009) Thinking Aloud Together: A teacher's semiotic mediation of a whole-class conversation about percents, *Educational Studies in Mathematics*, 73, pp. 21–53

Smith, D. (2005) Deleuze on Leibniz: Difference, continuity and the calculus, in: S. H. Daniel (ed.), *Current Continental Theory and Modern Philosophy* (Evanston, IL, Northwestern University Press).

Stockero, S. L. & Van Zoest, L. R. (2011) Making Student Thinking Public, *Mathematics Teacher*, 104:9, pp. 704–709.

Swain, M. (2006) Languaging, Agency and Collaboration in Advanced Second Language Proficiency, in: H. Byrnes (ed.), *Advanced Language Learning: The contribution of Halliday and Vygotsky* (New York, Continuum), pp. 95–108.

Van Zoest, L., Stockero, S. L. & Kratky, J. (2010) Beginning Mathematics Teachers' Purposes for Making Student Thinking Public, *Research in Mathematics Education*, 12:1, pp. 37–52.

Vygotsky, L. S. (1986) *Thought and Language* (Cambridge, MA, MIT Press).

Whitin, P. & Whitin, D. J. (2002), Promoting Communication in the Mathematics Classroom, *Mathematics Teaching in the Middle Grades*, 9:4, pp. 205–210.

Chapter 7

(Re)Visioning the Centre
Education Reform and the 'Ideal' Citizen of the Future

Linda J. Graham

Reprinted by permission of Taylor & Francis Ltd, http://www.tandfonline.com, on behalf of © Philosophy of Education Society of Australasia.

Editors' Introduction

Discourses of public education reform, like that exemplified within the Queensland Government's future vision document, position schooling as a panacea to pervasive social instability and a means to achieve a new consensus. However, in unravelling the many conflicting statements that conjoin to form education policy and inform related literature, it becomes clear that education reform discourse is polyvalent. Alongside visionary statements that speak of public education as a vehicle for social justice are the (re)visionary or those reflecting neoliberal individualism and a conservative politics. In this chapter, it is argued that the latter coagulate to form strategic discursive practices which work to (re)secure dominant relations of power. The casualties of this (re)vision and the refusal to investigate the pathologies of 'traditional' schooling are the children who, for whatever reason, do not conform to the norm of the desired school child as an 'ideal' citizen-in-the-making and who become relegated to alternative educational settings. Graham's objective is to elucidate statements that work to present a particular view of the world and in doing so, prepare the ground for the 'practices that derive from them, in the social relations that they form, or, through those relations, modify' (Foucault, 1972, p. 139). Statements presented in this chapter form discursive dividing practices which prepare the ground for the exclusion of non-deserving students who have denied themselves the right to an ostensibly inclusive educational system. This works to legitimise their subjection to arcane behaviour modification practices and naturalises the gendered and socio-economically-loaded life opportunities afforded to them.

Introduction

In the traditionally conservative Australian state of Queensland, it appears that 'the pressures of difference have begun to knock on the door' (McCarthy, 2003, p. 133). Population increase in the tropical north-eastern state from both domestic and international migration is causing some unrest due to the increased cost of real estate, dwindling natural resources, inadequacy of existing infrastructure, traffic and lifestyle change and the effects of multiculturalism upon 'Queenslanders'

(Graymore *et al.*, 2002; BCC, 2005; Cole, 2005; Murdoch, 2005). In 2000, the Queensland government released the education future vision document, *Queensland State Education-2010* (QSE-2010) to provide, in the words of Premier Peter Beattie, 'a broad description of the future for Education Queensland' (Education Queensland, 2000, p. 3). The aim of QSE-2010 was to question via community consultation what the purposes of schooling in the first decade of the 21st century might be and provide a vision statement to underpin a reform agenda in accordance with those purposes. QSE-2010 reflects anxieties and priorities that are similar in nature to many expressed by governments in other nations (see Edwards & Nicoll, 2001). In line with OECD objectives (2003; 2004), education reform discourse within QSE-2010 speaks to democratic participation, active citizenship, life-long learning and social cohesion. *But this is not all it does . . .*

QSE-2010 generically describes forces for change by discussing changes in family structure, multiculturalism, economic instability, information technology and the devolution of government (Education Queensland, 2000). Five years after the launch of QSE-2010 and mid-way through its life-cycle, I question how this policy and its off-shoots, which have informed a suite of reforms to education in Queensland, might be operating as a form of strategic rhetoric (Nakayama & Krizek, 1995); in that statements within the QSE-2010 vision may be working to privilege dominant perspectives and in doing so, (re) secure existing relations of power. The analysis here questions the effects of this (re)visioning and the apparent rejection of children who do not conform to the 2010 vision. These are the children who become described as 'not suited to traditional schooling' (Education Queensland, 2002), and who end up referred to 'alternative education programs and settings for students who have difficulty in conventional school and disciplinary structures' (Education Queensland, 2000, p. 16).

Turning to Literary versus Literal Versions of Truth

Discourse analysis consistent with a Foucauldian notion of discourse does not seek to reveal the true meaning by what is said or not said (Foucault, 1972). Instead, when 'doing' discourse analysis within a Foucauldian framework, one looks to statements not so much for what they say but what they *do*; that is, one questions what the constitutive or political effects of saying this instead of that might be? As Foucault (1972, p. 134) argues, 'there is no subtext'. The analyst's job 'does not consist therefore in rediscovering the unsaid whose place [the statement] occupies' (Foucault, 1972, p. 134). Instead, Foucault (1972, p. 134) maintains that 'every*thing* is never said' and that the task is to determine, in all the possible enunciations that could be made on a particular subject, why it is that certain statements emerged to the exclusion of all others. There is not the scope within this paper to look to conditions of possibility. Of interest here is more the function of these statements; not how they appeared and came to dominate but what it is that they now *do* (Culler, 1997).

In the context of this paper then, discourse analysis is read as a exercise in explicating statements that function to place a discursive frame around a particular political position; that is, statements which coagulate and form rhetorical constructions that present a strategic reading of social texts to (re)secure existing relations of power (Foucault, 1972; Nakayama & Krizek, 1995). The intention is to demonstrate how such statements, in eliding other competing positions, come to present a particular view of the world and in doing so, prepare the ground for the 'practices that derive from them, in the social relations that they form, or, through those relations, modify' (Foucault, 1972, p. 139).

This paper progresses with four layers of analysis. The first provides a discussion of 'the problems of the present' as articulated by education reform discourse in Queensland. In the second layer, I retreat to paint a Foucauldian backdrop highlighting discursive motifs inherent to the modern art of government and development of liberal democratic society as a 'sovereignty of the good' (Foucault, 1988, p. 61). The third moves to consider how it is that exclusion can come to be rearticulated as a result of 'good/bad choices' and 'good/bad choosers'. The final layer of analysis (re)turns to the present as a symptom of the future, isolating similar discursive motifs in education department literature. These reflect not only the view that 'in order to change 'the future' or 'society' one must change the child' (Baker, 2005, p. 69), but also sanction the use of exclusion and force against those who do not/cannot/will not conform to the social norms established by and through existing relations of power.

I. (Un)clear and Present Danger

The structure and character of the family is changing in ways that are unprecedented. With new patterns of employment and underemployment, greater mobility and new concentrations of poverty, families are shifting in configuration from nuclear families. Parents are older and working more. Children have fewer siblings in smaller families and they move more often.

The nurturing family of recent decades, based on consensus that the Australian dream surrounded every child, has melted away. Teachers see the signs of family disruption in students—anxiety, depression, lack of discipline, aggression, inadequate literacy outcomes and a greater need for adult role models, particularly male role models.

This places new pressures on schools and teachers to provide children with high levels of social support. It makes it more difficult for some parents to help their children achieve in school. It creates the need for parenting education, the need for a safe, accepting and disciplined environment in schools and for new links with communities to rebuild a new consensus.

(Education Queensland, 2000, p. 4)

To support an education reform agenda, the opening paragraphs to QSE-2010 point to the problems of the present, describing changes in family structure and the challenge to schooling when faced with 'the signs of family disruption in students' (Education Queensland, 2000, p. 4). According to the Queensland Government this creates the need for discipline in schools, a new consensus and a (re)consolidation of the Australian identity. However, Foucault argues that identity is not fixed by some predetermined naturalised essence. Instead, it should be regarded as formulated, constituted, derived and inherently weak. He maintains, 'this rather weak identity, which we attempt to support and to unify under a mask, is in itself only a parody: it is plural, countless spirits dispute its possession' (Foucault, 1984, p. 94).

But plurality (and dispute) begets anxiety. If we historically (re)situate ourselves to recall the political imperatives leading to the constitution of the ethical pact said to underpin the ideal of a liberal democratic consensus (Foucault, 1988), we can start to grasp that plurality is not entirely consistent with consensus, and that consensus is entirely necessary to solidify a pact. When faced with 'a complex system of distinct and multiple elements, unable to be mastered by the powers of synthesis' (Foucault, 1984, p. 94), society turns to techniques of discipline and methods of subjection in order to secure that mastery; that is, modern society (re)turns to techniques of discipline-normalisation that Foucault (1975c) argues arose as a response to the threat of plague.

2. Turning to/from History . . .

In his College de France lectures, Foucault described a historical shift in the art of governing and the development of a productive form of power by juxtaposing two models of contagion control: the exclusion of lepers against the inclusion of plague victims (Foucault, 1975c). The methods used to manage the epidemics of leprosy and plague were different although each disease presented a similar problem. Both were highly contagious and deadly. The model of contagion control relating to leprosy though, led to the leper's exclusion where these unfortunate individuals were expelled from the community in an attempt to purify it (Foucault, 1975b). However, despite the virtual disappearance of leprosy towards the end of the Middle Ages, this model utilising the techniques of exclusion and banishment continued; albeit with a new object of concern.

> Leprosy disappeared, the leper vanished, or almost, from memory; these structures remained. Often, in these same places, the formulas of exclusion would be repeated, strangely similar two or three centuries later. Poor vagabonds, criminals, and 'deranged minds' would take the part played by the leper.
>
> (Foucault, 1988, p. 7)

Madness and Unreason

Among those confined there was distinction leading to the segregation and differential treatment of those characterised by 'unreason' and those who were considered truly 'mad'. 'Unreason' was conceptually aligned with indolence and idleness, immorality and debauchery and banished lest the unreasoned infect others with their 'contagious example of transgression and immorality' (Foucault, 1988, p. 81). Madness, on the other hand, was aligned with baseness, bestiality, a regression to animalism marked by the complete absence of those faculties of Reason which were taken to distinguish man from beast and the merely bad from the completely mad.

As Foucault (1975a, b, c; 1977) argues however, exclusion, banishment and confinement resulted in a negative form of power, a power that subtracted from itself because the community suffered the loss of human utility or, in Marxist terms, the 'surplus-value' that could be extracted from these individuals. Hence, institutions of refuse and waste became workhouses where labour 'assumed its ethical meaning: since sloth had become the absolute form of rebellion, the idle would be forced to work' (Foucault, 1988, p. 57). Although the great houses of confinement attempted to be economically independent through forced labour and industry, the competition they presented led to protests from private enterprise (Foucault, 1988). Thus 'unreason' as manifest in idleness, poverty, immorality and dependence needed a self-sustaining solution.

Inclusion and Plague: Educate, Reform, Cure . . .

During the classical age, the problem of unreason culminated in an ethical project which saw 'interest in cure and exclusion coincide' (Foucault, 1988, p. 10). This seemingly antithetical coupling deriving from the political dream of a 'sovereignty of the good' resulted in an effort towards the production of an 'ideal' citizenry through the use of sophisticated techniques of discipline. Foucault (1975b) discusses plague control as a historical event intrinsic to the development of the modern disciplinary society and the strategic control of human multiplicities, not through the techniques of banishment and forced exclusion, but through a forced and ever more strange *inclusion*. Individual positioning was determined through the development of methods of examination through which were established a personal itinerary of particularity. In distinguishing the exclusion of lepers from the inclusion of the plague victim, Foucault (emphasis added, 1975b, p. 46) states:

> It is not exclusion but quarantine. It is not a question of driving out individuals but rather of establishing and fixing them, of giving them their own place, of assigning places and of defining presences . . . Not rejection but *inclusion*.

The birth of the modern disciplinary society and the development of a strategic, productive form of power led to the displacement of overt forms of coercion and punishment, which by their violent nature were in danger of bringing about organised revolt and the destruction of the desired social order. This new 'governmentality' was the commencement of a shift to the *regulation of self* that was made possible via the recuperative properties of psychological discourse.

Discourse of Right versus Denial of Right

Ever more sophisticated methods of population control began to characterise the modern age. This refinement was necessitated by the apparent schism between two irreconcilable forces, the overt discourse of right and the covert denial of rights, where ignoble coercive disciplines work in opposition to the promise of freedom put forward by the formal egalitarian framework of the sovereignty of the good (Foucault, 1980). However, the apparent schism arising from the conflict between these 'two absolutely heterogeneous types of discourse' (Foucault, 1980, p. 107)—sovereign right versus disciplinary coercion—necessitated the unifying, collusive intervention of an arbitrating discourse that was successful via its claim to scientific objectivity. The need to reconcile the dissonance arising between the *discourse of right* and systematic *denial of rights* is what Foucault (1980, p. 107) maintains, 'rendered the discourse of the human sciences possible', for psychological discourse acts as a coherent relay between these 'mechanisms of discipline and the principle of right'.

As Foucault (1988, p. 106) points out though, the discourse of discipline is incongruent with 'that of law, rule, or sovereign will'. Instead of enabling access to the promise of freedom inherent to the discourse of right, modern disciplines silently and remotely imprison 'by means of the techniques propounded by the experts of the soul' (Rose, 1990, p. 11). These techniques bring about the seemingly voluntary management of the self by the self in order to prevent 'the weakening of discipline and the relaxation of morals' (Foucault, 1988, p. 59), strengthening the ethical pact underpinning the sovereignty of the good. It is no accident that psychological discourse has as its object the recalcitrant, the disordered and the unruly. In reconciling the irreconcilable, psychology acts to calm both dissonance *and* dissonants through the rule of the norm, as both a discursive domain and a grid of intelligibility for use in the interrogation and rectification of unsanctioned forms of difference.

The normative project culminates in the perpetual reinvestment of disciplinary power through techniques of normalisation engendered towards the production of the sovereign citizen, the self-governing individual, the self-regulated learner (Popkewitz, 2001). This modern art of governing can be characterised by its focus on the individual and preoccupation with governing the soul (Rose, 1990). Interestingly, in the effort to (re)claim the unreasoned, psychological discourses that speak to self-regulation and reason disseminate universalising theories of cognition and development that exclude through 'systems of recognition, divisions, and distinctions that construct reason and "the reasonable person"' (Popkewitz, 2001, p. 336). The generation of this power/knowledge has resulted in an impenetrable but 'fundamentally positive power that fashions, observes, knows and multiplies itself on the basis of its own effects' (Foucault, 1975b, p. 48). It is a knowledge cloaked in benevolence and inordinately difficult to resist.

Knowledge and Mastery

The imperative towards constructing a sovereignty of the good resulted in the transformation of houses of banishment to moral institutions and thus instead of purification through banishment or torture, the move to purify through curative practice was conceived (Foucault, 1988). It could be argued that the aim itself was virtuous and engendered towards the common good; to render unruly bodies productive whilst inculcating a desire to conform to the 'great ethical pact of human existence' (Foucault, 1988, p. 58). Integral to the functioning of this 'consensus' to underpin the modern disciplinary society, was what Foucault (1977, p. 26) termed a 'political technology of the body' constituted by two lines of force; namely, 'a *knowledge* of the body that is not exactly the science of its functioning, and a *mastery* of its forces that is more than the ability to conquer them' (Foucault, 1977, p. 26, emphasis added). These lines of force—knowledge and mastery, truth and discipline—traverse the modern socio-political landscape through their embodiment within relations of power to constitute a diffuse but cohesive network of power. The interrelation and reciprocity of these lines of force is illustrated in Foucault's coining of the term 'power/knowledge'.

Disciplinary power functions by way of disseminating knowledge as *truth*. These truths come to be dispersed via discourses or enunciations of particular truth-claims and sustained by a system of disciplinary technologies; seemingly insignificant practices that penetrate the social body to regard individuals, generating knowledge of individual particularity which then circulates to (re)produce and (re)inforce such claims to truth. Knowledge and mastery—truth and discipline, frame the socio-political dream of this republic of the good by providing a means to secure the submission of forces and bodies (Foucault, 1977). This occurs through the deployment of these two methods of observation and description, which produce a way of knowing and ordering that can be used to neutralise the potential political force of human multiplicities (Foucault, 1977).

Schools and Discipline

The imperative of good supported by the impetus of coercion led to the expansion of social institutions—prisons, factories, hospitals and schools—operating as sites for the exercise of disciplinary power. Childhood, albeit considered predictive of adult pathology, was seen as more amenable to cure. These two factors assured that 'children were to become favoured objects and targets' (Rose, 1990, p. 132) in the will to know and govern individuals. As a result, schooling became a privileged disciplinary site for the individualisation and socialisation of the child as a desirable future citizen (Synott & Symes, 1995) and ever more sophisticated methods were developed to know and master the school child. These methods— both technological and discursive—operate as the 'means of visualisation and techniques of inscription' (Rose, 1990, p. 134) and are deployed within social institutions, such as the schooling system, to fix and to know the individual 'within a single common plane of sight' (Rose, 1990, p. 132). As such, schooling operates as a field of application for the inculcation of social and moral principles (Synott & Symes, 1995), forming a net-like organisation in which relations of power become exercised, (re)informed and strengthened (Foucault, 1980).

The intersection of these techniques of enunciation and visibility (Deleuze, 1992) construct a pedagogical net which acts to capture, sort, spatialise and rehabilitate individual school children (Graham, 2006). The pedagogical categorisation of difference creates disciplinary spaces into which individuals become distributed through methods of examination that utilise 'grids of specification' (Foucault, 1972, p. 46) constituted by relative domains of knowledge; such as special education or educational psychology. As Rose (1990, p. 134) argues, the emergence of the individual within the field of knowledge came about 'not through any abstract leap of the philosophical imagination, but through the mundane operation of bureaucratic documentation'. Statistical tallies of populations tabulating births, deaths, and marriages graduated to the complex of aptitudes, disinclinations, areas of weakness, learning styles, processing speed, short-term memory, spatial abilities, word recognition, sociometric statuses and so on—transforming the work of the humble statistician into an enterprise of individualisation.

In the modern schooling institution, this new-found knowledge has come to be deployed palliatively with repression only coming into play as a lateral effect (Foucault, 1975a), obscuring the other work done in the name of schooling through those ignoble practices that occur on 'the underside of the law' (Foucault, 1976, p. 93f in Marshall, 2001, p. 35). Whilst the discourse of discipline is incongruent with the notion of autonomous freedom, this is disguised through the seemingly benign notion of meritocracy and the 'positing of a faculty of choice' (Marshall, 2001, p. 295). This brings about the appearance of autonomy with the implication that we are masters of our own destiny and hence, victims of our own folly. Arguably, these notions obscure the conditions of our own production (Olssen, 2005) and how our subjectivity has been formed via the constitutive pressure of technological and discursive forces.

These forces are heavily implicated in the practices of schooling. Instead of enabling access to the promise of freedom inherent to the discourse of right, schooling aids to imprison the soul by taking up the persuasive humanism of psychological discourse to construct the school child as an autonomous individual who is imbued with a 'faculty of choice' (Marshall, 2001, p. 295). However, the insertion of a capacity to 'choose' brings with it an assertion of not only choosing *to* but also choosing *not to*. It is to the trap within this notion that I now turn.

3. The Chimera of Choice and The Chains of Freedom

Ironically, 'freedom' has become compulsory in that the citizen is enchained by or even *contracted to* a particular illusion of freedom that is consistent with the aspirations of government. Central to the success of this 'art of governing' is the production of the citizen who believes they are free (Olssen, 2005). The artifice inherent to this notion becomes evident when the imposition of force on bodies is masked by the seductive humanism of psychology and ensuing technologies of the self. This culminates in the constitution of an ideal subject/citizen who 'chooses' to uphold the terms of the social contract in the belief that, *in this at least,* they are exercising both the faculty and right to choose (Marshall, 1997b; 2001).

Political liberalist ideology, together with conceptualisations of personal autonomy, becomes articulated in and through the discourse of cosmopolitanism, which Popkewitz (2004, p. 189) describes as the relationship engendered 'between the freedom and will of the individual and the political liberty and will of the nation'. The power of political liberalism—and its idealised notion of the 'autonomous chooser' (Marshall, 1997b), disseminated through the discourse of cosmopolitan reason (Popkewitz, 2004)—is in its *reasonableness.* It is hard to resist concepts such as individual rights, personal autonomy and rule by consensus, however poststructural critique is not simply levelled at the concept but how concepts come to be taken up and used in disciplinary ways.

For example, Olssen (2005, p. 372, emphasis added) objects to how the concept of autonomy 'misrepresents and distorts the character of social existence . . . in a way that distorts the overall frame of reference in a *particular political direction*'. The misrepresentation noted by Olssen is in the suggestion that an individual can choose from a variety of options *of their own making,* resulting in conceptualisations of 'the personally autonomous individual who was free and *could* choose' (Marshall, 1997b, p. 33, emphasis in original). Marshall (1997b, p. 33) though, argues that the personally autonomous individual has been supplanted by 'the notion of the autonomous chooser—an individual capable of choosing correctly from a variety of free choices'. This does not mean that the 'autonomous chooser' *is free* for an individual can only ever hope to choose from choices that are or have been made available to him/her and this again is within the constraints of circumstance. Therefore, it is reasonable to argue that both our freedom and capacity to 'choose' has already been delimited by factors outside our control.

Existing relations of power and an individual's position within those relations determine the degree to which they can exert control over their own lives. So whilst we might be able to choose from the options available, we may not have the power, control or faculty to choose what we actually want. In this regard, Marshall (2001, p. 295, emphasis added) distinguishes personal autonomy as 'being able to *decide for oneself*' from strategic conceptualisations of the 'autonomous chooser' supposedly imbued with 'a *faculty of choice*'. The difference here is subtle and oscillates around being the author of one's own choices as opposed to choosing within the limits prescribed and organised towards a particular strategic end by others. Marshall (1997b, p. 47, emphasis in original), in a phrase that speaks to the argument I make with respect to education reform discourse in Queensland, explains:

> It is not just that the insertion of the economic into the social *structures* the choices of the individual, but that, also, in behaviouristic fashion it

manipulates the individual by penetrating the very notion of the self, structuring the individual's choices, and thereby, in so far as one's life is just the individual economic enterprise, the lives of individuals.

Contributing to Marshall's (2001, p. 294) discussion of the problem of in/dependence for the autonomous chooser in delineating freedom *from* and freedom *to*,[1] I argue that the insertion of a faculty of choice is strategic for an additional reason: in that it allows for the assertion of personal responsibility; that is, to be both responsible *to* and responsible *for*. This is not just the responsibility *to* 'make continuous choices' (Marshall, 2001, p. 295) consistent with the ideal of the 'unfinished cosmopolitan' (Popkewitz, 2004). If we unpack the obligations of cosmopolitan citizenship we find; first, the responsibility *to* choose good choices; second, to take responsibility *for* the consequences of those choices; and third, being responsible *for making* those choices. This culminates in a situation whereby one becomes characterisable by the things one has or has not done, whence the individual becomes known and marked by an identity conceived around the 'choices' s/he has supposedly made. Thus, a second objectionable aspect of the concept of autonomy comes into play when the rhetoric of the autonomous individual with an ability to choose is used to construct a binary of *good/bad choices* and thus, *good/bad choosers.*

If one really did have the freedom and 'right' to choose, then surely there would be not be consequences for exercising that choice either way? Also any emphasis on 'opportunity' and 'choice' suggests a level playing field and that the 'choices' available are the same for all (see Marshall, 2001, p. 294). It seems the bitter pill masked by the discourse of cosmopolitanism is that the common good is only good for some. Not those who are capable of exercising autonomy, for arguably 'nobody is autonomous in this sense' (Olssen, 2005, p. 373), but good for those who both have the capacity and are content to choose from *approved* choices, in order to cultivate a civic self that can compete in 'a race where there is no finishing line' (Popkewitz, 2004, p. 207).

4. Getting Back to the Future . . .

Queensland State Education-2010 is a textual demonstration of strategic discursive positioning that weighs concerns with social justice against the demands of globalised economic imperative. The narrative deploring decay to the social fabric is an exercise in refusal that hides the responsibilities of government behind the discourse of neoliberal individualism (Davies, 2005). This becomes apparent in statements like:

> There is a challenge facing education in Queensland as we move into an era where knowledge supersedes information and technology transforms long-standing relationships of time and space. It is to become a learning society—the Smart State—in which global forces *favour the adaptable.*
>
> (Education Queensland, 2000, p. 8, emphasis added)

Pausing to think outside the current spin, Davies (2005, p. 9) remarks sagely that whilst, 'it feels good to be flexible and adaptable . . . it also feels terrible when we realize we cannot afford to stop'. Similarly, Lambeir (2005) argues that through the application of this rationality, to *be* 'a human being is to choose to learn this and to learn that for the rest of one's natural life' (p. 353). Like Davies (but unlike the Queensland Government), he questions 'whether this is the kind of life we *want* to live for a lifetime' (p. 350). It appears that what the individual may want is important only in so long as it benefits *certain* others, therefore desire is stimulated in accordance with dominant objectives. In effect, neoliberal individualism makes it incumbent upon the desirable citizen to cultivate an 'adaptable' or cosmopolitan self, so as to avoid burdening the republic of the good. Here again, Olssen (2005, p. 373, emphasis in original) is instructive in arguing that:

> To define the perfection of the state in terms of such a value therefore will obviously short-change many groups. To make it the foundation value of the state also potentially exonerates the state from responsibility to assist its citizens when in need. It is not so much of a slippage, after all, from arguing that 'the state should assist people to become autonomous' to arguing 'they expect all to *be* autonomous'.

Not only is Queensland education reform discourse in danger of the slippage to which Olssen refers but the discursive practices within constitute a correlative object (Foucault, 1972; Deleuze, 1988); the dissonant citizen at the root of civic dissonance. This is the 'unreasoned' individual who fails to capitalise on educational opportunities because they do not choose in accordance with the 'proper' choice put forward by dominant paradigms (Lambeir, 2005). It appears that in a contemporary individualistic society, we are free *only* in so long as we 'choose' to adhere to the narrow parameters of the social norms established by and through existing relations of power. In the educational context, approved choices are presented as 'opportunities' that the 'good chooser,' as an ideal citizen-in-the-making, should properly and promptly avail themselves.

Assigning Places and Defining Presences

Those who either do not/cannot/will not position themselves to take advantage of 'opportunity' become positioned themselves. Once constituted as an object of a particular sort, individuals can be dispersed into disciplinary spaces and, from there, become subject to particular discourses and practices that Butler (1997, pp. 358–359) argues results in, 'the "on-going" subjugation that is the very operation of interpellation, that (continually repeated) action of discourse by which subjects are formed'. Through this process, individuals not only come to occupy *spaces* at different points in the social hierarchy but, through their continual subjugation, come to know and accept their *place*. Such processes and practices of exclusion are described benevolently in departmental literature:

State schools should provide a safe, tolerant and disciplined environment that allows *all* students the *opportunity* to learn. This means: developing alternative education programs and settings for students who have difficulty in conventional school and disciplinary structures.

(Education Queensland, 2000, p. 16, emphasis added)

Importantly, non-adherence is also perceived as a *choice* that brings with it a suggestion of personal responsibility and culpability. More subtly, this contributes to the constitution of a recognizable object of discourse—the *punishable* 'chooser'—upon whom the therapeutic force of the good must be directed and if necessary, intensified (Foucault, 1972; 1975c; 1977; Ewald, 1992). These manoeuvres become articulated in educational reform discourse, thus:

This reform is about engaging young people in learning. It is not about forcing reluctant or disruptive students to remain in classrooms or lowering the standards of behaviour we expect from young people. Processes for dealing with disruptive behaviour, such as suspension and exclusion, will continue. Extra career guidance and personal support, and more flexible learning options will be provided for these young people to continue their learning *in different environments.*

(Education Queensland, 2002, p. 7, emphasis added)

However, these 'different environments' are not all benign. In Queensland, school suspension that is longer than five days in duration or repeated suspensions can also result in enrolment in alternative site placement units running intensive behaviour modification programs. Depending upon the school district, age, gender and profile of the child, enrolment in these programs can be for a few weeks[2] or up to six months (Bouhours *et al.*, 2003).[3]

The Object of Choice

The concept of personal autonomy posits a faculty of choice which (dis)places responsibility and allows for the assertion of 'good/bad choices' and 'good/bad choosers'. Such constructions of the individual subject are dependent upon the discourse of the human sciences, particularly the appeal to reason and the ability to choose *reasonably.* 'Bad choosers' end up referred to and become the domain of cognitive and behavioural psychologists (Ollendick & Hersen, 1998; Powell & Inglis-Powell, 1999; Wallace, 1999),

Please find below some suggestions to deal with Candy's [a pseudonym] behaviour . . . If consistently applied across all situations, Candy will be more likely to learn how her choices (actions) result in a consequence (effect). The aim is for Candy to learn that it is her choices that determine a consequence (reward/punishment), not her parents . . .

> EG: 'The rules are we go forward on the escalator. If you get hurt that is your choice'. Then if she tantrums, 'You can scream but the rules are the same. The tantrum won't work. You chose to walk the wrong way so you chose to get hurt'.
> (Letter from Psychologist, 2003, pp. 1–2, Researcher Archive)

Traces of psychological discourse can also be found in Queensland Government education policy, school management documents and media releases. For example, in *Education Views,* published by Education Queensland, an article entitled 'Alternative Program Helps At-risk Pupils', states:

> Mr Wells said the Government's approach to behaviour management issues was to have students who displayed unacceptable behaviours face up to the consequences of their actions.
> (Currie, 2000, p. 2)

In *Schools + Parents* magazine, another Education Queensland publication, an article entitled 'Dealing with Misbehaviour in the Early Years', states:

> Mr O'Brien recommends parents reinforce that their child is responsible for his or her own behaviour ('I can see you put your toys away yourself today!') and appeal to their child's own sense of self ('When did you discover how to do that?) . . . Mr O'Brien suggests parents *seek help* from their child's teacher, guidance officer or principal if the behaviour persists.
> (Education Queensland, 2005, pp. 18, 19, emphasis added)

We can see clearly how the discourse of the human sciences manifests as discursive, dividing practice in an example of a Behaviour Management Plan available on the Education Queensland website. The plan outlines responsibilities and consequences for primary school students and sets out levels of conformity, described as 'Discipline Levels' that move from Gold, Silver or Bronze, to levels of nonconformity that slide from Level 1 to Level 5. From Level 2, pejorative discourse is invoked in statements such as, '*You* have failed to improve your standards' (Education Queensland, 1995, p. 15, emphasis added). At Level 5, the student is informed:

> Unfortunately, *you* have not shown any willingness to improve at this School. As a result *you have denied yourself the right* to be a student at Swayneville State School. *You* will be officially suspended from this School. The Director General of Education will determine *your* future primary education.
> (Education Queensland 1995, p. 15, emphasis added)

Aptly illustrating the schism arising between the discourse of rights and the coercive denial of those rights, following this excerpt is a statement that reads: 'A right is something which belongs to you and cannot be taken away by anyone' (Education Queensland, 1995, p. 15). Since 'the good' cannot be seen to be taking away the rights of a child, psychological discourse acts to reconcile the irreconcilable by positioning the child as 'having denied themselves that right'. The use of 'you' also has individualising effects. It is a discursive tactic that firmly positions the incorrigible child as the site of the educational problem (Slee, 1994; 1995), demarcating between children who 'choose' to conform to prevailing norms and those who supposedly choose otherwise. This suggests not only equality of choice but that the 'approved' choices are relevant and desirous to all. Ironically, it could be argued that the child who 'chooses' otherwise is demonstrating more autonomy than the child who chooses the choice already made for him/her. Such is the chimera of 'choice'.

Reconciling the Irreconcilable

Despite the promise of freedom in neo-liberalist rhetoric, leaking through behaviour management policy discourse is the coercive subordination of the rights belonging to the supposedly 'autonomous' individual to the republic of the good (Foucault, 1988). This subordination is evident in phrases like '[a] supportive school environment is where school *community* members feel safe and valued' (Education Queensland, 1995, p. 4, emphasis added). Here the responsibility of the individual is to the 'community' and the interests of the community are paramount, however, the neoliberal twist on community and responsibility is that the individual is responsible to the community but there is diminishing obligation by return and the dominant interests are economic (Davies, 2005). Traditionally, those with the least influence (economic and social) have had little say in the constitution of 'community,' or what should be considered as acceptable social norms. Typically, this group—the poor, the disadvantaged, the disabled, and migrant populations—benefits least from the unequal structural arrangements such a 'consensus' upholds.

Olssen (2005, p. 374) maintains that, 'in individualistic cultures . . . people are 'responsibilized' through strategies of 'power-knowledge' to believe they are freer than they really are' for 'underpinning the determinations of individuals is a mix of shaping and conditioning forces and necessities'. The forces and necessities to which Olssen refers are what Popkewitz (2004, p. 193) describes as 'regulatory norms of participation' and these contribute to inclusion and exclusion by constituting both centre and margin (see Graham & Slee, in press). Psychological discourse acts to rearticulate the conditions of such exclusions by establishing a causal link within the recalcitrant, uncooperative 'unreasoned' child-citizen who 'chooses' to make the wrong choices. In this, the discourse of cosmopolitan reason acts to reconcile the irreconcilable; masking the schism that arises between the discourse of rights and the coercive denial of those rights when, for example, a child is excluded from an education to which our justice system states they have a legal right. The cosmopolitan discourse of choice, autonomy and responsibility rearticulates that problematic by positing the child as having *denied themselves* that right.

An Illusory Interiority

Psychological discourses that speak to self-regulation and reason disseminate universalising theories of cognition and development that exclude through 'systems of recognition, divisions, and distinctions that construct reason and "the reasonable person"' (Popkewitz, 2001, p. 336). The child who does not choose *reasonably* is constructed as behaving outside of those regulatory norms of participation constituting a liberal democratic consensus (Popkewitz, 2004). In this way, the arbitrating discourse of cosmopolitan reason works to construct both centre and margin by defining and universalising 'tacit standards from which specific others can then be declared to deviate' (Ferguson, 1990, p. 9). At the centre is the self-regulated child who learns according to the dominant paradigms that speak to 'proper' approaches to learning in order to 'calculate the "proper" dispositions and sensitivities of reason so that children . . . become "reasonable" citizens of the future' (Popkewitz, 2004, p. 207).

Dispersed to the margins is the 'improper' child; the 'at-risk' child who comes to be described in deficit discourses and targeted with 'equity programs that focus on the right for all students to access education that leads to learning outcomes consistent with their potential' (Education Queensland, 2000, p. 17). Whilst the 'exclusions appear as a quest for greater inclusion' (Popkewitz, 2004, p. 211), this results in an illusory interiority; an ever more strange inclusion where the maintenance of notions relating to normal and mainstream ensures that certain children exist as the *included* Other (Graham & Slee, in press). This results in an uncontested, naturalised domain at centre, offering up particular individuals to the full force of the gaze whilst leaving others in the relative but contingent safety of the shade.[4]

In conceptualising the tear in the social fabric that supposedly once fashioned the Australian dream, QSE-2010 refers to the need for schools to promote social cohesion, harmony and sense of community, emphasising that 'schools where there are high proportions of students at risk will need special support' (Education Queensland, 2000, pp. 4, 6). The Government pledges that it will provide resources to do so, however, this promising social justice ethic is doused by later clarification that this is simply to avoid 'the need for higher expenditure on remedial welfare later' (Education Queensland, 2000, p. 13). This resonates with Olssen's (2005, p. 382) warning that 'autonomy is a strategy for decreasing the role of the state and increasing individual responsibility for welfare'. He cautions that the pursuit of personal autonomy leads not to liberation but 'unfreedom' (Marshall, 1996, p. 83) for agency is a political skill that comes more easily to some than to Others (Olssen, 2005).

Conclusion

By privileging autonomy and individualism, education reform discourse in Queensland such as that found within the future vision document, *Queensland State Education-2010*, firmly positions particular types of children as *outside of centre* whilst indicating from where the threat to the new consensus may come. Popkewitz (1988, p. 77) describes clarion calls for educational reform as rhetoric that 'directs attention to schools as responding to people's most cherished beliefs about developing a good society'. This rhetoric also works to absolve the school from failure by delivering:

> a warning about the threats of moral and cultural disorganization as embodied in the characteristics of the child who is placed outside of the values that order the composite of the *all* children, the child who does not choose, chase desire, and become a life-long learner.
>
> (Popkewitz, 2004, p. 211, emphasis in original)

The effect of this discursive positioning of centre is to naturalise traditional and privileged contemporary cultural norms as the 'proper' way of being in the schooling context. QSE-2010 has been used as a blue print for a suite of reforms to education in Queensland from the introduction of a preparatory year, to a new focus on middle years and the development of alternative pathways in the senior years with vocational options. These developments are not necessarily bad but, if retaining a Foucauldian reticence, one must be cognisant of potential danger.

The analysis here is restricted to the reconceptualisation of the senior years through QSE-2010 and the resultant *Education Training Reforms for the Future,* which markets the flexible VET schooling option as 'alternative education programs and settings for students who have difficulty in conventional school and disciplinary structures' (Education Queensland, 2000, p. 16). These options are described enthusiastically despite the restriction and location of each of these alternative sites to significantly socioeconomically depressed areas, erroneously suggesting that only working-class kids hate school.[5] Alternative pathways are problematic if they produce bodies as 'adaptable' (but still disposable) cogs in a conscience-free market economy (Marshall, 1997a). Or, if they happen to lead in particular directions by offering 'choices' that reinforce socioeconomic and gender stratification. The argument goes that these options are a sensible offering that are more relevant to those students 'not suited to traditional schooling'. What seems to go *without* saying however, is that the problem resides within the deviant student and that there is nothing wrong with traditional schooling.

I stated at the beginning of this paper that my objective was to elucidate statements that work to present a particular view of the world and in doing so, prepare the ground for the 'practices that derive from them, in the social relations that they form, or, through those relations, modify' (Foucault, 1972, p. 139). Education reform discourse in Queensland positions students who either cannot or do not conform to rigid contemporary norms as deviant individuals. Statements like those elucidated in this paper coagulate to form discursive dividing practices which prepare the ground for the exclusion of non-deserving students who have denied themselves the right to an ostensibly inclusive educational system. This works to legitimise their subjection to arcane behaviour modification practices and naturalises the gendered and socioeconomically-loaded life opportunities afforded to them.

Interrogation of the strategic rhetoric (Nakayama & Krizek, 1995) within discourses that work to (re)secure a normative centre may make visible constructions that have become naturalised, privileging particular ways of living in the world. Naturalisation effaces. In naturalising a particular mode of existence, we construct a universalised space free from interrogation (Nakayama & Krizek, 1995); a ghostly centre which eludes critical analysis and thus recognition of the power relations embodied within notions of normalcy which exert influence over other ways of being (Graham & Slee, in press). When we particularise students as 'not suited to traditional schooling', we work to maintain power imbalances and structural inequity by naturalising attributes that carry social, political and cultural currency, such as those said to characterise the cosmopolitan child (Popkewitz, 2004). This works to remove the scene of schooling from the field of investigation into reasons for schooling failure. In describing and reifying characteristics of the life-long learner as citizen of the future 'sovereignty of the good' (Foucault, 1988), Queensland education reform discourse effectively fashions a scapegoat for social and systemic problems—the difficult child, the unruly body, the *un*cosmopolitan child—as the product of global instability and family disruption who has failed to adapt and take up the opportunity to participate in the consolidation of Queensland as the 'Smart State' of Australia.

Notes

1 See Marshall (2001, p. 294): 'Thereby, in relation to *choice* it might be argued that choice presupposes autonomy, and therefore some notion of understanding about the ability to choose and the range of choices available. . . . Also, autonomy presupposes that the autonomous chooser is independent and has not been influenced, manipulated or determined to choose in certain general directions. It can be argued that if genuine autonomy is implied in the notions of choice by neoliberals that in fact there is a limited and imposed sense of autonomy operating in this notion of the autonomous chooser. Nor is freedom to be interpreted as merely freedom *from* constraints, that is in a negative sense, because there is also positive freedom, or freedom *to*'.

2 Such as LASER and NICKLIN, short-term programs run in the Education Queensland Stafford District.

3 Queensland does have longer stay alternative site placement centres where the child usually remains enrolled and engages in an intensive behaviour modification program for a period of six months. After this period, the child does not typically return to the suspending school but is instead relocated to another school in the area. In Corinda District, in Brisbane's south west region, enrolment is almost exclusively boys. This is not the result of policy but the result of referral and the nature of the behaviour. It appears that more boys engage in aggressive, physical behaviour than girls. This is considered more seriously and results in more serious responses; i.e. referral to long-stay programs rather than short-term.

4 In referring to shade here, I do not claim that those at centre are immune to the gaze nor reside in the safety of darkness. Instead, consistent with Foucault's discussion of 'intensification' and 'redoubled insistence' (Foucault, 1977; Ewald, 1992), the suggestion is that there are proximal-zones of scrutiny and that the force of the gaze and intensity of light increases incrementally upon one's deviance from the 'norm'.

5 I find it problematic that each of the areas named, i.e. Logan, Ipswich, Deception Bay and so on, are areas characterised by lower socioeconomic circumstances and high non-English speaking immigrant populations. Much educational discourse unquestioningly positions the socially and economically disadvantaged as the problem and not the schooling practices that might appear irrelevant or alienating to young people.

References

Baker, B. (2005) State Formation, Teaching Techniques, and Globalisation as Aporia, *Discourse: Studies in the Cultural Politics of Education*, 26.1, pp. 45–77.

BCC (2005) Neighbourhood Planning: Fact Sheet 7—Planning Basics—The Shape of the Future. (Brisbane, Brisbane City Council) pp. 1–8.

Bouhours, T., Bryer, F. & Fleming, S. (2003) Exclusion of Primary School Students: Archival analysis of school records over a 30-year period, in: B. Bartlett, F. Bryer & D. Roebuck, *Re-imagining Practice—Researching Change* (Brisbane, School of Cognition, Language and Special Education, Griffith University) vol. 1, pp. 102–114.

Butler, J. (1997) Sovereign Performatives in the Contemporary Scene of Utterance. *Critical Inquiry*, 23.2, pp. 350–377.

Cole, M. (2005) Queensland on the Road to Ruin—System Ageing, Clogged, *The Courier Mail*, Brisbane. 7th February 2005, p. 4.

Culler, J. (1997) *Literary Theory: A very short introduction.* (Oxford, Oxford University Press).

Currie, E. (2000) Alternative Program Helps At-risk Pupils, *Education Views.*

Davies, B. (2005) The (Im)possibility of Intellectual Work in Neoliberal Regimes, *Discourse: Studies in the Cultural Politics of Education*, 26.1, pp. 1–14.

Deleuze, G. (1988) *Foucault.* (Minneapolis, MN, University of Minnesota Press).

Deleuze, G. (1992) What is a Dispositif*?, in: T. J. Armstrong (ed.), *Michel Foucault: Philosopher.* (New York, Harvester Wheatsheaf): pp. 159–168.

Education Queensland (1995) Swayneville State School Supportive Environment Management Plan, *Management of Behaviour in a Supportive School Environment: A School Review* (Education Queensland, Queensland Government).

Education Queensland (2000) Queensland State Education—2010 (QSE-2010). (Brisbane, Education Queensland, Queensland Government).

Education Queensland (2002) Education and Training Reforms for the Future: A White Paper (ETRF). (Brisbane, Queensland Government, 2004).

Education Queensland (2005) Dealing with misbehaviour in the early years, *Schools + Parents* (Brisbane, Corporate Communication and Marketing Branch, Department of Education and the Arts). 1.

Edwards, R. & Nicoll, K. (2001) Researching the Rhetoric of Lifelong Learning, *Journal of Education Policy*, 16.2, pp. 103–112.

Ewald, F. (1992) A Power Without an Exterior, in: T. J. Armstrong (ed.), *Michel Foucault: Philosopher.* (New York, Harvester Wheatsheaf) pp. 169–175.

Ferguson, R. (1990) Introduction: Invisible Centre, in: R. Ferguson (ed.), *Out There: Marginalization and contemporary cultures.* (New York and Cambridge, New Museum of Contemporary Art and MIT Press) pp. 9–14.

Foucault, M. (1972) *The Archaeology of Knowledge* (New York, Pantheon Books).

Foucault, M. (1975a) 12 February 1975, in: V. Marchetti, A. Salomoni, F. Ewald & A. Fontana (eds), *Abnormal: Lectures at the College de France 1974–1975.* (London, Verso) pp. 137–166.

Foucault, M. (1975b) 15 January 1975, in: V. Marchetti, A. Salomoni, F. Ewald & A. Fontana (eds), *Abnormal: Lectures at the College de France 1974–1975.* (London, Verso): pp. 31–54.

Foucault, M. (1975c) *Abnormal: Lectures at the College de France 1974–1975.* (London, Verso).

Foucault, M. (1977) *Discipline and Punish: The birth of the prison* (London, Penguin Books).

Foucault, M. (1980) Two Lectures, in: C. Gordon (ed.), *Power/Knowledge: Selected Interviews & Other Writings 1972–1977* (New York, Pantheon Books) pp. 78–108.

Foucault, M. (1984) Nietzsche, Genealogy, History, in: P. Rabinow (ed.), *The Foucault Reader* (New York, Pantheon Books) pp. 76–100.

Foucault, M. (1988) *Madness and Civilization: A history of insanity in the age of unreason* (New York, Vintage Books).

Graham, L. (2006) Caught in the Net: A Foucaultian interrogation of the incidental effects of limited notions of 'inclusion', *International Journal of Inclusive Education,* 10.1, pp. 3–24.

Graham, L. and Slee, R. (in press) An Illusory Interiority: Interrogating the discourse/s of inclusion, *Educational Philosophy and Theory.*

Graymore, M., Sipe, N., Rickson, R. & Shaw, R. (2002) South East Queensland's Sustainable Human Carrying Capacity, *Coast to Coast 2002* (Queensland).

Lambeir, B. (2005) Education as Liberation: The politics and techniques of lifelong learning, *Educational Philosophy and Theory,* 37.3, pp. 349–355.

Marshall, J. D. (1997a) Dewey and the New 'Vocationalism', *Philosophy of Education Society Yearbook,* 28th September 2005. Available at: http://www.ed.uiuc.edu/EPS/PES-Yearbook/97_docs/97contents.html

Marshall, J. D. (1997b) Michel Foucault: Problematising the individual and constituting 'the' self, *Educational Philosophy and Theory,* 29.1, pp. 32–49.

Marshall, J. D. (2001) Varieties of Neo-liberalism: A Foucaultian perspective, *Educational Philosophy and Theory,* 33.3 & 4, pp. 293–304.

McCarthy, C. (2003) Contradictions of Power and Identity: Whiteness studies and the call of teacher education, *Qualitative Studies in Education,* 16.1, pp. 127–133.

Murdoch, S. (2005) Brisbane Escapes Housing Downfall, *The Courier Mail,* Brisbane. 2nd September 2005, p. 3.

Nakayama, T. K. & Krizek, R. L. (1995) Whiteness: A Strategic Rhetoric, *Quarterly Journal of Speech,* 81, pp. 291–309.

OECD (2003) OECD Educational Policy Analysis 2003. Available at: http://education.qld.gov.au/corporate/professional_exchange/docs/oecdfiles/ed-pol-anal2003.pdf

OECD (2004) Completing the Foundation for Lifelong Learning: An OECD survey of upper secondary schools (Paris, OECD).

Ollendick, T. H. & Hersen, M. (1998) *Handbook of Child Psychopathology.* (New York, London, Plenum Press).

Olssen, M. (2005) Foucault, Educational Research and the Issue of Autonomy, *Educational Philosophy and Theory,* 37.3, pp. 365–387.

Popkewitz, T. S. (1988) Educational Reform: Rhetoric, ritual and social interest, *Educational Theory,* 38.1, pp. 77–93.

Popkewitz, T. S. (2001) Dewey and Vygotsky: Ideas in historical spaces, in: T. S. Popkewitz, B. M. Franklin & M. A. Pereyra (eds), *Cultural History and Education: Critical essays on knowledge and schooling* (New York, RoutledgeFarmer).

Popkewitz, T. S. (2004) The Reason of Reason: Cosmopolitanism and the government of schooling, in: B. M. Baker & K. E. Heyning (eds), *Dangerous Coagulations: The uses of Foucault in the study of education* (New York, Peter Lang).

Powell, P. & Inglis-Powell, B. (1999) *Raising Difficult Children: Realistic behaviour management for difficult children including those with attention deficit/hyperactivity disorder* (North Parramatta, Gouldian Press).

Psychologist (2003) Specific Suggestions. L. Tomes. (Sydney: Report/Letter from Child Psychologist).

Rose, N. (1990) *Governing the Soul: The shaping of the private self* (London, Routledge).

Slee, R. (1994) Finding a Student Voice in School Reform: Student disaffection, pathologies of disruption and educational control, *International Studies in Sociology of Education,* 4.2, pp. 147–172.

Slee, R. (1995) *Changing Theories and Practices of Discipline* (London, The Falmer Press).

Synott, J. and Symes, C. (1995) The Genealogy of the School: An iconography of badges and mottoes, *British Journal of Sociology of Education,* 16.1, pp. 139–152.

Wallace, I. (1999) *You and Your ADD Child: Practical strategies for coping with everyday problems* (Sydney, HarperCollins).

Chapter 8

Biopolitical Utopianism in Educational Theory

Tyson Lewis

Editors' Introduction

In this chapter, Lewis shifts the center of utopian debates away from questions of ideology towards the question of power. As a new point of departure, he analyzes Foucault's notion of biopower as well as Hardt and Negri's theory of biopolitics. Arguing for a new hermeneutic of biopolitics in education, Lewis then applies this lens to evaluate the educational philosophy of John Dewey. In conclusion, the chapter suggests that while Hardt and Negri are missing an educational theory, John Dewey is missing a concept of democracy adequate to the biopolitical struggles of the multitude. Thus, Lewis calls for a synthesis of Dewey and Hardt and Negri in order to generate a biopedagogical practice beyond both traditional models of education as well as current standardization. In this chapter it is argued that, for Dewey, education can serve the function of allowing the multitude to recognize itself as the multitude, as a public whose interests lie in the continual production of a global common and whose desires are immanently democratic. This indictment of contemporary political theory for its lack of concern for educational problematics is not in the end a 'guarantee' in which education solves all social problems: education, in other words, is not sufficient but necessary. The function education within schools can come to play is the cultivation of constitutive power necessary to risk social exit into the absolute opening of a dystopian-utopia both inside yet anterior to the Empire.

Introduction

What is the status of utopian thinking in education today? Within the last several years there has been a surprising return to the theme of utopia in educational philosophy. Authors ranging from liberal curricular reformists (Halpin, 2003) to critical pedagogues (Giroux, 2002) have asserted the primacy of utopian thinking in order to overcome a variety of educational deadlocks, including teacher apathy, student resignation, and the oppressive reproduction of social inequalities through schooling practices. In fact, a recent issue of the journal *Policy Futures in Education* was dedicated solely to the theme of educational utopianism, drawing on a variety of perspectives through which utopia was both problematized and revitalized. And lastly, the anthology entitled *Edutopias: New Utopian Thinking in Education* (2006) makes a strong case for putting utopian thinking back at the center of educational philosophy.

While asserting various (if not contradictory) definitions of utopia, all these authors tend to frame their discussions in relation to ideology and ideological critique. Of course, such discussions are of paramount importance and have a long and rich history outside the field of educational philosophy. Yet by focusing on the relation between utopia and ideology (and thus on the level of the imaginary), another dimension remains obscured: that existing between utopia and power. As such, my first goal in this essay is to redirect the discussion of utopia towards the analysis of power and, in particular, power over life or biopower (Foucault, 1990). It is my contention that understanding utopia in relation to biopower is of pressing importance, for questions concerning the relation between *zoe* (life in general, natural life) and *bios* (political life) are the central problematic of all utopian projects. Drawing on the later work of Michel Foucault as a new point of departure for theorizing utopia in education, I will then argue that without recognizing biopower within utopian projects, the continued existence of sovereign force will remain a constant threat in utopian experiments as well as in radical classrooms.

As opposed to biopower (as the domination of life from above), Michael Hardt and Antonio Negri (2005, pp. 94–95) offer a new concept—biopolitics—that recognizes the immanent power of production to form new notions of collectivity that can and do create the preconditions for a universal democracy. Thus, my second goal expands upon the first and articulates the need for utopian education with Hardt and Negri's theory of biopolitics. While Hardt and Negri focus specifically on the biopolitical nature of the multitude, I will argue here that their analysis is missing an important element: an educational theory. Drawing on the biopolitical demands of the multitude, I speculate what this education might look like. Such speculative thinking is meant to ignite our collective educational imaginations by articulating educational philosophy with historical tendencies that result from the push and pull within Empire. Here it will be useful to analyze the writings of John Dewey as a test run for the interpretive power of biopolitics as a new educational hermeneutic. In conclusion, I will suggest that a dual reading enables us both to critique Dewey (and the residual elements of biopower at work in his philosophy) and to provide a pedagogical mandate for the postutopian (or as Negri argues 'dystopian') utopian insurgencies of the multitude.

From Ideological Critique to a Critique of Utopian Power

The vast scholarship on utopia has focused on its relationship to ideology and thus with questions of true versus false consciousness. The intellectual lineage of this particular strand of utopian analysis begins with Marx and Engels and their comments concerning the fate of classical utopian socialism. In the *Manifesto of the Communist Party* for instance, Marx and Engels write a scathing critique of utopianism as 'always ludicrous in its effect, through total incapacity to comprehend the march of modern history' (Tucker, 1978, p. 491). As class struggle progressively develops in opposition to industrialized capitalism, utopianism, according to Marx and Engels, becomes a mystification of the real conditions of historical transformation. Here utopia is completely subsumed under ideology as a distortion/deception and thus set opposed to the science of historical materialism. In a later essay, Engels once again returns to this debate in order to argue that utopia is a form of bourgeois false consciousness lacking the scientific validity of Marx's mature theory of capitalism. As Engels writes, 'Not one of them [the classic utopias of Saint-Simon, Robert Owen, and Charles Fourier] appears as a representative of the interests of that proletariat which historical development had, in the meantime, produced' (ibid., p. 685). As such, utopia drifts into individual fantasy tainted by conservative sentiments. Like Marx's inversion of Hegel, so too must scientific socialism flip utopian socialism on its head and ground it in an understanding of the objective relations of production. While there are extensive debates in Marxism concerning the relation between Marx himself and utopia—see for instance the opposing conclusions drawn by Vincent Geoghegan (1988) and Darren Webb (2000)—what I want to emphasize here is that such debates concern the fundamental relation between ideology and utopia.

Karl Mannheim's now famous book *Ideology and Utopia* (1985) furthers this debate. Briefly stated, Mannheim posits ideology as a set of ideas that obscure the present and focus on the past while utopia transcends the present and is oriented towards the future. Here utopia and ideology are both similar yet different. On the one hand, both speak to a certain discontinuity with the present. Yet on the other hand, the nature of this discontinuity is unique to each. In terms of ideology, such ideas can never be fully realized in the present and are thus impossible. In terms of utopia, these ideas are in fact realizable and therefore capable of transforming social relations through the project of revolution. Here the distinction between utopia and ideology becomes clear: utopia is oppositional to the status quo while ideology is conservative. Thus Mannheim positions utopia and ideology within a shared problematic of discontinuity, effectively replacing Marx and Engels's opposition, which relied on the category of distortion. Again my point here is that with Mannheim, the central focus of utopian thinking is further correlated with the problematic of ideology and thus with truth claims concerning the nature of reality and the reality to come.

Fredric Jameson stakes out a rather different approach to the question of utopia and ideology. In *Seeds of Time* (1994) Jameson eloquently writes that utopia reveals 'the miring of our imaginations in the mode of production itself, the mud of the present age in which the winged Utopian shoes stick' (p. 75). In other words, utopia forces us to recognize the limits of our cognitive capacities to transcend the problematics of capitalism and the ideological closure of our imaginations. Here the positive function of utopia is precisely its failure, for in that failure, the subject becomes aware of ideological limits. As such, utopias are not simply ideological (for they contain an element of critique even in their failure) nor are they simply concerned with the realizability of any one particular claim in a possible future (for in essence they are reflections on the present). In another formulation, Jameson argues that utopias are always positioned within particular ideological standpoints, each of which is unique and as such cannot be sublated into an 'authentic' utopian synthesis (2004). The positive function of these various utopias is thus not their individual content but rather their ability to critique or negate one another. The goal is not synthesis but rather the creation of a constellation, which holds each difference in itself without collapsing one imagined world into the other. The tension arising between these competing visions of alternative future trajectories in the end speaks to the boundaries of the imagination mentioned above, to our inability to escape our own ideological situatedness. A third articulation draws heavily on the work of Ernst Bloch whose saw utopia as manifest throughout all of popular culture. Adapting Bloch's utopian hermeneutic, Jameson argues that we must read utopian content in even the crassest and most debased forms of media culture while likewise reading the ideological dimension in even the most utopian texts (Jameson, 1982). Stated differently, all cultural artifacts or political movements have an ideological manifest content and a utopian latent content. It is through the manifest content of its cultural articulation that ideology distorts the latent utopianism, thus transforming hopes for a 'perfect' civilization into Nazism, or plans for population health into eugenics programs. Overall, Jameson sees utopia and ideology as dialectically interdependent wherein every ideology contains a utopian bribe, and every utopia is always already politically tainted by the ideology of the present.

In the field of educational philosophy, the relation between utopia and ideology has also dominated discussions. Henry Giroux argues that a central field of struggle for educators is to critique the conservative ideology that has completely appropriated and reworked leftist utopian aspirations in education (2002). Here utopianism has been co-opted by a right-wing agenda that transforms critical hope into a dystopian utopian hope through which neoconservative ideologies are justified and legitimated. Quoting Giroux, 'As a radical deflection, hope is packaged as the promise of neoliberal capitalism, substituting the celebration of wealth, privilege, and greed for notions of hope grounded in an opposition to economic injustice, racism, domination, and diverse forms of oppression' (ibid., p. 111). Thus utopianism is reduced to market-logics and privatization. For Giroux both the left and the right are to blame for this predicament. Leftists all too quickly abandoned the utopian tradition that the right promptly incorporated into their conservative agenda. Drawing on the utopian thinkers discussed above, Giroux argues that one of the main tasks today is to locate the utopian kernel within supposedly 'anti-utopian' political fantasies and reclaim it for liberatory educational and social movements.

Zeus Leonardo offers another educational intervention into utopian and ideological debates (2003). For Leonardo, there is an inherently utopian moment in the process of ideological critique. Rather than simply negative, Leonardo draws on Lenin and Lukacs to suggest the positive function of a 'socialist ideology' or a 'mature workers' ideology', which locates utopia in the immanent movement of critique against exploitation. For Leonardo as with Giroux, the terrain of struggle between ideology and utopia is located on the level of the imaginary. In other words, both authors focus on the level of conscious (or unconscious) utopian articulations in right-wing and left-wing struggles for political hegemony.

While emphasis on the ideological level of utopianism is important, the analysis of the imaginary has to a large extent eclipsed an analysis of utopia and power, especially within critical theory traditions. Such an analysis focuses less on the level of consciousness or unconsciousness and more on the level of the body and of material relations between subjects—the ontological level of being as it is historically conditioned. Opening up this dimension is crucial, for utopian ideology (or utopian interests) might not necessarily coincide with on-going power relations. A transitional figure here is Paul Ricoeur whose theory of ideology and utopia argues that their relationship concerns the question of legitimization and therefore power. According to Ricoeur (1986), 'what is at stake in ideology and in utopia is power' (p. 298). Ideology attempts to fill in a gap between the beliefs of the people in leadership and the excessive claims made by the leader. Utopia on the other hand exposes this function of ideology, which conceals the disjuncture between authority and the necessary belief in the rightfulness of that authority. According to Ricoeur, 'All utopias finally come to grips with the problem of authority. They try to show ways people may be governed other than by the state, because each state is the heir of some other state' (ibid.). Interestingly, Ricoeur argues that Marxism's emphatic emphasis on the economic mode of production and less on the question of power is directly responsible for the corruption of the Soviet Union. Here, the question of surplus-value was solved yet the question of 'surplus-power' remained operative through Stalinism (ibid., p. 201). Thus Ricoeur positions the question of power at the center of both utopia and ideology. In short, Ricoeur extends the debate beyond Marx who positioned ideology/utopia against science and beyond Mannheim who argued that ideology and utopia were both constituted through disjunction with the present.

Yet his analysis of power is limited. For instance, in Ricoeur's model, power only exerts itself in relations of rule (subjective belief) and not in relations of social integration. Thus, below the level of power relations there exists for Ricoeur a more fundamental level through which ideology is not simply concerned with authority claims but rather with social collectivity, with the maintenance of identity. Here at its most elemental level, power is external to the preservation of social traditions. Thus power is locked within a juridical framework between the one (the sovereign) and the many (the people). As opposed to this model, Michel Foucault would argue that power is much more complex, existing within the question of legitimacy but also beyond it. For Foucault (1990), the concept of power is more expansive, constituting social relations and, in the last instance, life as such, hence the term biopower. In Foucault's theory, power operates on the micro-level of disciplinary normalization (through which individuals are constructed) as well as on the macro-level of biopower (through which the health and security of populations are policed by the nation-state). While for Ricoeur power remains between people and their leader, for Foucault, power in the modern era functions between a biological population and various apparatuses of governmentality. Because of its more comprehensive nature, it is to Foucault and his theory of power that we must now turn in order to fully explicate the ramifications of Ricoeur's own theory of utopia.

In the recently published series of lectures titled '*Society Must Be Defended*' (2003), Foucault ends with an account of racism and its connections with biopower. Like Ricoeur, Foucault clearly sees that both capitalist democracies and socialist societies reproduce dystopian practices because they have not adequately addressed the issue of power. For Foucault, the ultimate problem resides in the unacknowledged reliance and acceptance of biopower as a power over life. This power over life defines life through and through in order to make survive. Yet, at the very heart of biopower resides the kernel of death in the form of genocide (Foucault, 1990). To make survive, biopower engages in various eugenics projects to eliminate all biological threats. The question becomes: How do various societies justify killing through this technology of biopower? For Foucault (2003), racism 'is primarily a way of introducing a break into the domain of life that is under power's control: the break between what must live and what must die' (p. 254). Racism allows the state to wage war not only on the external other but also on those within society itself labeled as 'other'. As such, racism is an inherent and central mechanism allowing biopower to regulate the population. It is racism that reinscribes the sovereign's right to kill within governmentality. While Nazism is in Foucault's genealogy the apex of intensified biopower, democracy and socialism are not exempt from his overall condemnation of racism. As Foucault argues, 'Socialism has made no critique of the theme of biopower . . . it has in fact taken it up, developed, reimplanted, and modified it in certain respects, but it has certainly not reexamined its basis or its modes of working' (ibid., p. 261). Expanding Foucault's argument, could we not say that utopianism in general is implicated here? Because utopia is an attempt to reconfigure power in relation to life, is it not inherently liked to biopower and thus the immanent possibilities of either banal normalization or sovereign violence?

Here we clearly see the danger of ignoring the question of power in relation to utopian political (and educational) projects. Ideological critique is simply not enough. A new *practice* of power must accompany the cognitive mapping of utopia. Otherwise the return of the sovereign's ban over life will haunt utopian projects. Such warnings abound in utopian and dystopian literature. Novels like Margaret Atwood's *The Handmaid's Tale* (1985) function less on the level of ideological critique of utopianism and more on the level of power, exposing the continued existence of biopower over the decision to grant life or take it away in utopian worlds of tomorrow. Likewise, Kim Stanley Robinson's *Mars Trilogy* (1993–1996) is an epic struggle concerning the ultimate politicization of life: terraforming Mars. While agreeing with noted utopian scholar Tom Moylan (2000) that these novels offer warnings concerning the possibility of future violence, it is the exact nature of this warning that must be specified. It is my contention that these 'critical dystopias,' to use Moylan's language, offer a warning against the persistent life of sovereign force within utopia as the ultimate manifestation (or fantasy) of biopower. The same can be said of 'utopian' educational practices. As Daniel Cho and I have argued (2006), the critique of ideological interests does not necessarily mean that unconscious investments into certain forms of power relations will necessarily cease to operate even in the most radical of classrooms; hence the oft-heard feminist charge that the critical classroom does not feel empowering (Ellsworth, 1989). While rhetorically posing as critical, such classrooms become oppressive on the level of biopower itself, on the level of power that determines the form of educational ontology.

These questions have become even more pressing in the current historical situation. Giorgio Agamben (1998) has recently argued that the sovereign right over death at the heart of biopower has expanded to include multiple new locations including airports, hospitals, etc. This expansion of the violent kernel of biopower is manifest in the current global state of exception wherein a sovereign force (the United States acting as exception) has called forth a war against terror through which rights of citizens are suspended and interment camps are built outside of legal regulation (Agamben, 2005). Michael Hardt and Antonio Negri also speak of the universalization of war. They state, '[W]ar has gone from an instrument of politics, used in the last resort, to the foundation of politics, the basis for discipline and control' (Hardt & Negri, 2005, p. 334). Here in the extended state of emergency, capitalism and sovereignty coincide perfectly in the reemergence of Empire. In relation to schooling, I have suggested (2006) that Empire has returned as a 'just war' against inner city youth through zero tolerance measures that reconstruct the school less as a disciplinary mechanism and more as a state of emergency. Thus the dialectic of biopower between the preservation of life and its symbolic or physical destruction is being felt on an increasing level.

Such a diagnosis of global politics might seem at first glance to be radically disheartening, yet Jameson (2004) has argued that the present is also ripe with utopian possibilities. Analyzing the material and political preconditions for the utopian imagination, Jameson suggests that utopias were written during 'periods of great social ferment but seemingly rudderless, without any agency or direction; reality seems malleable, but not the system; and it is that very distance of the unchangeable system from the turbulent restlessness of the real world that seems to open up a moment of ideational and utopian-creative *free play* in the mind itself or in the political imagination' (ibid., pp. 45–6). Postmodernism is precisely such a political condition, generating the calm before the storm necessary for utopian speculation. How are we to mediate these two positions (the absolutization of a sovereign decision and the material preconditions for utopian imagining)? And what forms of power are involved in Jameson's notion of utopian free play? For if utopian dreaming is more than a simple retreat into daydreams, it must operate on the level of power relations existing in institutions and between acting subjects. In the next section I will suggest that Hardt and Negri's theory of the multitude offers a possible alternative to the dialectic of biopower.

The Biopolitics of the Multitude

As Hardt and Negri describe (2000; 2005), emergent Empire is a proverbial noplace through which utopian possibilities and dystopian terrors are immanent. Here, the dialectic of Empire becomes clear. On the one hand, Empire is a form of capitalist deterritorialization beyond the boundaries of the nation-state, creating new forms of exploitation and oppression. On the other hand, Empire is also the result of the insurgent movement of a democratic and cosmopolitan multitude and thus a progressive advance beyond the sovereignty of the one (the state) over the many. Empire is a space of global exception, a space of war wherein the multitude express their universalizing claims to democracy and where capitalism in the form of transnational corporations and banks appropriates the labor of the multitude and refashions it in terms of surplus-value. This battle is waged on the level of the *biopolitical,* for what is at stake in the production of democracy and in the reproduction of capitalism is life itself.

But before I give a positive definition of the multitude, it might be easiest to first describe what the multitude is not. The multitude is not a people, for a people is a homogenous group united through a shared identity (Hardt & Negri, 2000, p. 103). For the multitude, collectivity is mediated not through a national identity (the One of the sovereign) but rather through the One of the desire of democracy, which is decentered and deterritorializing. Nor is the multitude the industrial working class. In Empire, 'all forms of labor tend to be proletarianized' (ibid., p. 256), and as such the proletariat has become a universal category no longer restricted to factory production—an empty signifier that addresses all those who live and work within Empire. In other words, immaterial labor, social labor, affective labor, and reproductive labor are all capitalized, expanding the breadth of the term to include the world's poor. Here the distinctions that defined the proletariat dissipate as unemployment/employment, labor/non-labor take on shared characteristics (Virno, 2004). Thirdly, the multitude is not organized strictly in terms of postmodern identity politics (Hardt & Negri, 2000, pp. 142–143). Such identity politics argue against binary logic and inside/outside dichotomies. Because there is no longer a constitutive outside in Empire, such political strategies miss their mark, and in the worst case, legitimate the flexible inclusivity driving Empire. Thus from the perspective of the multitude, postmodern identity politics can all too easily become a symptom of Empire rather than a real rupture with sovereignty. And finally, the multitude is distinct from the notion of a crowd (ibid., p. 100). As opposed to the people, the crowd has no shared elements, no common, and as such must be externally led by a sovereign who unites them by imposing laws and orders from above. In contrast to these social formulations, the multitude is self-organizing in such a way as to resist either collapse into a people or into the mob mentality of the crowd.

So what is this new social formation that is both the motor of Empire as well as its key combatant? The multitude is characterized by several features: singularity, commonality, immaterial labor, swarm intelligence, and the desire for democracy. First, in the multitude, the contradiction between identity and difference (which marks modern social movements) is replaced with the complementary paring of singularity and commonality (Hardt & Negri, 2005, pp. 217–218). In a network model of social production, singularity and commonality break with the two dominant models of resistance politics: either forming a people or party united under the leadership of the One or radical separation into fragmented, single issue movements. In the network model 'each local struggle functions as a node that communicates with all other nodes without any hub or center of intelligence. Each struggle remains singular and tied to its local conditions but at the same time is immersed in the common web' (ibid., p. 217). Thus singularity refers to 'a social subject whose difference cannot be reduced to sameness, a difference that remains different' (ibid., p. 99). A singularity is not a deviation from a standard (or a norm) but is rather different in itself without being predicated on a comparison between self and other. Here—as opposed to the liberal tradition of political theory—individuality (now freed from the constraints of the modernist, property-owning, statist subject) emerges only after a more basic process of collectivity is constituted through shared biological faculties, linguistic practices, and historical conditions.

The common is generated and expanded through various forms of immaterial labor that produce immaterial goods (affects, knowledge, etc.), services, and communication. In other words, labor is purely biopolitical not simply producing tangible goods but social life in all its complex dimensions, in all of its singular manifestations. Through virtual or immaterial labor, cooperation becomes immanent to the field of production and the network model of labor has a tendency to replace the assembly line (Hardt & Negri, 2000, p. 294). From within the very structure of network production there emerges a form of the common, which in the end is a positive name for the productive and generative capabilities of the multitude working together, creating new forms of communication and new notions of collective production. As Hardt and Negri argue, 'The commons is the incarnation, the production, and the liberation of the multitude' (2000, p. 303). Or stated differently, 'Producing communication, affective relationships, and knowledges, in contrast to cards and typewriters, can directly expand the realm of what we share in common' (Hardt & Negri, 2005, p. 114). This common field of social relations both accelerates the spread of Empire, and at the same time also produces a new possibility for a new public sphere (without a people), a new republic inside but against capitalism (Virno, 2004, p. 40).

Network production produces a new form of ever expanding general intellect in the form of accumulated knowledge. Such knowledge is no longer restricted to intelligence as a faculty of the mind but is also corporeal and thus biopolitical

(Hardt & Negri, 2000, p. 364). This new form of social intelligence is called 'swarm intelligence' (Hardt & Negri, 2005, p. 91). In the swarm, intelligence is collective, general, and equally distributed throughout a web of social relations lacking a center. Creativity comes from multiple directions, surging through the network of immaterial labor in the seemingly formless movements of the multitude. Again, while superficially chaotic, if not anarchistic, Hardt and Negri insist that this swarm intelligence is organized. The key here is that the organization does not come from sovereign force or a form of compulsive disciplinary normalization but from the immanent desire of the multitude for democracy. The democratic political struggle of the multitude against sovereignty can be summarized in a series of demands guided by swarm intelligence. First, the multitude demand global citizenship, or stated differently the ability to move across all borders without impediments (Hardt & Negri, 2000, p. 400). Here migration is not only the plight of disempowered masses escaping from the tyranny of sovereign nation-states but also a form of transformative politics: a desire for cosmopolitan freedom. The appropriation of space from the territorialization of the nation-state is coupled with the need to appropriate time (ibid., p. 401). Time must become one with the internally cooperative movement of the collective as it labors in global networks. Finally, a social wage must be guaranteed for all, and the mode of production has to be controlled by the multitude. This means not only hardware and communication systems but also the ability to reconfigure such systems to meet the needs of the collective. This last demand is central for realizing the freedom present in Empire yet incapable of articulating itself in terms of material social relations. Furthermore, the redistribution of the means of production guards Hardt and Negri against the potential charge of reducing the revolutionary possibilities of Marxism to simple economic reformism. These demands represent a new form of global, absolute democracy in which the multitude becomes fully self-organizing. As such we see a movement from biopower (statist, hierarchical, territorialized, etc.) to biopolitics (as the immanent production and cooperation of the multitude in a new post-Fordist, transnational space). Overall the insurgent movement, organization, and productivity of the multitude replace Agamben's *homo sacer* or bare life as the negative surface of biopower with that of '*homohomo*' as the generative life of collective biopolitics (ibid., p. 204).

Homohomo is the subject of constituent power as an expansive, creative, revolutionary power set against the constituted (or territorialized) power of the state (Negri, 1999). The constituted power of the state fears productive, biopolitical power, and as such gentrifies, normalizes, bureaucratizes, and polices the multitude. Thus *homohomo* is a subject outside the state. As Negri states, 'Subjectivity is not something that subsists: it is—on the contrary—produced' by the productive, innovative time of the body (Negri, 2003, p. 173). It is not subjectivity that is the bearer of constitutive power but rather the body as the ontological base of the biopolitical movement of the multitude through work and communication networks. But it must be emphasized that this ontology is not linked to an essential Being but is linked with historical change. As such, *homohomo* as a 'full ontology' is linked with the new nature of productive labor released by Empire but also set against it. It is an ontology free from metaphysics and more or less aligned with Spinoza's theory of 'self-presence'—a self-presence that directly incorporates into itself capitalism as a historically specified ontological ground for biopolitics.

Hardt and Negri argue that now is the first time in history when absolute democracy is possible, yet I would temper their claims in one very significant way. Perhaps democracy is immanent, yet without *authentic democratic education,* such potentials will remain abstract without actualization. The question becomes: who are the educational theorists who can help us flesh out this vision of education beyond biopower and its internal contradictions? In the next section I will suggest that John Dewey offers a unique avenue for demonstrating the push and pull of education between biopower/state/the people and biopolitics/globalization/the multitude. Agreeing with Richard Brosio (1994), I suggest that Dewey lacked a theory of historical agency necessary to promote and embody his call to democracy. As such, his philosophy was transformed into a reformist political platform incapable of realizing democracy within a capitalist economy. The following section attempts precisely to locate Dewey in relation not simply to working class struggle against capitalism (as presented in Brosio's argument) but rather to resituate Dewey in terms of the insurgent momentum of the multitude against Empire. While Hardt and Negri might provide Dewey with a political model capable of embodying his democratic aspirations, Dewey provides Hardt and Negri with a needed social theory of education. It is my contention that the reason why the multitude tends to become a mythological and/or allegorical figure in Hardt and Negri's writing is that they lack a theory of education necessary to cultivate the constitutive power of the multitude. Without such an educational theory the ambiguities of the multitude—its internal 'acquiescence and conflict, servility and freedom' (Virno, 2004, p. 26)—dominate, and the utopian thrust of Hardt and Negri's manifesto becomes an empty prophesy. Thus a theory of immanent education is an important form of revolutionary planning which some have found lacking in Hardt and Negri's writings (Brennan, 2003). In short, Dewey provides the multitude with a tentative pedagogical outline of democratic education, and the multitude provide us with the political demands necessary to reassess Dewey in terms of contemporary biopolitical struggles. Overall, this reading provides Dewey and Hardt and Negri with further resources for realizing a form of utopianism that no longer rests solely on the critique of ideological interests but also and more fundamentally on the restructuring of power relations.

Dewey and Biopolitics

Educational life has always been a paradoxical formulation in school reform for it would seem that family or private life necessarily must be banned in order for the good life of the polis (as a political life of deliberative action) to be secured.[1]

Framed in terms of this relation, Dewey's project is located squarely on the plane of life itself, on the plane of educational ontology. At stake for Dewey is redefining how educational life is to be constructed through experience. Thus Dewey's educational mandate against the 'wasting' of a child's life (1980, p. 39) is a biopolitical ethic through which the various aspects of schooling are integrated into the life of the child. Education in other words must break down barriers that result in education's 'isolation from life' (ibid., p. 46). Dewey creates a new relation between life as such and educational life that is not predicated on fundamental disjunctures in which educated life separates itself from the private life of the child and in which the mind separates from the body. Dewey writes, 'The advance of physiology and the psychology associated with it have shown the connection of mental activity with that of the nervous system' (1997a, p. 336) leading to a new theory of sensual or embodied reason. These continuities are further enacted on the macro-level of social relations as well. Just as the biopolitical migrations of the multitude break down barriers separating nation-states, labor from non-labor, and employment from non-employment so too should educational biopolitics break down a series of barriers separating the life of the child from school life. Dewey advocated that schools should encourage continual social interaction to produce new modes of communication, the cultivation of voluntary dispositions rather than submission to externally imposed standards of practice, the deconstruction of barriers separating classes and races, and finally an expansion of shared concerns with the simultaneous 'liberation of grater diversity of personal capacities' (1997a, p. 87). As such, Dewey's great insight is that the reconstruction of education must take into account both a critique of epistemology (how we think) and a reconstruction of life. Here, education becomes the continuous construction of Being and is therefore immanently biopolitical.

Dewey fundamentally ruptures the conception of the 'child' as an ontological category. The child is a notion inherent in the operation of biopower as a power over life from above in the form of a sovereign decision. The child's life—the physical body of the senses and the psychic life of the passions—is defined in relation to this sovereign decision. For instance, in *Emile*, Rousseau articulates a subtle and covert strategy of manipulation behind which lies a transcendent center of power: the tutor (as the one who holds the knowledge of natural education). Thus childhood for Rousseau is effectively a mediation point between the immanence of disciplinary control (with the 'freedom' to discipline one's self as a form of self-governance) and sovereignty (as a command issued from a centralized source). Hence the contradictory nature of Rousseau's pedagogy, which speaks equally to the autonomy of the child and the absolute mastery of the tutor. Rousseau thus authors both of the following statements without irony: 'The first of all goods is not authority but freedom . . . That is my fundamental maxim. It need only be applied to childhood for all the rules of education to flow from it' (1762/1979, p. 84) and 'Let him [the pupil] always believe he is the master and let it always be you who are in control' (ibid., p. 120). In short, the student must be forced to be free.

What we see in Dewey is the effective erasure of the transcendent command of the sovereign (verticality) with the immanent exercise of discipline emerging from within the intellectual labor of education itself (horizontality). This is a shift from biopower towards a biopolitical concept of educational production that replaces 'the child' with what I would describe as 'youthfulness' (the child liberated from the objectifying properties of childhood) as a new ontological category. If Dewey's theory of education is opposed fundamentally to biopower, it is also equally opposed to a new form of sovereign control: educational standardization. Standards have replaced the ontology of the child with a new ontology of the student as a quantifiable statistic dependent on *control* in the form of *instruction*. If for Hardt and Negri, biopolitics represents a hybrid union between sovereignty (now virtualized in terms of immanent control over the production of subjectivities) and capitalism, then standardization in schools is the proper educational logic of Empire. Here administration does not seek to unify diversity as it does to manage individual diversity through particularizing itself according to the needs of local singularities. Thus when proponents of standardization argue that leftist critiques underestimate the flexibility of the standards movement, they are in fact revealing the tight connections between standards and Empire which leftists miss. Also, when standardization movements include mandates such as 'critical thinking' this should not be dismissed as a mere rhetorical or ideological ploy but rather as a way of incorporating the autonomy of the subject into an overall neo-liberal view of self-regulation, competition, and managerial independence inherent in new forms of biopolitics. Furthermore, the control unique to current standardization is itself a mixed constitution, pulling its ideological resources equally from military strategy (hence the intimate relation between standardization and certain forms of zero tolerance measures [Lewis, 2006; Saltman & Gabbard, 2003]), economic logics (where students are seen as potential social investments [Simons, 2006]), and communications technologies (hence the drive for new media literacies to overcome a digital divide). With the rise of standardization, management of performance as a measure of productivity has replaced the more modernist notion of a subject striving to realize genuine and personally meaningful beliefs through practice (Ball, 2003). Through the management of performance within the control networks of standardization, biopolitics is intended to operate as biopower which invests in students who have potential (an economic logic) but also determines new forms of abandonment for those whose lives are deemed unworthy of being educated. In other words, biopolitics functions as a power that constitutes *bios* in accordance with neo-liberalism and an overall police logic (Negri, 2004).

For Dewey, the role of the teacher is not to master or control but rather to guide a process tied to student experience. Dewey writes that the teacher assists by cooperating with the 'natural capacities of the individuals guided' (Dewey, 1997a, p. 23). Discipline here is determined by *bios* as a power of singularities (the teacher included in this network as one of many) investigating a collective project. Dewey describes such activity in the following manner: 'They are doing a variety of things, and there is the confusion, the bustle, that results from activity. But out of the occupation, out of doing things that are to produce results, and out of doing these in a social and cooperative way, there is born a discipline of its own kind and type' (Dewey, 1980, p. 12). In other words, educational discipline is fostered through what Dewey refers to as 'attention' (1997b, p. 52), which is internal to educational experimentation and guided by teacher facilitation. As such, the role of the teacher shifts from that of enforcing a sovereign decision (as in Rousseau's covert manipulation of Emile) or performative control (as with No Child Left Behind) to that of directing youth towards the attention necessary to actively produce a new, collective way of being in the world. In this formulation, education both starts from and ends with the reproduction of the common, not as a unified people but as a dynamic ensemble or what Dewey would most likely refer to as a proto-democratic 'public' (1988). Within the public, singularity is not necessarily absorbed into a centered unity (as in a people bound by a notion of national sovereignty or an irrational crowd hypnotized by a leader). Rather singularities are maintained (if not produced) within the overall movement of the common. In Dewey's language, 'individual variation' remains 'precious' even as the school fosters a sense of collectivity (1997a, p. 305). Thus the goals of democratic education attempt to strike a dynamic and productive balance between the common and the singular, cultivating an eighth form of intelligence: swarm intelligence. Such intelligence is enacted through education at the singular and collective levels and is summarized in Dewey's theory of habit. As Hardt and Negri argue (2004, p. 198), the multitude emerges from this pragmatist notion of habit as a mediation between internal impulses/interests/capacities and collectivities.

Overall, each educational experience leads to more experiences without eviscerating the internal potentials of youth to create and to discover (Dewey, 1997b). Just as meaning is enriched through the continuation of experimentation, so too is the constitutive power of youth renewed through each actualization of itself. Thus the youthful body is *homohomo* as a generative life constructing and reconstructing itself over and above the limit case of sovereign mastery or standardized control. What prevents this theory of education from simply toppling over into a new form of 'life-long learning', which is linked intimately with a neo-liberal ideology of entrepreneurial enterprise and risk management (Simons, 2006), is precisely the role of the teacher who selects experiences that both appeal to students and/or community needs but also and importantly are guided by democratic criteria. As such, experience is not educative if it leads to anti-social outcomes such as atomism, selfish/narrow interests, or limitations on the possibility of future experiences. Experience is educative when it leads to democratic ends: shared interests, a collective sense of responsibility, the powers to debate, question, problematize, invent, etc.

From Dewey's perspective, the constitutive powers of the multitude must be given direction towards democracy at a young age if they are to struggle effectively to realize expanding freedom. While Hardt and Negri might be correct in the argument that the material preconditions exists for true, global democracy, constitutive power is always under threat of transforming back into sovereign power unless the multitude recognizes itself as multitude, as a networked swarm whose desire is that of democracy and whose intelligence is always collective and embodied. In other words, democratic education helps transform constitutive powers into a purpose/demand to wage a fight against new forms of exploitation and subjugation. Education acts as a mediation between the manifesto of the multitude presented by Hardt and Negri and the actual practices of the multitude as they labor within and against Empire. Importantly, the transformation of constitutive impulse into a directed purpose is not simply the imposition of adult, political ends onto into the experiential continuum of youth. As Dewey states, this situation is to be avoided through 'a co-operative enterprise' (1997b, p. 72) that manages the particular singularities of youth with the long-term gestation of the multitude coming into existence as a multitude.

This analysis helps us understand why it is to Dewey that we must turn for an educational theory of the multitude rather than proponents of progressive education such as A. S. Neill. At first blush, it would seem that the proper educational model for the multitude would be Neill's Summerhill (1992). Neill allows youth to experience a form of freedom that is not territorialized by particular forms of structure, standards, or normalization. Here Neill basically argues that freedom must be experienced from the earliest stages of life if the young are to become truly self-regulating adults. Underlying this conviction is that education in a negative sense (as removing obstacles) ultimately leads to a democratic organization of the students by their own powers. Such a theory of education equates the constitutive power of youth with the spontaneously democratic constitutive powers of the multitude.

Yet we cannot easily endorse the Summerhill model without serious reservations. For instance, the constitutive powers of youth can only emerge against the background of the past, and as such there would be some responsibility of the teacher to introduce the student to such a backdrop.[2] Without this guidance, constitutive power as a creative rupture would not be recognized as such, nor would the force and strength (not to mention dangers) of such power be reckoned with reasonably. Yet what form of reason is needed here? Education must work to cultivate a 'new rationality' (Negri, 1999, p. 328) which consists of (a) a form of abstraction arriving from within the communication networks of living labor and learning, (b) creative versatility, (c) a rethinking of measure outside of norms and normalization, (d) a rejection of process for immanent procedure, (e) equality as a principle of action against all forms of privilege, (f) cooperative as opposed to command logic. The new rationality is in others words the cognitive component to swarm intelligence which in sum is collective and embodied. This new rationality might in fact be determined by the ontology of the multitude and its collective/spontaneous strength (or as the case might be, by students working collaboratively), but without a democratic form of education guided by a teacher (as a singularity within the contingent network of education), such reason will not necessarily mature into a revolutionary form adequate to meet the demands of constitutive powers (which could overflow its limits) or to the co-opting power of Empire (which routes such powers back into capitalist channels of production). Neill's own complaint concerning problem children newly introduced to educational freedom speaks directly to this point. Some students, argues Neill, have lived stultified lives (or have cultivated 'passionate attachments' to unfreedom [Cho & Lewis, 2006]) and thus when introduced to freedom react violently, producing chaos and undo disruption at Summerhill. Rather than act to cultivate a new rationality capable of understanding the productive powers unleashed by the Summerhill experience, Neill simply refuses to intercede, and these students are voted out of the school. Dewey's approach, on the other hand, mediates internal impulses of youth with democratic long-term interests, cultivating the constitutive powers of collective educational experiments in ways that Neill only can begin to approximate.

Likewise, Ivan Illich's theory of deschooling (2004) is equally problematic as an educational vision equal to the multitude. Certainly Hardt and Negri would accept Illich's critique of (a) compulsory schooling, (b) the cult of the expert, (c) the centrality of school as *the* privileged site of education. Taking into account these criticisms as well as Illich's ingenious expansion of education through learning webs, I would nevertheless argue that Dewey surpasses Illich in both his rigorous theory of education and his imaginative reconstruction of schools as key (though not exclusive) locations of education. Missing in Illich is the guided relation between the cultivation of interest and a new rationality found within swarm intelligence. Hence the worry that learning webs could just as easily lead towards global networks of critical and utopian insurgency as they could lead to homogenous enclaves sealed off from larger movements.

Yet there are distinct ambiguities in Dewey's work that speak to the continued presence of biopower within his anticipatory biopolitical agenda. This is not to dismiss Dewey but rather to highlight his own historical positionality and to speak to his great foresight in imagining an 'untimely pedagogy' speaking to the needs and demands of the multitude. As such the residual effects of biopower in Dewey's writings on education indicate not so much a lack in his own educational imagination but rather speak to the objective ambiguities of his historical location in industrial capitalism and imperialism. It is only now in an age of Empire that we can begin to tease out the intricate relations between biopower and biopolitics in Dewey's educational philosophy. As such the following comments are an attempt to understand how it is that Dewey relates to the present and in turn how his work may (or may not) be revitalized as the missing pedagogical theory of the multitude.

For instance, we should look carefully at Dewey's comments concerning education and nationalism. On the one hand Dewey wants to break down barriers not only between classes and races but also between national territories (1997a, p. 87). He is admittedly opposed to nationalistic education, which subordinates the student to national sovereignty (as in 19th century idealist concepts of education) (ibid., p. 94). The nation-state is obsessed with its own security, territory, and economy, thus denying the transnational movements of communication, science, and commerce. Thus there is a push and pull in education between national aims (which are limited to the construction of a people) and the aims of the public, or the common (which is expansive and highly pluralistic). Thus education must place emphasis on 'whatever binds people together in cooperative human pursuits and results, apart from geographical limitations' (ibid.).

Yet the historical conditions were not yet ripe for a full critique of the nation-state. Dewey advocated that a 'secondary and provisional character of national sovereignty' be 'instilled as a working disposition of mind' in the young (1997a, p. 98). This endorsement of the nation-state itself represents the tension between biopower and biopolitics in Dewey's ideas. On the one hand, Dewey argues that the nation-state forms the logical culmination of expanding human interaction, which results in the need to regulate the broad effects of these actions on others (1988, p. 12). While his notion of socio-political activism remains locked within the horizon of the state, so too his utopian theory of the 'Great Community'—as the realization of the democratic potentials unleashed by the 'Great Society'—falls within a general theory of the state, and in particular a certain US exceptionalism (ibid., p. 148). On the other hand, the afterword to *The Public and its Problems* suggests that a new horizon has appeared: one that reorients the problem of the public towards a transnational, post-WWII reality populated by international organizations like the United Nations. While Hardt and Negri would agree with Dewey's theory of American exceptionalism (in relation to the unique qualities of the US constitution), nevertheless today we see a heightening of the conflict appearing not so much between nation-states and cosmopolitanism but rather between the transnational movement of Empire and its equally global counterpart: the multitude. Both sides stand against the nation-state as a territorializing force constricting the constitutive power of the multitude. Thus Dewey's pedagogy is poised at a historical juncture that both moves towards the multitude and globalization while retaining its hold on the concept of the 'good' sovereignty of the nation-state. Certainly Hardt and Negri would argue the state is one important node in the overall network form of global sovereignty, yet this role is not so much as a safeguard of democracy as it is a historical attempt to solve the problem of the multitude through either discipline or control. As such, the 'good' sovereignty of Dewey's American ideal cannot be historically or theoretically justified. It is our job in the present to question the centrality of this problematic and to realize the historical thrust of Dewey's pedagogy by situating democratic education within and against Empire. As such, American history, as described by Dewey in *The School and Society* (1980), cannot end with a sense of US triumphalism or evolutionism that culminates in the nation-state form and the constitutional contract of American democracy. Rather US history must be decentered by the histories of insurgency both within and against the US as well as non-European counter-narratives that complicate Dewey's linear and heroic historical model, western ideology.

Second, there is the question of *which form* of democracy should act as a guiding principle of education. For Dewey democracy is ultimately a form of social interaction that builds or fosters shared interests, continual social readjustment to changing circumstances, and a pluralistic notion that welcomes diversity of opinion while using critical inquiry to build consensus (1997a, p. 87). Yet is this the only definition of democracy possible? According to Hardt and Negri, such features are largely antithetical to democracy, or at least must be balanced against the disruptive and destabilizing horizon of democracy found in the demands of the multitude. If one emphasizes consensus building, then the other emphasizes antagonism as a break with dominant forms of common sense. If one sees democracy as reform through continuity, then the other sees it as rupture and discensus. As Negri argues, constitutive power 'bursts apart, breaks, interrupts, unhinges any preexisting equilibrium and any possible continuity' (1999, p. 10). Thus if continuity is to be valued by Hardt and Negri, it is less the reconstructive growth of experience in accordance with a reasonable evaluation of changing social pressures and more with the continual rupture of revolution.

These political debates must in the end inform a new notion of democratic education, orienting us from democracy as a pluralistic vision of 'harmonious' consensus building to an absolute form of democracy (deterritorializing and revolutionizing). In educational terms, this would mean that Dewey's theme of growth through experience and critical reflection would have to accept the possibility of 'absolute openings' (Negri, 1999) or rather disruptions in the flow of experiences by educational events.[3] If the two components of experience are continuity (temporal) and interaction between internal capacities, needs, and interests and the external environment (spatial) then events inaugurate discontinuity and the formation of new subjectivities that cannot be measured against past habits of mind or past rationalities. These events are not simply experiences among others but are rather short-circuits in the fabric of experience that introduce new starting points. In other words, the effect of the event in education is not cumulative but rather inaugural.

The event as rupture does not come from a void or lack but rather from the *excess* of constitutive power inherent in the exercise of education.[4] In other words, the productive capacities of youth out-step the limits of experience as a recognizable (though problematic) and cognizable phenomenon, provoking radically new evental horizons. It is this constitutive power as overflow that in the event becomes a theoretical question open for critical reflection, and it is precisely here that education for insurgency begins. While Dewey would not perhaps discount the occurrence of educational events, the worry is that his overriding emphasis on the educational continuum will reduce the significance of the event, or even worse misrecognize the possibility of its happening in the classroom. Without the educational event, the constitutive power of youth would never offer the educative moment for cultivating a new rationality, and constitutive powers would never become subjectivized as a dangerous yet powerfully productive possibility. In other words, young men and women would fail to see themselves as subjects of constitutive power. Thus if Dewey brings a new educational vision to the politics of the multitude then Hardt and Negri bring a new, radicalized potential to Dewey's guiding vision of democracy.

Biopolitics and Utopia in Education

Overall, a biopolitical pedagogy works to transform student life into *homohomo* or productive, generative life through which new notions of democratic community can evolve. As opposed to the emptying out of student life before the One of biopower, youthful life as a potentiality should be recognized for its constitutive powers of creation, its movement towards the common, and its utopian and democratic possibilities. Here Dewey's pedagogy becomes a *biopedagogy* against the various levels of corruption emanating from within Empire. His creed enables us to think through youthfulness as a life stage emanating from within the multitude, and the multitude enables us to think the political horizon of Dewey's pedagogy. My personal educational wager is that the folding of biopolitical insurgencies back into biopower (and thus the horizontality of sovereign force) can be overcome through a democratic education whose experimentation cultivates a new rationality in light of the event of constitutive rupture. As such, it is a major oversight of Hardt and Negri's manifesto that universal education is left off of their list of democratic demands. Here it is important to remember that for Dewey education can serve the function of allowing the multitude to recognize itself as the multitude, as a public whose interests lie in the continual production of a global common and whose desires are immanently democratic. This indictment of contemporary political theory for its lack of concern for educational problematics is not in the end a 'guarantee' in which education solves all social problems. Education in other words is not sufficient but necessary. The function education within schools can come to play is the cultivation of constitutive power necessary to risk social exit into the absolute opening of a dystopian-utopia both inside yet anterior to Empire.

Acknowledgements

I would like to thank Richard Kahn and David Kennedy for their insightful criticisms of this paper and for their invaluable friendship.

Notes

1 Perhaps the classic example of this sovereign ban is to be found in Hegel's *Philosophy of Right* (1967). Here the private sphere of the family cultivates a child's sense of independence, and schooling submits this freedom to the universal law of the state in the form of an obligation to obey. Hence, private freedom exists only as an exclusion constituting educational life.
2 Hannah Arendt has argued as such (1993).

3 Although Hardt and Negri argue that there is no outside of Empire, this does not mean that there are no absolute openings. As a logical consequence of their thesis, we can also argue that there is no inside of Empire either. Rather there is only a zone of indistinction between the inside and the outside that is pure potential, where the logic of capital and the logic of resistance exist simultaneously on the same field of social relations.

4 In other words, Alain Badiou's theory of the event (2002) will remain a 'miracle' as long as its biopolitical roots in the constitutive powers of the multitude (embodied and collective yet running in surplus of any ideologically territorialized notion of self, society, or law) are not recognized.

References

Arendt, H. (1993) *Between Past and Future* (New York, Penguin Books).

Agamben, G. (2005) *State of Exception* (Chicago, IL, University of Chicago Press).

Agamben, G. (1998) *Homo Sacer: Sovereign power and bare life* (Stanford, CA, Stanford University Press).

Atwood, M. (1998) *The Handmaid's Tale* (New York, Anchor Books).

Badiou, A. (2002) *Ethics: An essay on the understanding of evil* (London, Verso).

Ball, S. (2003) The Teacher's Soul and the Terrors of Performativity, *Journal of Educational Policy,* 18:2, pp. 215–228.

Brennan, T. (2003) The Italian Ideology, in: G. Balakrishnan (ed.) *Debating Empire* (London, Verso).

Brosio, R. (1994) Dewey as the Schoolmaster for Marx's Radical Democracy, *Educational Philosophy 1994* (Urbana-Champaign, IL, Philosophy of Education Society).

Cho, D., & Lewis, T. (2006) The Persistent Life of Oppression: The unconscious, power, and subjectivity, *Interchange,* 36:3, pp. 313–29.

Dewey, J. (1980) *The School and Society* (London, Southern Illinois University Press).

Dewey, J. (1988) *The Public and its Problems* (Chicago, Swallow Press).

Dewey, J. (1997a) *Democracy and Education* (New York, Free Press).

Dewey, J. (1997b) *Experience and Education* (New York, Touchstone).

Ellsworth, E. (1989) Why Doesn't This Feel Empowering? Working through the repressive myths of critical pedagogy, *Harvard Educational Review,* 59:3, pp. 297–324.

Foucault, M. (1990) *History of Sexuality: An introduction* (New York, Vintage Books).

Foucault, M. (2003) '*Society Must be Defended*' (New York, Picador).

Geoghegan, V. (1988) *Utopianism and Marxism* (London, Routledge, Kegan, and Paul).

Giroux, H. (2002) *Public Spaces, Private Lives* (London, Rowman & Littlefield).

Halpin, D. (2003) Hope and Education: The role of the utopian imagination (London, RoutledgeFalmer).

Hardt, M. & Negri, A. (2000) *Empire* (Cambridge, MA, Harvard University Press).

Hardt, M. & Negri, A. (2005) *Multitude: War and democracy in the age of empire* (New York, Penguin Press).

Hegel, G. W. F. (1967) *Philosophy of Right* (Oxford, Oxford University Press).

Illich, I. (2004) *Deschooling Society* (New York, Marion Boyars).

Jameson, F. (1982) *The Political Unconscious: Narrative as a socially symbolic act* (Ithaca, NY, Cornell University Press).

Jameson, F. (1994) *Seeds of Time* (New York, Columbia University Press).

Jameson, F. (2004) The Politics of Utopia, *New Left Review,* 25, pp. 35–54.

Leonardo, Z. (2003) Reality on Trial: Notes on ideology, education, and utopia, *Policy Futures in Education,* 1:3, pp. 504–25.

Lewis, T. (2006) The School as an Exceptional Space: Rethinking education from the perspective of the biopedagogical, *Educational Theory,* 56:2, pp. 159–176.

Mannheim, K. (1985) *Utopia and Ideology: An introduction to the sociology of knowledge* (San Diego, CA, Harcourt Brace Jovanovich).

Moylan, T. (2000) *Scraps of the Untainted Sky* (Boulder, CO, Westview Press).

Negri, A. (1999) *Insurgencies: Constituent power and the modern state* (Minneapolis, MN, Minnesota Press).

Negri, A. (2003) *Time for Revolution* (New York, Continuum).

Negri, A. (2004) It's a Powerful Life: A conversation on contemporary philosophy, *Cultural Critique,* 57, pp. 151–183.

Neill, A. S. (1992) *Summerhill School: A new view of childhood* (New York, St. Martin's Griffin).

Ricoeur, P. (1986) *Lectures on Ideology and Utopia* (New York, Columbia University Press).

Robinson, K. S. (1993–1996) *The Mars Trilogy* (New York, Bantam Books).

Rousseau, J. J. (1762/1979) *Emile* (New York, Basic Books).

Saltman, K. & Gabbard, D. (eds) (2003) *Education as Enforcement: The militarization and corporatization of schools* (London, RoutledgeFalmer).

Simons, M. (2006). Learning as Investment: Notes on governmentality and biopolitics, *Educational Philosophy and Theory,* 38:4, pp. 523–540.

Tucker, R. (ed.) (1978) *The Marx-Engels Reader* (New York, W. W. Norton and Company).

Virno, P. (2004) *A Grammar of the Multitude* (New York, Semiotext).

Webb, D. (2000) *Marx, Marxism, and Utopia* (Aldershot, Ashgate).

Chapter 9

A Place Pedagogy for 'Global Contemporaneity'

Margaret J. Somerville

Reprinted by permission of Taylor & Francis Ltd, http://www.tandfonline.com, on behalf of © Philosophy of Education Society of Australasia.

Editors' Introduction

Somerville in her chapter argues that around the globe people are confronted daily with intransigent problems of space and place. Educators have historically called for place-based or place-conscious education to introduce pedagogies that will address such questions as how to develop sustainable communities and places. These calls for place-conscious education have included liberal humanist approaches and critical place-based approaches such as those advocated by David Gruenewald. In this chapter she proposes a reconceptualized framework of place as a pedagogical practice that draws on contemporary feminist poststructural and postcolonial philosophies as a basis for an alternative place pedagogy for global contemporaneity. Within this reconceptualized concept of place Somerville outlines three key principles for a reconceptualised place pedagogy: our relationship to place is constituted in stories and other representations; place learning is local and embodied; and deep place learning occurs in a contact zone of contestation. These principles give rise to new emergent arts-based methodologies for developing and practising place-responsive pedagogies. Somerville proposes an ontology of becoming-other as an extension of feminist poststructural work about the subject in process. This becoming-other is a relational ontology that includes the non-human and inanimate 'flesh of the world' as well as human others. Within this ontology of becoming-other there is an epistemology that includes all of the technologies that we use to create representations—including language, computers, and paper, but also clay, brushes, paint, fabric—all of the artefacts we use to create. Each individual representation is conceived as a pause in an iterative process of representation and reflection, and as contributing to assemblages of such artefacts whose meanings are intertextual. Any pedagogy of place must remain open and dynamic, responsive to the interaction between specific people and their local places.

Introduction

Clouds

Early morning walk with dogs down through the roundabout on the edge of town. Here the world of suburban houses opens out and there is a wonderful big puff of clouds licked pink from the sunrise against a pale blue sky. But as the street opens out the view I can see the six chimneys of the power station, two by two by two, with a thin trail of umbilical vapour connected to the big cloud. It's a power station cloud. I run back home to get my camera, worried that by the time I get back to this spot it will have gone. Dogs running, camera slung around my neck, only a few minutes—and yes, it has changed. Pink tinge gone, it is lit bright in the early morning light, more normalised, a bright daytime cloud in a bright blue day. I have to take a photo so you will understand. Space, place and time, weather, climate change, culture and nature, the significance of that moment of representation.

We are linked in this moment of 'global contemporaneity' (Carter, 2006, p. 683). Around the globe intransigent problems confront us. Daily we are presented with news about global warming, climate change, rapid loss of endangered species, and devastating catastrophes of weather. In Australia the local and the global have powerfully intersected in ways that make attention to global/local issues of greenhouse gas emissions, climate change, drought, increasing problems of water scarcity and local negotiations about water use, an imperative. A global report on climate change produced by 700 world scientists is presented by the UN. The Australian government reluctantly acknowledges the phenomena of climate change and the relationship between greenhouse gas emissions, the use of fossil fuels to produce energy, and the current crippling water crisis. The response to these problems has largely been framed in terms of the techno-scientific solutions of modernity—moving water, building more dams, desalination plants—combined with a neoliberal economic approach—water trading, carbon trading, economic sanctions. But what might be an adequate educational response?

In this paper I want to think through these as issues of space and place. I use the twin terms 'space and place' (Hubbard et al., 2004) because in considering the multiple definitions of 'place' it became clear that space and place are so deeply implicated in one another it is impossible to consider one without the other. The choice of term for particular theorists depends on their theoretical locations and research questions. I have used both space and place in my own work. In this paper, however, I want to focus on the question of our attachments to our local places, so I will be using the notion of place. I want to consider what sort of education might produce a different response to the natural world than one that promotes such profoundly disturbing solutions to these critical issues of climate change and drought. I want to ask, How might we educate a generation of children 'growing up global' (Power, 2007) to be attached to their local places, to inhabit, and to know place differently? These are questions I will take up in the body of this paper.

I think science education is one useful beginning point in this thinking because of the hegemony of Western science in these solutions. A recent special edition of *Educational Philosophy and Theory* provides a starting point in questioning the philosophical bases of science education from several different perspectives. Three articles, in particular, engage with the epistemological and ontological bases of science and the relationship of science education to non-Western knowledges. Gough takes as his starting point Harding's critique of the Eurocentrism and androcentrism of scientific knowledge: 'Both popular/media culture and non-Western knowings tend to be ignored or devalued within many forms of Western science education. These exclusions contribute to what Sandra Harding (1993) calls an increasingly visible form of scientific illiteracy' (Gough, 2006, p. 626). Lyn Carter draws on postcolonial scholarship for her critique and proposes a border epistemology (Mignolo, 2000) in an attempt to move to 'other thinking' (Carter, 2006, p. 683). This, she believes, will recover 'critical spaces for oppositional thinking and practice' (Carter, 2006, p. 679). Similarly, Fendler and Tuckey (2006) aim to unsettle the certainties of scientific knowledge by asking what it means to combine literacy with science in a deconstructive textual practice. Again they focus on the problem of the binary assumptions of western science, in particular, 'certain fundamental categories—life versus non-life, objective versus subjective, and scientific versus cultural' (Fendler & Tuckey, 2006, p. 602).

These deconstructive approaches are methods in themselves and offer strategies for reading science and science education as a textual, political and socio-cultural practice. The underpinning critiques of Eurocentrism and androcentrism are not new and it is important to take these further. However, it is the potential of Gough's method of a 'nomadic geophilosophy of science education' that I want to take up here. I believe that this structure of his nomadic geophilosophy is revealed through a passage in which Gough begins with the name of a song, *Shaking the Tree*, a song that signifies 'taking action . . . to resolve local situations':

> Peter Gabriel and Youssou N'Dour's song, *Shaking the Tree*, is in several ways emblematic of my project. It is a call to change and enhance lives composed in a spirit which complements Deleuze and Guattari's (1994) practical 'geophilosophy' (p. 95), which seeks to describe the relations between particular spatial configurations and locations and the philosophical formations that arise therein. Both Gabriel and N'Dour compose and perform songs about taking action to solve particular problems in the world, and Deleuze (1994) believes that concepts should intervene to resolve local situations' (p. xx).
>
> (Gough, 2006, p. 625)

This richly layered metaphorical passage works on several levels and I would like to briefly reflect on these. *Shaking the Tree* is a song, so we begin with a metaphor of singing, sound and the human voice, of creative expression in song, a move between a metaphysics of logics and of poetics. This denotes not only a different approach to writing, but to academic thought. This different approach has both practical and metaphysical implications. The image of 'shaking the tree' is connected with Deleuzian notions of the problematic of the tree-as-structure as opposed to the rhizome as a metaphor of thought. The tree represents the certainties and hierarchies of western science and the paper is Gough's rhizomatic song, a song that is both practical and located, metaphysical and transformational. He names the variety of assemblages available to shake the tree of modern Western science: 'arts, artefacts, disciplines, technologies, projects, practices, theories and social strategies' (Gough, 2006, p. 626). This approach is not mere theoretical artifice. These are the essential elements of thinking, and writing, differently.

Through this paper I would like to take up some of these strategies in different ways, not only as deconstruction or critique, but to propose a possible beginning point for creating something different. I write from a particular embodied, material and temporal location, from my own particular histories as a white Australian female anglo migrant, about the question of what might be an adequate educational response to intransigent global problems. I have tried, but I cannot write otherwise. So the bits that I gather like a bowerbird are the ones that help me to make these global connections, to interrogate my own histories, producing new assemblages and rhizomatic thought. I enter the space of Carter's postcolonial coming-into-being to open up 'possibilities for living within all the complexities of postcolonial and reflexive contemporaneity' (Carter, 2006, p. 684).

This takes me back to the clouds. In entering this space/time conjunction of global contemporaneity I write from the specific location of my new home in Latrobe Valley, Churchill, Victoria, the home of Victoria's brown coal fired power stations. By writing from the multiple and contested places in Latrobe Valley, I write not only against its stereotypical representations, but against the notion of place as either constructed or natural. I use this strategy to disrupt the taken for granted and romantic binaries that construct wilderness and the natural world as distinct from human artefacts. The cloud passage at the beginning, for example connects to the significance of clouds in climate change:

> Although it is a greenhouse gas, water vapour is also an enigma in the climate change arena, for it forms clouds, and clouds can both reflect light energy and trap heat. By trapping more heat than reflecting light, high thin clouds tend to warm the planet, while low thick clouds have the reverse effect. No single factor contributes more to our uncertainty of future climate change predictions.
> (Flannery, 2005, p. 27)

The clouds that I see on my morning walk are even more disruptive of our taken-for-granted binaries of the natural and cultural because these clouds are in fact produced by the power stations. They open us to the enigma and challenge of place.

Place

Walking out of the scrub at the edge of the playing field there's a big puddle of water lying since recent rains. My heart rises the first time I see this water appear after drought. The second time there is already an amazing chorus of frogs. My son tells me they sing in chorus so the females can choose a mate. But where do they come from? There have been no frogs singing since that first day at dawn. Why aren't they singing? Is it the time, or are they all gone again? It's Sunday morning so I wander over to the little wetland. I think about knowing a place day in and day out, over seasons and years to really know what is going on, I think about how places teach us. I crouch down beside the water in the pose of the child, crouching down beside this place just to see what I can see. I smell the rank smell of childhood water holes filled with water after rain. Peering in to the shallow pool I enter a still, tea coloured world of decaying leaves and grass, tiny creatures minutely disturbing with their movements. But there are no tadpoles at the edges of this water. Why, I do not know. I walk a little further, feet squelching in the mud, looking for telltale signs of frog's eggs with their tiny black dots of tadpoles coming into being, the sort of clear gelatinous globs on the smooth surface of the water. How did I learn that these were baby tadpoles?

My own work in dealing with 'the complexities of postcolonial and reflexive contemporaneity' began in another time and place. In 1988 an Armidale Aboriginal woman, Patsy Cohen, approached me to help her do some research about 'Ingelba and the five black matriarchs'. I had no idea what she meant, why she wanted to do this research, where, who she was talking about, or how we might go about it. The focus of Patsy's research was a bare parcel of land tucked into a bend of a cold high country river about forty kilometres from the town where we were living. Her research methods were to gather together, for a day, all the people who had lived at Ingelba, to photograph the day, and record the stories people told as they walked around and remembered. Patsy was recovering her lost heritage. Removed from her mother as a young child, she returned to Ingelba a stranger, a victim of our shared colonial histories. My ethnographic imagination was fashioned in the space between Patsy's desires and my imaginings (Cohen & Somerville, 1990). In order to collaborate in this research I was required to become the unknower, to think through imagination. Everything in this project was structured according to place. This place called Ingelba began for me as a barren, empty paddock. It became peopled with life as the physical place gathered around it the meanings of Patsy's individual life, her communities' collective meanings and the meanings of our shared colonial history.

Place, that is, both a specific local place and a metaphysical imaginary, was presented as an alternative lens through which to construct knowledge about the world. In my work with Aboriginal people place has come to offer a way of entering an in-between space where it is possible to hold different, and sometimes contradictory, ideas in productive tension. It is a meeting point for my own interests in ecology and body/landscape connection and Aboriginal ontologies and epistemologies based on land. Place has long been noted as an organising principle in Aboriginal ontologies and epistemologies by both Indigenous and non-Indigenous Australian scholars (Somerville, 1991; Rose, 1996; Behrendt & Thompson, 2003). 'Aboriginal Australians regard the land as a totality, connection to country being the very essence of their belief structure and subsequent social organisation' (Ward *et al.*, 2003, p. 29). This remains true despite dispossession, displacement, and genocide of Australian Aboriginal cultures since colonisation (Langton in Behrendt & Thompson, 2003) and has profound implications for an Australian understanding of relationship to place (Somerville, 1999). 'For Indigenous people, issues of community health, economic development, care for Country and culture are all intertwined' (Rose, in Ward *et al.*, p. 72). Australian scholars and researchers cannot begin to articulate a position about place without confronting the complex political realities of Indigenous/ non-Indigenous relationships in place. Possibly more than any other they are in a unique position to articulate what it means to learn about place in 'a postcolonial and reflexive contemporaneity' (Carter, 2006, p. 684).

Place is productive as a framework because it creates a space between grounded physical reality and the metaphysical space of representation. In my work with archaeologists, for example, the particular physical location enabled conversations between an epistemology based in direct access to a physical reality and an epistemology based in reality as accessed through representation (Beck & Somerville, 2005). The archaeologists I worked with approached the Aboriginal stories as either supporting or contradicting the archaeological evidence. We had many discussions about 'the story' of archaeology and how it could sit alongside Aboriginal oral place stories. This is an important issue in natural resource management where traditionally Aboriginal place knowledge can only be recognised to the extent that is can be incorporated into a scientific natural resource framework. This bridging of physical reality and representation has the potential to bring positivist paradigms from the physical sciences into conversation with post positivist research in the emerging field of 'ecological humanities' (Rose, 2004). Such a bridging of different disciplinary and subject areas is imperative in addressing intransigent problems of space and place such as the health of rivers and waterways. While research in the physical sciences has typically been seen as the solution for complex environmental problems, emerging research in the eco-humanities suggests that changing our relationship to our places is as important as techno-scientific solutions. In this way place can offer an important framework for an integrated educational curriculum which seeks to address environmental issues from a range of perspectives that could cross traditional subject boundaries of science, history, geography, creative arts and English.

Place also functions as a bridge between the local and the global. Without an intimate knowledge of local places that we love there is no beginning point. Without a concept of the local, action is not possible. However, under conditions of global contemporaneity, it is no longer possible to consider local problems, such as a drought that affects every local area in Australia in different and specific ways, as independent of global issues. Through place it is possible to understand the embodied effects of the global at a local level: 'Place in other words, fore-grounds a narrative of local and regional politics that is attuned to the particulari-ties of where people actually live, and that is connected to global development trends that impact local places' (Gruenewald, 2003b, p. 3). Place enables us to act on the local from the perspectives and understandings of the global (Soja, 2000), such as actions to repair the micro-habitat of endangered species. It can also enable us to intervene in the global on the basis of local knowledges, for example, in the case of climate change where reducing local emissions will impact globally (Somerville, 2003). Place has the potential to offer alternative storylines about who we are in the places where we live and work in an increasingly glo-balised world.

The discourses of Indigenous knowledge about place are one site for the inter-section of Western and non-Western epistemologies. Barbara Schroder describes the intersection of these discourses in walking with a local Indigenous woman in Ecuador 'As we walked she introduced me to an astonishing variety of medicinal plants, pointing them out and describing what they were good for'. She gives two significant and typical reasons for why, at the time, she took no notice. Firstly she was a student of 'medical anthropology' so it was outside her disciplinary area, and secondly, 'this traditional ecological knowledge seemed destined to vanish' (Schroder, 2006, p. 307), a common colonial assumption about Indigenous knowledges. She goes on to elaborate, however, the growing tradition of 'native science' in Ecuador and the epistemology that underpins this tradition:

- all forms of life are inseparably connected to one another
- individual groups of humans are inextricably connected to particular parts of the planet
- geographical features (mountains, rivers, plains) are living beings
- human experience is unitary with technology, education, spirituality, politics, and the arts all different expressions of same underlying truths
- cycles and circles are predominant metaphors for life and reality (Schroder, 2006, p. 308).

While these sorts of characterisations have their own problems of essentialism, they also offer some key points for reflection. In remembering my own experi-ence as a child, and in watching my own four children growing up, it seemed that these characteristics are a potential for all of our knowing the world and our place in it. In pondering on each of these points, I wondered if they could equally be applied to all young children, at least as a potential. If this was the case, then the challenge is to educate these characteristics of an epistemology into, rather than out of, our educational pedagogies. Social theory, however, has been typically characterised by a 'lack of interest in place, material context, and specifically the land. Social science usually prefers context free generalisation' (Connell, 2007, p. 196). Modernity is about the achievement of placelessness, and schooling is the quintessential project of modernity. Postmodernity, on the other hand, requires us to recognise the multiplicity of places. This then becomes the challenge for teacher educators (Green, 2007).

Schroder indirectly takes up the idea of this potential of early childhood by describing an exercise by Peat (2002) that 'highlights the primacy of place in human experience':

> He invited us to close our eyes and remember, first the bedroom of our child-hood, then the house, and then the neighbourhood. . . . [w]e will be able to recreate the landscape in amazing concrete detail (p. 106). The strong visceral feelings that accompany this exercise attest to the primal connections that even contemporary, urban Westerners have with particular places.
>
> (Schroder, 2006, p. 312)

I have written previously that inside the house of my childhood is a dark, empty space (Somerville, 1999). We do not all have benign childhood memories. There is no essential primal experience here. But perhaps because of these dark inside spaces, the outside of my memories is filled with colour and light. Even though I grew up in the suburbs of the major city of Sydney, I remember the lurky places in the gully that fronted the houses in my street as a micro world of rocks, caves and cliffs, uncleared bush, eucalyptus trees and tea-tree scrub, storm water and bush fires.

Place Pedagogies

Mostly when it rains we head down to the stormwater drain to catch the rush of foamy water in the concrete canal. But later I crawl through tunnels of tea-tree scrub to the tadpole holes. They are there longer, long after the stormwater drain has dwindled to its usual trickle. Crouching beside tea-tree water, in the rank smell of decaying plants, blobs of clear jelly appear with tiny dark spots. Day by day the black specks grow into baby tadpoles. Tiny tadpoles that flicker in the stillness of leaves and debris. Then huge ones, slow and sluggish, stirring clouds of mud, growing legs. Losing their tails, turning into frogs, something exquisitely exciting about this change of form. They are the prize ones. I collect them in jars and take them home to watch. I know when the tadpole holes come and go, that after rain they fill up, frogs' eggs appear, baby tadpoles grow and turn into frogs. Then they dry up again and other things take my attention. Finding new red gum tips or velvety nasturtiums to take home for my mum.

For a long time I hadn't understood my work about relationship to place as spe-cifically pedagogical, although I was located in the discipline of adult and com-munity education. I was more concerned to develop appropriate methodologies and ways of writing to express the complex relationships to places and people that were created in the spaces of my work with Indigenous people. There was always, however, a strong underlying motivation to tell the stories of their places for others, to make them available for a wide, popular audience. In more recent work we had begun to develop a more explicit educational agenda with the production of educational materials for use with both Aboriginal and non-Aboriginal schools and communities. In this work new pedagogies, and alternative ontologies and epistemologies, were being created in that in-between space. I made a leap forward into conceptualising this work as a developing place pedagogy when I read David Gruenewald's 2003 articles calling for a place conscious education. I was aware, however, that this work was grounded in a different place and philosophy and it was important to locate it in a genealogy of place based education.

The emergence of calls for a place based-education 'to better serve the social and ecological well-being of particular places' is related to 'an ecologised humanist tradition' in the US (Ball & Lai, 2006, p. 262). In particular, Kentucky farmer Wendell Berry (e.g. Berry, 1981), is identified as representative of the 'ecohumanist' approach underlying this tradition. Berry's, and subsequent scholarship in this tradition, critiques the role of educational institutions in ignoring the 'infinitely particular world of watersheds, growing seasons and ecological niches' (Zency, 1996, in Ball & Lai, 2006, p. 265). These writers foreground the significance of local places in educational processes. Philosophically, this 'ecologised humanist tradition' is underpinned by an enlightenment philosophy and the autonomous, rational subject of liberal humanism (Weedon, 1997). The development of a critical place-conscious education is linked to David Gruenewald, and his response to 'the romantic excesses of ecohumanists' (Ball & Lai, 2006, p. 270).

> Critical perspectives on place-based education provide a corrective to the romantic excesses of ecohumanists, which generally lead to a depoliticization of place, community, and the local. . . . They suggest a central importance even in place-based education for teaching and learning of critical tools for understanding and generating mechanisms for larger-than-local socio-ecological transformation.
>
> (Ball & Lai, 2006, p. 270)

Gruenewald's (2003a, 2003b) articles radically transformed my thinking because of the explicit linking of *place* and *pedagogy*. 'Place', according to Gruenewald, is 'profoundly pedagogical': 'as centers of experience, places teach us about how the world works, and how our lives fit into the spaces we occupy. Further places make us: As occupants of particular places with particular attributes, our identity and our possibilities are shaped' (Gruenwald, 2003b, p. 647). I immediately identified with his description of 'decolonisation' and 're-inhabitation' as the two broad and interrelated objectives of a critical place pedagogy (Gruenewald, 2003a). Decolonisation involves developing the ability to recognise ways of thinking 'that injure and exploit other people and place' (Gruenewald, 2003a, p. 9). Reinhabitation involves 'identifying, affirming, conserving, and creating those forms of cultural knowledge that nurture and protect people and ecosystems' (Gruenewald, 2003a, p. 9). I was interested to explore how these ideas enabled an articulation of the pedagogical qualities of my past fifteen years of place research. I was also aware, however, that my methodologies, developed within a feminist poststructural and postcolonial perspective, and in collaboration with Australian Aboriginal people, differed philosophically and practically from Gruenewald's ideas.

In Australia the linking of ecological concerns and studies in the humanities, has been interpreted differently to the 'ecohumanists' of the US. The birth of the term 'ecohumanities' was marked by the introduction of a special section of *Australian Humanities Review*:

> The ecological humanities works across the great binaries of western thought. We work in a time of rapid social and environmental change, and are committed to cross cutting the divides that impede our understanding and action. The commitment has a parallel in our work toward social and ecological justice and the future of life. Those of us settler society scholars have another ethical imperative here: to be responsive to Indigenous people knowledges and aspirations for justice.
>
> (Rose, 2004)

The linking of ecology and humanities is here related to crossing the 'great binaries of western thought'. Philosophically this locates ecological humanities in a poststructural rather than an enlightenment paradigm. Ecological concerns have previously been dominated by the physical sciences and a scientific, positivist paradigm. Rose is a long term scholar of contemporary Indigenous cultures, in particular, Indigenous relationship to the environment (see for example, *Nourishing Terrains*, 1996). While Rose's interest is not specifically pedagogical, she writes about the Aboriginal people she collaborates with as her 'teachers' and works to translate Indigenous understandings and practices of place into broader debates about how we relate to the environment in Australia.

Writing in place studies in Australia has been characterised by an interdisciplinary approach, a necessary engagement with the relationship between Indigenous and non-Indigenous people and knowledges, and the use of alternative genres of writing. This thrust is partly pedagogical in itself in the motivation to reach a broad audience with these alternative views. Examples of these alternative modes of place writing can be seen in the writings of Larissa Behrendt (*Home*, 2004), Tom Griffiths (*Forests of Ash*, 2001), Mark Mackenna (*Looking for Blackfella's Point*, 2002), and Peter Read (*Belonging*, 2000). The focus on how non-Indigenous people can understand and practice place differently through a relationship to Indigenous knowledges introduces an important dimension into the broader debates about place and environment. Part of this process of research is developing a language and (inter)disciplinary practice that makes this conversation possible. It now seems important, however, even urgent, for educational practitioners to engage with these conversations, specifically in relation to the formulation of alternative place pedagogies.

Elements of a Place Pedagogy

It's just on dusk, mid Autumn. A half full moon and cool wind blows over Morwell River Wetlands as we walk with the teacher before dark falls. The Freeway hums in front and the Hazelwood Power Station behind. Here in the wetlands the frog chorus begins. Partly natural, partly artificial, the original river somewhere nearby, old logs and tree stumps placed in pools by the power company to bring life into these wetlands. Frogs' skin is a permeable membrane between inside and out, so they are a good measure of a place. John and Jim, ten-year-old twins, run down the road to join us, followed by their mum, and then Jacinta, one of seven children, with her Dad. Last month, drought, no Community Frog Watch because snakes hide in the giant open cracks. Tonight, after recent rains, we make our way through frog calls, along the softening cracked edges of the water under the rising moon. Kids cavort, playfully using digital camera/recorders to take photos and record the sounds. We hear a whistling tree frog, a common frog, a bell frog, and on the ground we read the telltale signs of fox, wallaby and kangaroo. The photos will go onto the website with stories, and scientific names to beam across to Oregon where kids in schools in the United States monitor wetlands in an opposite hemisphere and season. Kids making places.

In response to Gruenewald's call for a critical place based education, I began to formulate the key elements of a pedagogy of place based on feminist post-structural and postcolonial theorising. This place pedagogy is empirical in the sense that it derives from qualitative empirical studies. It is underpinned by my own learning. Over twenty years of collaborative research with Australian Aboriginal people, and working through the lens of feminist post-structural theory, I had learned to think through place. What was this process and what were its essential elements? In the following section I outline the key elements that together form a conceptual framework for this place pedagogy:—*our relationship to place is constituted in stories (and other representations); the body is at the centre of our experience of place*; and *place is a contact zone of cultural contact.* These elements must all be simultaneously present and do not have any hierarchical ordering.

Our Relationship to Places is Constituted in Stories (and Other Representations)

The first key concept that I am proposing for a place pedagogy is that our relationship to place is communicated in stories. If Patsy had not communicated her stories of Ingelba to me, for example, I would still see Ingelba as an empty, barren landscape. Here I understand story as a basic unit of meaning making: 'Stories bring nature into culture and ascribe meaning to places, species and processes which would otherwise remain silent to the human ear' (Sinclair, 2001, p. 22). At Ingelba, place storytelling had many dimensions. It was oral, visual, performative, collective, and emplaced. It had many modes of representation—audio recordings, written transcripts, photos, drawings, and maps—which were assembled and re-assembled to produce different forms. The concept of story can be usefully enlarged to embrace the expressions of visual artists, sculptors, and poets, as well as scientists, policy makers and agriculturalists. Each discipline and artistic modality has its own forms and genres of place stories.

The analytical strategy of storylines, as developed in feminist poststructuralism (Davies, 2000; Sondergaard, 2002), can be used deconstructively to analyse how stories function to shape places: 'A storyline is a condensed version of a natural-ized and conventional cultural narrative, one that is often used as the explanatory framework of one's own and other's practices and sequences of action' (Son-dergaard, 2002, p. 191). Dominant storylines of place 'deny our connection to earthly phenomena, . . . [and] construct places as objects or sites on a map to be economically exploited' (Gruenewald, 2003b, p. 624). Deconstructing such storylines is therefore part of the process of 'decolonization' through which we can analyse ways of thinking that injure and exploit other people and places (Gru-enewald, 2003a, p. 9). In Australia, for example, Sinclair describes stories about the Murray River as participating in a 'broader cultural and political narrative of technological and agricultural progress'. Such stories are shaped by 'the vision of a barren land being made productive; of a silent and timeless place being trans-formed and brought into history by the energy of an industrious and resourceful society' (Sinclair, 2001, p. 43). The Murray River is now generally recognized as being in ecological crisis. These dominant storylines depend for their justification and legitimation on the suppression of alternative stories that already exist, often as the shadow side of dominant stories.

The concept of story and storylines can also be used reconstructively to seek out previously invisible place stories or to generate new stories about place. Changing our relationship to places means changing the stories we tell about places: 'If human beings are responsible for place making, then we must become conscious of ourselves as place makers and participants in the sociopolitical pro-cess of place making' (Gruenewald, 2003b, p. 627). Storylines 'are realised and created/changed in the more or less fragmented ways they are taken up by sub-jects as they develop their own narratives' (Sondergaard, 2002, p. 191). They are made and changed in community, and, as Davies (2000, p. 79) reminds us, the task of generating alternative storylines 'that have the power to displace the old is extraordinarily complex'. According to Rose (2004) the major shift in 'ecological humanities' has been to introduce new storylines of embodied connection.

Place Learning is Necessarily Embodied and Local

Of the three elements of a place pedagogy, this is the most radical, transformative, and challenging. After two major collaborative place projects with Aboriginal communities I became aware that the Aboriginal people I worked with were dif-ferently embodied in the landscapes of their stories. I imagined my relationship to these landscapes as a shadow, present in all the stories, but unable to articulate my presence (Somerville *et al.*, 1994). The feminist poststructural emphasis on lan-guage, and the concept of place as constituted through language, were no longer adequate by themselves. In many strands of place research, the subject/object binary is regarded as the problematic basis of the separation between subject and object on which environmental exploitation is founded. I regard the mind/body binary as primary, and foundational to Western language and thought. I began to do some in-depth work around the body and body/place connections, addressing the mind/body binary as it applies to place (Somerville, 1999). In *Volatile Bodies,* feminist philosopher Liz Grosz proposed to interrogate philosophy by 'putting the body at the centre of our notion of subjectivity' (Grosz, 1994, p. 5). I applied this strategy to place, revisiting a series of place projects and experiences, and putting the body, my body, at the centre (Somerville, 1999).

The first process in my own body/place learning was to work with a massage practitioner who believed that massage—the touch of skin on skin by another— could surface awareness of body-in-place embedded in bodily tissue (Carmont, 1996). This tissue awareness surfaced in images spoken during the massage, and recalled later to write them down. I then started to respond with this body/ place writing as an immediate sensory response to the landscapes of my research, a different version of journal writing based on the sensory experience of the body-in-place at any particular moment. Much of Grosz's theorising, especially in relation to Lacanian psychoanalysis and French feminist philosophies, was central to this reconceptualisation of body/place connections. Lacan, following on from Freud, offered a possible way of theorising the emergence of the embodied subject into language in the 'mirror stage', the point at which binary oppositions are created (Lacan, 1977). Focussing on this moment of becoming, the French feminists variously take this up as a generative space for writing and theorising the body. Again, I took this up in relation to body/place connections with important methodological consequences for thinking about place pedagogies.

Methodologically the body, as a meta-category, can be used to identify absences in dominant storylines and to construct new stories of place. A sense of embodied connection to place was represented in Aboriginal stories of everyday life in local places—collecting water and food, moving through, and dwelling in, places in a daily, embodied way, over years and generations. We learn about place through embodied connections in particular local places. Rose (2002, p. 311) describes this sense of embodied connection between people and place as 'ecological connectivity', based on 'dialogical interpenetration between people and place'. She believes this dialogical relationship between people and place opens Aboriginal and non Aboriginal people alike to the embodied materiality of places: 'The country that gets into people's blood invariably contains the blood and sweat of Aboriginal people as well as settlers. It may contain convict blood, and the remains of the dead. It will contain the blood of childbirth, and the blood and bones of massacres' (Rose, 2002, p. 321).

As a non-Aboriginal Australian, working with Aboriginal people and their places, has required me to open myself to the materiality of places as well as their stories. Experiences of body/place connection led me to see the landscape itself as the third subject, present in all of my research. In Gruenewald's words, place is profoundly pedagogical. It is primarily the materiality of a particular place that is pedagogical for me. This learning demands an attentiveness to place from the whole body: 'the body, and not only the ear, is a trembling flame, a vibrating surface, ruffled water. The body does not photograph the world, but filters it across permeable membranes' (Carter, 1992, p. 129). The weather, and the quality of the air and clouds, the sound of the frogs, the smell of the tadpole holes, and the day by day growing into frogs. It is place learning that derives from a deep, embodied intimacy. This place learning gives rise to a different ontology, an ontology of self becoming-other in the space between self and a natural world, composed of humans and non-human others, animate and inanimate; animals and plants, weather, rocks, trees.

Place is a Contact Zone of Cultural Contact

Over many years of collaborative place research I came to realize that specific local places offer a material and metaphysical in-between space for the intersection of multiple and contested stories. This characteristic of place as providing a site for the intersection of multiple and contested stories is especially significant in the relationship between indigenous, and other subjugated knowledges, and Western academic thought. It is also a useful concept when considering the multiplicity of different stories about the same place such as scientific stories, oral histories of place, popular responses to place, immigrant experiences of place and so on. This characteristic of place has been theorized as 'the contact zone' (Pratt, 1992, 1999). In contact zone theorising it is important to hold these different stories in productive tension. Carter maintains that the main function of the in-between space of the contact zone is to preserve difference, even to the point of suspending meaning (Carter, 1992). The idea of the contact zone is importantly different than conceptualisations of the third space (e.g. Bhabha, 1994; Soja, 2000) because it focuses primarily on difference rather than hybridity.

My collaborative research about place with Aboriginal people participated in a contact zone requiring all researchers to refuse easy answers, to confront the difficult questions, and to move beyond their comfort zone, in order to engage with an enabling pedagogy of place. In the middle of a large and long term collaborative project, for example, the team of three Aboriginal and three non-Aboriginal researchers recorded a series of conversations about the politics of place representation. In an analysis of these conversations we identified different sorts of 'borderwork' that were critical to our negotiations in what we called the 'discomfort zone' of cultural contact in the research (Somerville & Perkins, 2003). The 'borderwork' critical to negotiating difference in the contact zone (Somerville & Perkins, 2003) was precarious, risky and difficult emotional work (Anzaldua, 1987; hooks, 1990). Some of this involved maintaining boundaries, making clear important differences and protocols. But much of the essential work of collaboration involved moving between, and across, boundaries. We found the discomfort zone to be a place of productive tension based on difference and characterised by mobile and shifting boundaries constructed within this emotional and intellectual border work (Somerville & Perkins, 2003).

The areas where my place learning has been most slow and painful have been in regard to our shared colonial histories, such as place stories about children being removed, and massacre stories. My long relationship with Patsy Cohen was predicated on her early experiences of being taken from her mother and her desire to recover her lost stories of place through our mutual research. Years after our first initial emotional recording of Patsy's story, and the production of *Ingelba and the Five Black Matriarchs* (1990), she told me that she had never talked to anyone about these experiences before and that it had made a significant difference to her and to her family. Many times before and since, however, we faced the abyss, unable to reach across the space of our different positioning in these colonial histories. I have worked with many such stories and many times have faced this abyss.

Perhaps the most difficult, and also the most productive, has been my work with Tony Perkins about a massacre story which he presented as the lens through which to view all of the place stories of the Yarrawarra people. With very careful and detailed work, Tony and I recorded the massacre story over many years, each time moving closer to understanding what it meant for him to tell the story and what it meant for me to hear it, why this act of telling and listening in the contact zone was so significant (Somerville & Perkins, 2005). To have elided our difference in that telling and listening would have been to deny our different positions in relation to that colonial place story. It is only through entering that place of difference so deeply, with all of the ethical responsibilities that entails, that each of us is able to speak from the place between self and other, between Indigenous and non-Indigenous. Even then, we each speak from that place differently. I believe that this is what makes it possible for me to claim a pedagogy of place developed from the space in-between.

Emergent Arts Based Methodologies

A hot day, asphalt and cheap portable buildings. Crowded classroom and the stuffy smell of kids' bodies and old school lunches. Kids of all shapes and sizes navigate desks, tables, boxes, scientific equipment and hanging artworks. A girl with Down's Syndrome and Integration Aide moves awkwardly through the chaos. But that afternoon all is transformed. On the interactive screen I am treated to a preview of the end of year concert. Kids in groups of twos and threes, fingers splayed, arms and legs outstretched, move sometimes slow and ponderous, sometimes quick and light, to frog music. At the wetlands kids get to know the different frogs by their calls. They learn where each one likes to live, their habits and movements. Now their dance is choreographed to the sound of frog calls made music, moving in the rhythms of the different frogs. Often the centre of the camera's attention, Mary's awkwardness is subsumed by frog, her pleasure in dance and performance palpable and beautiful. Kids-becoming-frog in this frog dance.

A methodology for a place pedagogy needs to encompass the multiple forms in which alternative representations of place are expressed; the embodiment of experiences in place; and the multiple alternative voices and stories about any particular place. I have chosen temporarily, for want of a better alternative, to name this approach an *emergent arts-based methodology*. The methodology is *emergent*, because the emphasis is on undoing dominant stories of place (decolonisation) and the collective and relational making of new place stories (re-inhabitation). These stories are local and responsive. They cannot be pre-empted prior to creating the conditions for their telling; their emergence must be facilitated in the process. The methodology is *arts-based* in order to encompass the multiple forms in which alternative representations of place are possible. It requires bodily engagement with the materiality of specific local places and the conscious facilitation of the representation of alternative and invisible stories. Underpinning this methodology is a new ontology and epistemology.

An ontology and epistemology for this methodology of postmodern emergence (Somerville, 2007) is one of becoming, rather than one in which an essentialist liberal humanist subject finds its expression. The notion of the becoming self is well developed in feminist poststructural theory (Davies, 2000). The subject is reconceived from the fixed liberal humanist self to one that is in process, coming into being each time he or she is spoken into existence (Davies, 2004). The notion of becoming-other, including becoming-animal, is developed by Deleuze and Guattari (1987, p. 274) and further taken up by Grosz (1994) in her feminist critique of philosophy from the perspective of the body. Here, however, I want to explore becoming-other as a methodological and pedagogical strategy, an ontology of emergence (Somerville, 2007) arising out of this place based research. Such an ontology needs to incorporate elements of our past self history (ontogeny), who we imagine ourselves to be, and our embodied relationship with others. It also includes our participation as bodies in the 'flesh of the world' (Merleau-Ponty, 1962), a reciprocal relationship with objects and landscapes, weather, rocks and trees, sand, mud and water, animals and plants, an ontology founded in the bodies of things. In this ontology, bodies of things are dynamic, existing in relation to each other, and it is in the dynamic of this relationship that subjectivities are formed and transformed.

Within this ontology of becoming-other, there is an epistemological relationship with the objects and technologies, that we, in the process of becoming-other, can intentionally manipulate—stone, wood, and clay, pencils, crayons, brushes and paints, computers, words and paper, cloth, thread and scissors—among the myriad other things that we humans have chosen to use to create. Each time we make a single individual representation of our places it exists beside a proliferation of other representations, a pause in an iterative moment of representation and reflection (Somerville, 2007). These representations can be endlessly combined, thus creating assemblages, artefacts of place whose meaning lies in intertextuality, in the conversations created between each of the parts. Although digital technologies are not a precondition for these creations, they have made them far more possible. They allow the assembling and re-assembling of different representations combing different modalities such as the text, visual images and sound.

In asking about what place pedagogies are enacted within the Morwell River Wetlands project, for example, we can visit the web site constructed by the children and their teacher to see what we can find there. There is the history of the wetland, a quintessential postmodern place. Half created, half natural, a post-industrial wetland/wasteland, it declares its pedagogies to the world. It has its origins in the Morwell River itself, but is equally significantly in the work of International Power, the multinational corporation who now owns Hazelwood Power Station. The brown coal fired power stations in Latrobe Valley produce 85% of Melbourne's electricity and are represented on every news item about climate change, flashing across our televisions daily. But here on the wetlands website we also see children's drawings and photographs, sounds of frog calls identifying the different frogs, tables that compute the measure of water quality, and frog statistics that measure the health of the place by its frogs. The concatenation of voices is represented in Aboriginal stories, power station stories, the river's stories. I can know the Morwell River Wetlands as place far more deeply through my engagement with this assemblage of artefacts. On the other hand, the beginning point is always that particular local place, part natural, part artificial, in mid autumn, with a half full moon and a cool wind as the frog chorus begins.

Conclusion

The moment of 'global contemporaneity' seemed an important idea within which to situate a reconceptualized place studies. It signals the particular conjunctions of space, place and time in relation to the intransigent problems of space and place that we are presented with daily on the mass media. In responding to these problems I have asked: What might be an adequate educational response? and posed the question: How might we educate a generation of children 'growing up global', to be attached to their local places, to inhabit, and to know place differently? Because of the emphasis on techno-scientific and economic rationalist solutions, I suggest that a useful beginning point is critiques of science and science education. These critiques of the androcentrism and Eurocentrism of science (education) offer possible directions for a different approach. I take up Gough's (2006) challenge to think rhizomatically in order to 'reintroduce reality as dynamic, heterogeneous, and non-dichotomous' (Deleuze and Guattari, in Gough, 2006, p. 628).

I propose 'place' as a beginning point for thinking about these questions and trace my own thinking to a collaborative research project with an Indigenous woman who was the first to teach me to think through place. Place, as both a specific material terrain and a representational concept, disrupts the dichotomies of local/global, the real and representational, and Indigenous and non-Indigenous knowledges. In citing a typical listing of the qualities of an Indigenous relationship to place (Schroder, 2006), I begin to wonder if these qualities, at least in potential, apply to all children. The challenge then becomes one of pedagogy, how to incorporate these characteristics in to, rather than out of, our educational philosophies and practices.

A genealogy of place based, or place conscious education, identifies its origins in the liberal humanist tradition of Wendell Berry, later reconceptualized in the critical tradition by David Gruenewald. In Australia the linking of ecology and humanities, led by Deborah Bird Rose, specifically addresses 'the great binaries of western thought', locating it in a poststructural paradigm. There are elements of postcolonial/poststructural thinking in Gruenewald's approach, particularly in his central concepts of decolonisation and reinhabitation. The place pedagogy approach that I am proposing radically departs from Gruenewald's position in that it derives from feminist poststructural theorising and my empirical qualitative research with Australian Indigenous people. The elements of a place pedagogy outlined in this paper: *our relationship to place is constituted in stories and other representations; place learning is local and embodied; and deep place learning occurs in a contact zone of contestation* constitute an alternative pedagogy of place and through these essential elements, an alternative methodology is offered.

An alternative methodology for a place pedagogy is described as an emergent arts based methodology because it needs to encompass the multiple forms and alternative stories in which embodied experiences and representations of place emerge. I have proposed an ontology of becoming-other as an extension of feminist poststructural work about the subject in process. This becoming-other is a relational ontology that includes the non-human and inanimate 'flesh of the world' as well as human others. Within this ontology of becoming-other there is an epistemology that includes all of the technologies that we use to create representations—including language, computers, and paper, but also clay, brushes, paint, fabric—all of the artefacts we use to create. Each individual representation is conceived as a pause in an iterative process of representation and reflection, and as contributing to assemblages of such artefacts whose meanings are intertextual. Finally, in visiting the Morwell River Wetlands website, I acknowledge the fundamental underlying debt to particular local places, in a return to Gruenewald's statement that 'place is profoundly pedagogical'. Any pedagogy of place must remain open and dynamic, responsive to the interaction between specific people and their local places.

References

Anzaldua, G. (1987) *Borderlands/La Frontera: The new mestiza* (San Francisco, Spinsters/Aunt Lute).

Ball, E. L. & Lai, A. (2006) Place-Based Pedagogy for the Arts and Humanities, *Pedagogy: Critical Approaches to Teaching Literature, Language, Composition, and Culture*, 6:2, 261–287.

Beck, W. & Somerville, M. (2005) Conversations between Disciplines: Historical archaeology and oral history at Yarrawarra, *World Archaeology*, 37:3, 467–482.

Behrendt, J. & Thompson, P. (2003) *The Recognition and Protection of Aboriginal Interests in NSW Rivers* (Sydney, Healthy Rivers Commission).

Behrendt, L. (2004) *Home* (Brisbane, University of Queensland Press).

Berry, W. (1981) *The Gift of Good Land: Further essays cultural and agricultural* (San Francisco, North Point Press).

Bhabha, H. (1994) *The Location of Culture* (London, Routledge).

Carmont, C. (1996) *Tissue Talk*. Unpublished PhD Thesis, (Armidale, Department of Social, Cultural and Communication Studies, University of New England).

Carter, L. (2006) Postcolonial Interventions within Science Education: Using post-colonial ideas to reconsider cultural diversity scholarship, *Educational Philosophy and Theory*, 28:5, 677–691.

Carter, P. (1992) *The Sound in-Between: Voice, space, performance* (Sydney, University of New South Wales Press and New Endeavour Press).

Cohen, P. & Somerville, M. (1990) *Ingelba and the Five Black Matriarchs* (Sydney, Allen and Unwin).

Connell, R. (2007) *Southern Theory: The global dynamics of knowledge in social science* (Sydney, Allen and Unwin).

Davies, B. (2000) *A Body of Writing, 1990–1999* (Walnut Creek, CA, Altamira Press).

Davies, B. (2004) Introduction: Poststructuralist lines of flight in Australia, *International Journal of Qualitative Studies in Education*, 17:1, 3–9.

Deleuze, G. & Guattari, F. (1987) *A Thousand Plateaus: Capitalism and Schizophrenia*, B. Massumi, trans. (Minneapolis, University of Minnesota Press).

Fendler, L. & Tuckey, S. F. (2006) Whose Literacy? *Educational Philosophy and Theory*, 28:5, 677–691.

Flannery, T. (2005) *The weather makers: the history and future impact of climate change* (Melbourne, Text Publishing).

Gough, N. (2006) Shaking the Tree, Making a Rhizome: Towards a nomadic geophilosophy of science education, *Educational Philosophy and Theory*, 38:5, 625–645.

Green, B. (2007) *Teacher Education for Rural and Regional Sustainability, Seminar Presentation, Faculty of Education* (Gippsland, Monash University).

Griffiths, T. (2001) *Forests of Ash: An environmental history* (Cambridge, Cambridge University Press).

Grosz, E. (1994) *Volatile Bodies: Towards a corporeal feminism* (Sydney, Allen and Unwin).

Gruenewald, D. A. (2003a) The Best of Both Worlds: A critical pedagogy of place, *Educational Researcher*, 32:4, 3–12.

Gruenewald, D. A. (2003b) Foundations of Place: A multidisciplinary framework for place-conscious education, *American Educational Research Journal*, 40:3, 619–654.

hooks, b. (1990) Yearning: Race, Gender and Cultural Politics. South End Press, Boston.

Hubbard, P., Kitchin, R. *et al.* (eds) (2004) *Key Thinkers on Space and Place* (London, Sage Publications).

Lacan, J. (1977) *Ecrits: A selection* (London, Tavistock).

Mackenna, M. (2002) *Looking for Blackfella's Point* (Sydney, University of New South Wales Press).

Merleau-Ponty, M. (1962) *Phenomenology of Perception* (New York, Humanities Press).

Mignolo, W. (2000) *Local Histories/Global Designs: Coloniality, subaltern knowledges, and border thinking* (Princeton, NJ, Princeton University Press).

Peat, F. D. (2002) *Blackfoot Physics* (Grand Rapids, MI, Phanes Press).

Power, K. (2007) Pers. Comm. and title of Reconceptualising Early Childhood Education Conference, Hong Kong Institute of Education, December 2007.

Pratt, G. (1992) *Imperial Writing and Transculturalism* (London and New York, Routledge).

Pratt, G. (1999) Geographies of Identity and Difference, in: D. Massey *et al.* (eds), *Human Geography Today* (Cambridge, Polity Press).

Rose, D. B. (1996) *Nourishing Terrains: Australian aboriginal views of landscape and wilderness* (Canberra, Australian Heritage Commission).

Rose, D. B. (2002) Dialogue with Place: Toward an ecological body, *Journal of Narrative Theory*, 32:3, 311–325.

Rose, D. B. (2004) The Ecological Humanities in Action: An invitation, *Australian Humanities Review*, http://www.lib.latrobe.edu.au/AHR/archive/Issue-April-2004?rose.html, Accessed 7/1/05.

Schroder, B. (2006) Native Science, Intercultural Education and Place-conscious Education: An Ecuadorian example, *Educational Studies*, 32:3, 307–317.

Sinclair, P. (2001) *The Murray: A river and its people* (Melbourne, Melbourne University Press).

Soja, E. W. (2000) *Postmetropolis: Critical studies of cities and regions* (Oxford, Blackwell).

Somerville, M. (1991) Life History Writing: The relationship between talk and text, *Australian Feminist Studies*, 12.

Somerville, M. (1999) *Body/Landscape Journals* (Melbourne, Spinifex Press).

Somerville, M. (2007) Postmodern Emergence, *Qualitative Studies in Education*, 20:2, 225–243.

Somerville, M. & Perkins, T. (2003) Border Work in the Contact Zone: Thinking indigenous/non-indigenous collaboration spatially, *International Journal of Intercultural Studies*, 24:3, 253–266.

Somerville, M. & Perkins, T. (2005) (Re)membering in the Contact Zone: Telling, and listening to, a massacre story, *Altitude*, http://www.api-network.com/cgi-bin/altitude21c/fly

Somerville, M., Dundas, M., Mead, M., Oliver, J. & Sulter, M. (1994) *The Sun Dancin': People and place in Coonabarabran* (Canberra, Aboriginal Studies Press).

Sondergaard, D. M. (2002) Poststructural Approaches to Empirical Analysis, *Qualitative Studies in Education*, 15:2, 187–204.

Ward, N., Reys, S., Davies, J. & Roots, J. (2003) Scoping study on Aboriginal involvement in natural resource management decision making and the integration of Aboriginal cultural heritage considerations into relevant Murray-Darling Commission programs, Murray-Darling Basin Commission.

Weedon, C. (1997) *Feminist Practice and Poststructuralist Theory* (Oxford, Blackwell).

Chapter 10

Antonio Gramsci and Feminism

The Elusive Nature of Power

Margaret Ledwith

Reprinted by permission of Taylor & Francis Ltd, http://www.tandfonline.com, on behalf of © Philosophy of Education Society of Australasia.

Editors' Introduction

Ledwith's chapter argues from a feminist perspective for different 'women's ways of being and the relationship between knowledge, difference and power in a neo-liberal setting. She traces the relevance of Gramsci to her own feminist conscious-ness, and the part he played in her journey to praxis. She also addresses feminism's intellectual debts, most particularly in relation to the concept of hegemony. The intellectual context has shifted in emphasis from macro- to micro-narratives which reject Marxism as masculinist and dichotomous. The dilemma has been an over-emphasis on the personal-cultural at the expense of the collective-political, dis-tracting us from action for social justice at the same time as globalisation is creating escalating world crises of justice and sustainability. In conclusion, she advocates for a re-reading of Gramsci in the light of key feminist critiques of class and patriar-chy in order to develop analyses based on multiple sites of oppression and action which reaches from local to global through alliances to achieve a more integrated feminist praxis. Throughout, she uses 'dis'ability' and 'race' to denote the socially constructed nature of these concepts. In this way, the capital/labour contradiction which Gramsci extended to a 'national-popular', oppressor/oppressed dichotomy is extended to a local/global analysis, but within an analysis of difference which addresses the reach of global power into a diversity of personal lives.

My Journey to Praxis

Seamus Milne, in the 1980s, described Gramsci as 'the greatest intellectual influ-ence on the British Left' in a decade (Milne, undated). During that period of redis-covery of Gramsci, I was on my own parallel journey to praxis. Here, I want to trace that journey in its political context before exploring my central, burning question:

> What relevance have the ideas of Gramsci, forged by Sardism, poverty, 'dis'ability and the masculinity of his culture in the early 20th century, to my critical pedagogy as a White British woman today?

True to a philosophy of praxis, as well as to feminist pedagogy, I begin my inquiry in experience. It is short but apt, and traces the role of Gramsci in the development of my own political consciousness. My drive for consciousness came from dissonance in my practice; an inner discomfort that the reality I witnessed around me was not founded on justice and democracy. At that time, I was a classroom teacher who felt a certain discomfort at the young lives acted out before my eyes. I could see that the life chances of the children I taught were determined by their early experience far more than the innate 'cleverness' by which they were judged for academic success by the state. I could also see that the competitive nature of education reinforced a sense of failure in those whose self-esteem already faltered in the face of the harshness of their lives.

Take, for instance, the life of Jennifer O'Leary. Jennifer was a shy, slightly built 10-year-old when I met her. Her father had left the family, and she had lived in the local children's home together with her two brothers since her mother's new partner had made it clear that he did not want the children. In the same schoolroom, Paula Jones assumed superiority. She, by comparison, was the daughter of the house parents in the children's home in which Jennifer was cast into the role of 'orphan', and in that sense had status above Jennifer. Paula needed that status to survive her own oppressions. She was a girl child of mixed heritage in a racist society. Jennifer's brothers, Dermot and Devlin, were in classes older and younger than Jennifer. Every Friday, Dermot would stand on the outer step of the classroom anxiously looking for his mother who had told him that one weekend she would come and get them back. When his classmates taunted him, he screamed abuse, 'You *******, I know she'll come today!'

As a young teacher, in these ways, I witnessed hegemonic forces reaching into my classroom to construct personal lives. Yet, my teacher education had told me that this was an apolitical space, decontextualised from the real world. Jack, a colleague, rubbed his hands together in the staff room at the beginning of each new academic year proclaiming, 'Well that's got that lot sorted out: these will make it, and those don't stand a chance'. Life chances dichotomously reinforced by an agent of the state, acted out unconsciously; Jack played his part well. His words resonated inside me, and my discomfort grew. Teacher education had not provided me with any answers, so I got involved in the beginning of the national adult literacy campaign seeking to address the damage done by schooling (Ledwith, 2005).

Later, I found myself in Scotland working with Vietnamese refugees traumatised by the rejection of the Western world as they floated adrift on the South China Sea. They changed my worldview with their stories of giving birth on rusty landing craft, of being separated from their children, of hope and hopelessness. In my heart, I was desolate in the knowledge that they would be at the bottom of an unjust system, their hopes dashed. As they taught me more about life than I could ever teach them, my search led me to Edinburgh University and a master's degree in community development. It was David Alexander, the adult educator, whose passion in relation to Gramsci and Freire had a profound impact on me.

My engagement with both these thinkers touched me on an intellectual and emotional level. What Peter Mayo calls the 'fusion of reason and emotion' (Mayo, 2004, p. 10) contained in Freire touches people in a holistic way that reaches beyond the limitations of the intellect. At this point, I moved closer to a synthesis of action and reflection, of theory and practice, that gave me a glimpse of the potential of praxis to identify the forces of power and disempowerment. The hegemonic function of schooling, which had for so long eluded me, sat in stark relief. My naïveté shocked me; these ideas were so obvious I could not believe that false consciousness had stripped my mind of critical insight. Of course, it is not quite as simple as that. Gramsci emphasised the centrality of popular education in raising consciousness. He recognised that critical consciousness would not erupt spontaneously; false consciousness initially needs an external element to demystify the prevailing hegemony. David Alexander had played that role for me. This not only changed the nature of my understanding of the insidious nature of power, but it changed the nature of my engagement with the world. It was a powerful epistemological-ontological shift. From this point, my involvement in community development and in second-wave feminism expressed a greater unity of praxis (Ledwith, 2005).

The Concept of a Male Hegemony in Relation to Patriarchy

Here I want to acknowledge feminism's intellectual debt to Gramsci. He made an immense contribution to feminism without 'getting it'; such is the elusive nature of power and domination. His insightful analysis of *hegemony,* and the subtle nature of *consent,* offered feminists a conceptual lead on the *personal as political.*

After the Second World War, Simone de Beauvoir's *The Second Sex,* with its thrust on woman as Other, heralded what many feminists see as the real arrival of second-wave feminism in the 1960s, the decade of civil rights and student activism. The year 1968 saw a watershed in feminist consciousness and activism, which resonated, in my experience, into the early 1990s. In the UK, 'interest in Gramsci emphasized the need for ideological struggle to challenge ruling class hegemony' (Coole, 1993, p. 179) at the same time as Freire's *Pedagogy of the Oppressed,* with its Gramscian influence, brought inspiration to critical consciousness. Freire, on his return to Brazil from exile in 1979, 'began "relearning Brazil" by reading Gramsci and also "listening to the *popular Gramsci* in the *favelas*" ' [Brazilian shantytowns] (Torres, 1993, p. 135 in Ledwith, 2005). The two offered a powerful combination which Paula Allman saw at its most complementary in 'Freire's consideration of the political nature of education and in Gramsci's consideration of the educational nature of politics' (Allman, 1988, p. 92). But as the 1980s progressed, a powerful tide of neo-liberalism, together with feminism's and postmodernism's critiques of metanarratives with their masculinist bias, led Gramsci to fall out of favour. This marked an important shift in which debates around class and patriarchy eventually swayed in favour of feminism's emphasis on cultural identity and difference. Contradictorily, in relation to my debate on Gramsci and feminism, this neglected to integrate the economic nature of gender politics. In the UK, feminism's lack of political vigilance provided a smokescreen for Thatcherism's ideology of individualism, resulting in children and lone mothers imperceptibly replacing older people as most at risk of poverty (Oppenheim & Harker, 1996). Child poverty escalated from 14 per cent in 1979 to 34 per cent by 1996/7 (Flaherty *et al.*, 2004, p. 145), leaving the UK with one of the highest rates of child poverty compared with other countries facing similar economic trends—a situation which persists despite a raft of policies founded on the Blair/Brown government's political commitment to ending child poverty by 2020.

Clearly, there was a need for a more complex analysis which embraced difference but which did not reduce this to a single source of oppression, one which operated from multiple intersecting bases. During the 1970s, Juliet Mitchell began this process by identifying key structures for women's oppression: production, reproduction, sexuality and the socialisation of children.

> By arguing that each structure within the family has a certain autonomy in its capacity to subject women and that these structures themselves rebound on the economy, Mitchell was able to show that women's entry into the workforce would be insufficient to emancipate them since gains (such as working or controlling fertility) are compensated by losses elsewhere (such as renewed emphasis on mothers' socializing role)'.
>
> (Coole 1993, p. 180)

By the 1980s, Arnot was arguing that male hegemony consists of a multiplicity of moments which have persuaded women to accept a male dominated culture and their subordination within it (Kenway, 2001). The result is a constructed reality which is qualitatively different from that of men, in which women are diminished and exploited within a *common sense* patriarchal view of the world. Gramsci turned the key to the personal as political with his reinterpretation of the traditional Marxist concept of *hegemony*, opening our consciousness to the public/private divide and the way that domination permeates the most intimate aspects of our being through our interactions in civil society, for example, the family, community, schools and formal religions which remain key sites of male domination. This is the basis for Gramsci's acknowledged contribution to feminist thought which has provided a tool of analysis for understanding the sites of gendered oppression in society. By exploring the nature of consent, we come to see that hegemony is always in process, in continuous struggle, and we begin to see that feminist consciousness is the beginning of questioning the nature of that consent in relation to patriarchy.

These were the ideas that we were working with in community development practice in that period.

Hattersley Women for Change

The 1980s saw my own activism and professional practice informed by both femi-nism and Freirean-Gramscian thought in relation to popular education. It was a time of grassroots activism in which women came together in leaderless groups to explore consciousness from lived experience. We translated this into collective action for change based on a vision of social justice for all. For instance, in August 1981, a group of women who had never before been involved in political action, marched from Cardiff to Greenham to protest against the siting of cruise missiles in Britain. This was the start of the Greenham Women's Peace Movement, which 'highlighted the development of a new strand of community action' (Dominelli, 1990, p. 119). A praxis began to evolve with emphasis on lived experience as the basis of theoretical understanding.

In praxis, as a community worker, I worked in partnership with Wendy, a Hat-tersley woman and community activist. We had many discussions about Freire and Gramsci, and likened our roles in Hattersley to that of the *organic* and *traditional intellectual*. She lived the harsh reality of poverty pre-ordained by her working-class roots. Poverty had touched my life in many ways, and as women we shared many life themes, but I had been protected in the long term by my class privilege. Through experiences held in common, differentiated by class, we found a bond and shared a commitment to develop popular education for women in Hattersley. This was the mid-1980s, when the political context in the UK was being dra-matically reshaped by New Right ideology under Thatcherism, at the same time as new social movements, and second-wave feminism in particular, articulated a politics of difference. It was a time of activism and alliance, when the Women of Greenham Common and Women Against Pit Closures were supported by a network of local Greenham Support Groups and Miners' Support Groups. It was a time when, on a mission of solidarity, I travelled in Nicaragua, experiencing participatory democracy in action and linking community groups across our dif-ferent continents. I still feel the fear as I remember being caught up in a Contra raid, where women had been abducted and men were left injured; I still feel the tears of the mothers whose sons and daughters were missing, abducted from their activism in the outstanding literacy and health campaigns inspired by Freire; I still remember the shock of the sonic boom set off by American aircraft every evening over Managua in an attempt to assert the might of capitalism over this little coun-try's bid for true participatory democracy. It was a time of hope and inspiration when Nicaragua and Nelson Mandela were symbolic of peace and justice in the dawning of a wider political consciousness.

In communities like Hattersley, marked by a *culture of silence,* there was no tra-dition of meeting in groups. We waded through the apathy and disillusionment of local women. In this predominantly White, working-class community, we were faced with overt sexism, covert racism and vehement homophobia. Culturally, there was immense pressure to conform to working-class norms, which resulted in a denial of difference, at the same time as working-class solidarity was being eroded by individualism. People were pre-occupied with day-to-day survival of the harshness of their lives as poverty increased under high unemployment and the reactionary welfare policies implemented by the Thatcher government.

Wendy began the process by personally approaching women on the streets to set up a writing group as a route to critical consciousness. Local women slowly became more involved in community groups; problematising their everyday reality through a diversity of projects from Hattersley Women Writing to Woodwork for Women, they began to question from a more critical perspective. This was a triumph, but, as Freire (1972) would say, could not claim true critical consciousness unless it emerged as collective action. Moving from successful projects to a coherent movement for change was more problematic. Hattersley Forum, a democratic platform for debate in the community, provided an umbrella organisation for determining action for change. It occurred to me that Gramsci's notion of the *factory council* could be replaced by the community forum as a site of intervention where women could be central to the process of change. Key women activists had positioned themselves on the forum executive, but the forum meeting itself remained a male-dominated context where women in general felt intimidated by male power. We needed a space where women could start from the stories of their lived experience and examine the social, historical and cultural shaping of these narratives.

Gradually, we hit upon the idea of identifying a group of women who were already involved in community projects and inviting them to form a core group at the heart of Hattersley Women for Change. At the initial meeting, ten of us sat round tentatively sharing ideas. Of these, eight decided to meet weekly to explore the issues which were affecting women's lives through a local history project. From this, we would plan a popular education programme for local women. Ages ranged from twenty-three to sixty-eight, and amongst us there were varying differences of ability and ethnicity. At the same time as we were seeking answers to our questions, we were also seeking a strategy for developing critical consciousness on a level which had the potential for releasing the energy for collective change. We negotiated with Hattersley Forum to create Hattersley Women's Room in the community centre. This was a space where women could meet in a women-only environment in *culture circles*. We went out on the streets talking to women wherever they gathered in their community and eventually launched our programme in fine style with food and wine, inviting all women to come and celebrate, which they did! The response was encouraging. By the following week, I faced the realisation that it was not going to be that easy. No new faces had appeared inside the room, despite the fact that many peered in curiously from outside in the community centre snack bar.

As my hopes evaporated, Wendy, in her infinite wisdom, reminded me of the length of the process, of the fact that this sort of coming together was culturally outside their experience, of the need to reflect and perhaps reorganise. She was right of course! Things did not change until there was a critical incident. One morning I had a complaint that the children, left unsupervised, were using the enormous hall, the focal point of the community centre, as a race track, careering into the elderly, sight-impaired residents who were meeting that day. The tedium of yet another conflict situation in a community which raged *horizontal violence* at every tip and turn, exasperated me. As manager of the community centre, I had the responsibility to oversee these incidents, and I strode across determined to restore peace. The group of young mothers who spent most of their days in the centre's snack bar escaping from the harsh reality of their lives were either oblivious to or did not care about the havoc their children wreaked around them. Carole, angered by my perceived power and authority, screamed at her son as I approached, 'Freeze, Anthony, here she comes!'. Furious, and failing in the heat of the moment to locate my actions as political rather than personal, I rose to my full power and delivered a pronouncement about parental responsibility. A hush descended over every corner of this enormous space, and in that silence I pivoted in as dignified a way as I could muster, and left.

That afternoon, Carole appeared in my office for the first time. We talked on a personal level for the first time, sharing our feelings, our hopes, our despair, listening from the heart and soul. She told me that the incident that morning was the first time she had seen my calm exterior ruffled, that it broke the ice and made me human in a way that she understood. We parted friends. So, when I was approached by the local health visitor about concerns that women would not use the local clinic for ante-natal care, the first thought I had was to involve Carole. In dialogue, across barriers, we developed a health project in the community centre where Carole worked in partnership with the midwife. This encounter gave the Women's Room the seal of approval from local women. In relation to Hattersley Women for Change and wider collective action, it took a year to get the breakthrough we wanted. By then, many new women were getting involved in the administration and decision-making. This was just the beginning of women coming together to explore their consciousness through a wide range of activities and projects; a moving out from a core of women activists to extend confidence and understanding on a broader scale in the community. The aim was that, in time, these women would be taking action collectively and linking with others in communities everywhere through the credit union movement, the 'grey power' movement and women's networks. We witnessed the way in which men asserted power over this process using invasion of our women-only space, humiliation and ridicule. We also witnessed the hegemonic ways in which women's lives were put at risk by the public/private divide allowing domestic violence to be beyond the remit of police protection, exacerbated by class prejudice. Hattersley was a place where women 'got what they deserved' in the words of the police. Insight into *ideological persuasion,* and the way in which the dominant ideology reaches through the institutions of civil society into the minds of local people helped me to make sense of what often felt futile.

Patti Lather in her work, at this time in the mid-1980s, drew on Gramsci's notion of a *war of position* and the role of the *intellectuals* in relation to feminist political action. Lather takes Gramsci's emphasis on everyone's innate capacity to be philosophers and considers this in relation to the way that women have documented experience-based knowledge and acted to become prominent in all social institutions, claiming that this constitutes a *war of position*: 'many small revolutions . . . many small changes in relationships, behaviors, attitudes and experiences' (Kenway, 2001, p. 59). She places particular emphasis on the role of women as intellectuals in the tide of developing critical consciousness. In Hattersley, we recognised that we were part of women's knowledge in the making, of *women's ways of knowing* (Belenky *et al.*, 1997).

The Changing Theoretical and Political Context

In this section, I move into the changing intellectual and political context which accelerated from the 1980s into the new millenium.

> This interdependent world system is based on the exploitation of oppressed groups, but the system at the same time calls forth oppositional cultural forms that give voice to the conditions of these groups. White male bourgeois dominance is being challenged by Black people, women and other oppressed groups, who assert the validity of their own knowledge and demand social justice and equality in numerous political and cultural struggles . . . A major theoretical challenge to traditional Western knowledge systems is emerging from feminist theory, like other contemporary approaches, validates difference, challenges universal claims to truth, and seeks to create social transformation in a world of shifting and uncertain meanings.
>
> (Weiler in Holland & Blair, 1995, p. 23)

Paradoxically, the post-structuralist critiques of class metanarratives which laid the foundations for postmodernism from the mid-1980s, dislocated Gramsci in favour of 'mini-narratives rather than metanarratives, multiple identities rather than political identities, positioning rather than repositioning, discourse rather than the politics of discourse, performance rather than poverty, inscription rather than political mobilization, and deconstruction rather than reconstruction' (Kenway, 2001, p. 60). The paradox here is that Gramsci helped to provide the conceptual tools by which this became possible. Here I am mindful of bell hooks' acknowledgment of Freire. She found that Freire offered a structure within which she could define her experience of racism on a global level, when the radical struggle of Black women was not welcomed in the early, White, bourgeois feminist frame (hooks, 1993, p. 151). hooks refers to Freire's 'blind spot' to questions of gender, but acknowledges the ways in which his pedagogy gave her the conceptual tools that offered her insight into the nature of her own oppression as a Black American woman, helping her to see herself as a subject in resistance, thus locating a contradiction between White women and a third-world man (hooks, 1993, p. 150).

   In much the same way as metanarratives were derided by White feminists as obscuring male domination, early, White, second-wave feminists were in turn challenged by Black women on grounds of difference. In other words, White feminists stood accused of defining 'woman' from a White perspective, exposing a White power which has the arrogance to overlook other aspects of difference. This is a consequence of what bell hooks (1984) attributes to the either/ or dichotomous thinking so central to Western ideological thought, where a concept is only definable in relation to its perceived Other. Early second-wave feminists had defined 'woman' in relation to 'man' overlooking the ways in which 'race', class and gender intersect. These images are 'key in maintaining interlocking systems of race, class and gender oppression' (Hill Collins, 1990, p. 68).

The tide of neoliberalism that engulfed us in the 1980s provided a hothouse for germinating globalisation. Neoliberal globalisation is the 'market-organized and imposed expansion of production that emphasizes comparative advantage, free trade, export orientations, the social and spatial divisions of labour, and the absolute mobility of corporations' (Fisher & Ponniah, 2003, p. 28). This form of corporate capitalism, where the most powerful systems of the West dominate the world economically, invades other cultures with a Western worldview which works on political, cultural, racial, gendered, sexual, ecological and epistemological differences. In other words, in the name of a free market economy not only is labour exploited in the interests of capital (class), but the same structures of oppression which subordinate groups of people according to 'race', gender, age, sexuality, ethnicity, 'dis'ability are being reproduced on a global level.

> Neoloberal globalization is not simply economic domination of the world but also the imposition of a monolithic thought (pensamento unico) that consolidates vertical forms of difference and prohibits the public from imagining diversity in egalitarian, horizontal terms. Capitalism, imperialism, monoculturalism, patriarchy, white supremacism and the domination of biodiversity have coalesced under the current form of globalization. . . .
>
> (Fisher and Ponniah 2003, p. 10)

Wealth is increasingly transferred from poor to rich countries by exploiting the labour and resources of developing countries in order to feed the consumerist greed of the West. The consequences are increased social divisions both within and between countries. This has resulted in complex, convoluted, interlinking and overlapping oppressions which are poorly understood and therefore infrequently challenged. Yet, it is a fragile system, open to abuse as witnessed by the current crisis of capitalism triggered by banking practices, resulting in recession, and maybe full depression.

Clearly critical consciousness which solely looks to class is founded on Western cultural assumptions that subordinate indigenous belief systems. This reflects the cultural dominance that gave moral legitimacy to capitalism and continues to give economic superiority in the process of globalisation. Conversely, ecological thought acknowledges the way that cultures are founded on natural systems, and emphasises that diverse indigenous cultures have evolved in harmony with their natural environments. Cultural diversity thus becomes essential for biological diversity and histories based on local economic development offer alternatives for a future which reflects values other than consumer lifestyles: a harmonious co-existence between social justice and environmental justice.

Eco-feminism's embrace of the environment and sustainability arises from a critical connection between 'death of nature' and the rise of patriarchy, and can be explored through the work of such people as Charlene Spretnak, Carolyn Merchant and Vandana Shiva. The central argument from eco-feminism is that 'a historical, symbolic and political relationship exists between the denigration of nature and the female in Western cultures' (Spretnak, 1997, p. 181). Eco-feminism is rooted in principles of 'harmony, co-operation and interconnection' which challenge the perceived male principles of competition, 'discrimination, extremism and conflict' (Young, 1990, p. 33). This reaches beyond simple ideas of reformism to profoundly challenge capital's competitive worldview; exposing it as a system which elevates men over women and the natural world in ranked order importance, and, as such, is fundamentally corrupt. Eco-feminism calls for an alternative worldview based on harmony and cooperation, non-violence and dignity, a view which embraces both public and private, local and global, humanity and the natural world in equal measure. It reflects women's concerns for preserving harmonious life on earth over time and space. Crescy Cannan stresses that not only is the environmental crisis a crisis for us all, but it disproportionately affects both the poor and the South and so 'intensifies forms of inequality and threatens collective goods—thus it is a human crisis as well as a threat to the entire planet' (2000, p. 365).

In this respect, Fisher and Ponniah (2003) suggest that any counter-hegemony must tread that fine line of embracing a respect for difference at the same time as being able to create a common vision: 'If the global movements are to prosper, they have to produce a vision that allows them to maintain simultaneously both their convergence and their difference' (2003, p. 13).

Gramsci's Continuing Relevance to Feminism

The debate that centres on a view that 'Marxism and feminism are one, and that one is Marxism' has been problematic for feminism (Hartmann, 1981, p. 2). The relationship between capitalism and patriarchy as separate but interrelated systems in which dominant groups have a material interest began in the 1980s and still rages (Ferguson & Folbre, 1981, p. 314). The view that feminism is less important than class or even divisive of class is still argued by Marxists and has risen as a backlash against postmodernism arguing the primacy of class (Allman, 1999, 2001; Hill et al., 1999). Paula Allman (1999), for example, draws attention to the complex ways that global capitalism simultaneously cleaves divisions of poverty and wealth within and between countries and uses individualism as a smokescreen for its necessary illusion of progress, giving legitimacy to this juxtaposition of extremes of wealth and poverty.

In these times when private patriarchy has transcended the divide to public patriarchy giving a distorted vision of equality, Ferguson and Folbre argue: 'as historical factors change the rewards from and opportunities to control these goods and services, men's motives and abilities to control women vary, and the character and degree of patriarchal domination is modified' (1981, pp. 316–326). The contradiction between women's paid and unpaid work remains: 'the way the domestic sphere, the world of work and the state are interrelated dictate a battle on all fronts, a war of position in Gramsci's terms' (Showstack Sassoon, 1987, p. 174).

Returning to Arnot, 'male hegemony, [she] argues, should be perceived "as a whole series of separate moments through which women have come to accept a male dominated culture, its legality, and their subordination to it and in it . . . [which] together . . . comprise a pattern of female experience which is qualitatively different from that of men"' (Arnot, 1984, p. 64 in Kenway, 2001, p. 57).

Sylvia Walby (1992, 1994), in this same vein, argues the dangers of rejecting the centrality of patriarchy. In line with my focus on Gramsci, she sees the limitations of poststructuralism and postmodernism as 'a neglect of the social context of power relations' (1992, p. 16). Her position is that postmodernism has gone too far in fragmenting concepts of gender, 'race' and class, thereby overlooking structures which cleave these divisions. Marxism may have subsumed all forms of discrimination under class, but postmodernists stand accused of fragmenting overarching concepts. Walby emphasises three important issues raised by Black women: racist structures within the labour market; ethnic experience and racism; and locating the intersection of ethnicity and gender as an alternative site of analysis, both culturally and historically.

Walby (1994) offers six causal bases from which to analyse patriarchy: paid work, housework, sexuality, culture, violence and the state. By addressing the interrelationships between these structures, we avoid the trap of reductionism or essentialism. She warns that if we focus on disintegration, we are in danger of missing other patterns of re-organisation which offer insights into new forms of gender, ethnicity and class from a global dimension. For instance, the feminisation of labour in the UK is not only the result of industrial restructuring here, but the British economy depends on the exploitation of Third World women, thus 'there is a strong case for the interconnectedness of the exploitation of First and Third World women by patriarchal capitalism' (1994, p. 232). She cites Swasti Mitter's (1986) case for a 'common bond for women in the newly globalised economy' (Walby, 1994, p. 234) within a recognition of difference.

Peter Mayo points out that 'one has to go beyond Gramsci to avoid Eurocentrism and beyond both Gramsci and Freire to avoid patriarchal bias' (Mayo, 1999, p. 146). In this respect, Weiler refers to Gloria Anzaldua's conception of the *new mestiza* as a postcolonial feminist, warning that feminism can be an invasion of the self, unless patriarchy is critiqued from Western conceptions of *linear rationality, white privilege,* and *assumptions of universal truths.* Antiracist feminists educators have 'stressed that critical and feminist pedagogies, whilst claiming an opposition to oppression, are in danger of taking a kind of imperial and totalizing stance of knowing and "speaking for" those who are to be educated into truth' (Weiler, 2001, p. 72). Weiler rightly raises caution around concepts of *social identity* and *authority* in speaking for silenced others, and this is clearly an issue for global feminism.

In these times of globalisation, in order to avoid falling into a trap of what could be termed 'postcolonial feminism', we need more than ever to develop analyses of the interlocking oppressions of difference, context and level. Based on Walby's (1992, 1994) argument, I put the case for a three-dimensional model through which we can explore the intersections of oppressions, thereby identifying potential sites of liberation. These three dimensions are: i) **difference**: age, 'race', class, gender, sexual identity, 'dis'ability, ethnicity; ii) **contexts**: economic, cultural, intellectual, physical, environmental, historical, emotional, spiritual on another, and iii) **levels**: local, national, regional and global which form a complex set of interrelationships which not only interweave between axes, but which also intertwine on any one axis. (Ledwith, 2001, 2005). The basis of my argument relates to Gramsci's emphasis on critical education, history and culture, knowing who we are and what has shaped our reality on a multiplicity of dimensions in order to act together for change.

A transformative reach, from personal empowerment to collective global action, is vital to any critical analysis. 'The starting point of critical elaboration is knowing what one really is . . . as a product of the historical process to date which has deposited in you an infinity of traces, without leaving an inventory' (Gramsci, 1971, p. 324). In this respect, Mo Griffiths talks about the 'little stories' that link voice to narrative making that vital connection between the deeply personal and the profoundly political . . . 'by taking the particular perspective of an individual seriously; that is, the individual as situated in particular circumstances in all their complexity [and linking this] to grander concerns like education, social justice and power' (Griffiths, 2003, p. 81). Griffiths supports the idea that 'little stories' restore self-respect through dignity, mutuality and conviviality—but stresses that this is not transformative until it becomes a collective process.

Similarly, Darder talks about the way she provides learning contexts in which she resists giving answers, but encourages people 'to reach into themselves and back to their histories' (2002, p. 233). Using reflective writing to explore the inner depths of memory and history, she works with her students to analyse these from theoretical perspectives. This offers a past-present-future dynamic, 'moving between present and past with a view to contributing towards a transformed future' (Peter Mayo, 1999, p. 147). At the same time, it offers personal/political and local/global dynamics, such is the complexity of the power that we are struggling to identify and transform.

It is imperative that this inner-outer movement links people in alliance. My own research with Paula Asgill indicated that autonomy is a precursor of sustainable alliances across difference, in this case between Black and White women (Ledwith & Asgill, 2000, 2007). Without this understanding of who we are and what has shaped our reality, there is no basis for sustained action across difference. This, in turn, links to Doyal and Gough's (1991) notion of personal autonomy as a human need, and as a precursor of critical autonomy and collective action. This thinking connects with Gramsci's *war of position,* moving from personal to critical levels of consciousness and linking a diversity of social groups and organisations in alliance as a collective force for change.

To Return to My Original Question: What Relevance Have Gramsci's Ideas to Feminist Pedagogy Today?

Gramsci's impact on my own political consciousness, most particularly through the concept of hegemony, was profound in its analysis of the insidious nature of power and the role of consent. Retrospectively, I was able to understand schooling as hegemonic, and to see my own role as a young teacher as complicit in this process. Teacher education is conservative, and works well, albeit 'unconsciously', in training agents of the state to maintain the *status quo*. There are many 'Jacks' that it sends out into the formative lives of children. When I eventually discovered Gramsci, he gave me the conceptual tools to make sense of my own life and the experiences which had shaped me and those around me. He triggered my feminist consciousness.

Gramsci provided feminism with the tools with which to make sense of the personal as political through the concept of *hegemony* and female-specific forms of coercion and consent. Ironically, feminism turned on him as metanarrative and dichotomous in thought, provoking major debates between the relationship of patriarchy and capital. But, the insights that postmodern feminism contributed to an understanding of difference holds a tension for transformative action in times when we need to go beyond the self and engage in political action.

We face 'twin global crises of justice and sustainability' (Reason, 2002, p. 3), a context within which action is imperative. A rereading of Gramsci in relation to an analysis of power and difference could contribute to the theoretical foundation for a new-world view. The top-downness of our current system is, I believe, essentially corrupt and incapable of reform. We need to refocus our attention on a horizontal axis, one in which superiority and inferiority are replaced by difference and diversity, and in which humanity and the natural world can co-exist symbiotically.

The enriched insights into difference offered by postmodernism, reconsidered in the context of globalisation, offer immense potential for strategic change with critical education at its heart. This needs to be seen on an inner/outer continuum, which extends from personal to political in analysis, and from local to global in action.

Capital's transition from an industrial to a post-industrial global economy calls for a strongly defined self within a cultural-historical-political analysis which attends to difference and power. I see this as a form of critical autoethnography which locates the person within the power structures which shape experience, and which provokes consciousness of self as the basis of critical consciousness. It is a process which engages with personal autonomy as a precursor of critical, collective autonomy, thus bridging the individual and collective (Doyal & Gough, 1991). Doniger (1998) describes it as looking through the microscope at the thousands of details that bring our stories to life, and through the telescope to see the unifying themes. This was the nature of the identity politics which engaged me with Hattersley women as the basis of wider action for change.

It requires a fundamental shift of analysis to address the complex interconnectedness of a loci of oppressions (Ledwith, 2001, 2005). In these ways, a multiplicity of hegemonies is understood within the complex interrelatedness of oppressions. This not only offers insight into sites of intervention, but offer strategies for uniting 'social agents of unequal power' (Kenway, 2001, p. 58); a *war of position* in which the concept of alliance across difference get us beyond a simplistic structural analysis. In this way, the capital/labour contradiction which Gramsci extended to a 'national-popular', oppressor/oppressed dichotomy is extended to a local/global analysis, but within an analysis of difference which addresses the reach of global power into a diversity of personal lives.

References

Allman, P. (1988) Gramsci, Freire and Illich: Their contributions to education for socialism, in: T. Lovett (ed.), *Radical Approaches to Adult Education* (London, Routledge).

Allman, P. (1999) *Revolutionary Social Transformation: Democratic hopes, political possibilities, and critical education* (Westport, CT, Bergin & Garvey).

Allman, P. (2001) *Critical Education against Global Capitalism: Karl Marx and revolutionary critical education* (Westport, CT, Bergin & Garvey).

Belenky, M., Clinchy, B., Goldgerger, N. & Tarule, J. (1997) *Women's Ways of Knowing: The development of self, voice, and mind* (10th anniversary edn.) (New York, Basic Books).

Cannan, C. (2000) The Environmental Crisis, Greens and Community Development, *Community Development Journal*, 35:4 (October), pp. 365–376.

Coole, D. (1993) *Women in Political Theory: From ancient misogyny to contemporary feminism* (Hemel Hempstead, Harvester Wheatsheaf).

Darder, A. (2002) *Reinventing Paulo Freire: A pedagogy of love* (Oxford, Westview).

Dominelli, L. (1990) *Women and Community Action* (Birmingham, Venture Press).

Doniger, W. (1998) *The Implied Spider: Politics and theology in myth* (New York, Columbia University Press).

Doyal, L. & Gough, I. (1991) *A Theory of Human Need* (London, Macmillan).

Ferguson, A. & Folbre, N. (1981) The Unhappy marriage of Patriarchy and Capitalism, in: L. Sargent (ed.), *op cit.*

Fisher, W. F. & Ponniah, T. (2003) *Another World Is Possible: Popular alternatives to globalization at the world social forum* (London, Zed).

Flaherty, J., Veit-Wilson, J. & Dornan, P. (2004) *Poverty: The facts* (5th edn.) (London, Child Poverty Action Group).

Freire, P. (1972/82) *Pedagogy of the Oppressed* (Harmondsworth, Penguin).

Goldberger, N., Tarule, J., Clinchy, B. & Belenky, M. (eds) (1996) *Knowledge, Difference, and Power: Women's ways of knowing* (New York, Basic Books).

Gramsci, A. (1971) *Selections from Prison Notebooks* (London, Lawrence & Wishart).

Griffiths, M. (2003) *Action for Social Justice in Education: Fairly different* (Maidenhead, Open University Press).

Hartmann, H. (1981) The Unhappy Marriage of Marxism and Feminism: Towards a more progressive union, in: L. Sargent (ed.), *op cit.*

Hill Collins, P. (1990) *Black Feminist Thought: Knowledge, consciousness and the politics of empowerment* (London, Unwin Hyman).

Hill, D., McLaren, P., Cole, M. & Rikowski, G. (eds) (1999) *Postmodernism in Educational Theory: Education and the politics of human resistance* (London, The Tuffnell Press).

hooks, b. (1984) *Feminist Theory: From margin to center* (Boston, South End Press).

hooks, b. (1993) bell hooks Speaking about Paulo Freire—the Man, his Work, in: P. McLaren & P. Leonard (eds), *Paulo Freire: A critical encounter* (London, Routledge).

Kenway, J. (2001) Remembering and Regenerating Gramsci, in: K. Weiler (ed.), *Feminist Engagements: Reading, resisting and revisioning male theorists in education and cultural studies* (London, Routledge).

Ledwith, M. (2001) Community Work as Critical Pedagogy: Re-envisioning Freire and Gramsci, *Community Development Journal*, 36:3, pp. 171–182.

Ledwith, M. (2005) *Community development: A critical approach* (Bristol, Policy Press).

Ledwith, M. & Asgill, P. (2000) Critical alliance: Black and white women working together for social justice, *Community Development Journal*, 35:3, pp. 290–299.

Ledwith, M. & Asgill, P. (2007) Feminist, Anti-racist Community Development: Critical alliance, local to global, in: L. Dominelli (ed.), *Revitalising Communities in a Globalising World* (Aldershot, Ashgate).

Mayo, P. (1999) *Gramsci, Freire and Adult Education: Possibilities for transformative action* (London, Zed).

Mayo, P. (2004) *Liberating Praxis: Paulo Freire's legacy for radical education and politics* (London, Praeger).

Milne, S. (undated) *Fifty Years on, Labour Discovers a Guru* (London, The Guardian).

Oppenheim, C. & Harker, L. (1996) *Poverty: The Facts,* (London, Child Poverty Action Group).

Reason, P. (2002) *Justice, Sustainability and Participation,* available at http://www.bath.ac.uk/~mnspwr/.

Showstack Sassoon, A. (ed.) (1987) *Women and the State* (London, Hutchinson).

Spretnak, C. (1997) *The Resurgence of the Real: Body, nature and place in a hypermodern world* (Harlow, Addison-Wesley).

Torres, C. A. (1993) From the 'Pedagogy of the Oppressed' to a 'Luta Continua': the political pedagogy of Paulo Freire, in: P. McLaren and P. Leonard (eds), *Paulo Freire: A critical encounter* (London, Routledge).

Walby, S. (1992) *Theorizing Patriarchy* (Oxford, Blackwell).

Walby, S. (1994) Post-postmodernism? Theorizing Gender, *The Polity Reader in Social Theory* (Cambridge, Polity Press).

Weiler, K. (1995) A Feminist Pedagogy of Difference, in: J. Holland & M. Blair with S. Sheldon (eds), *Debates and Issues in Feminist Research and Pedagogy* (Clevedon, Multilingual Matters/The Open University).

Weiler, K. (2001) Rereading Paulo Freire, in: K. Weiler (ed.), *Feminist Engagements: Reading, resisting, and revisioning male theorists in education and cultural studies* (London, Routledge).

Young, A. (1990) *Femininity in Dissent* (London, Routledge).

Chapter 11

Foucault, Educational Research and the Issue of Autonomy

Mark Olssen

Reprinted by permission of Taylor & Francis Ltd, http://www.tandfonline.com, on behalf of © Philosophy of Education Society of Australasia.

Editors' Introduction

Olssen's chapter seeks to demonstrate an application of Foucault's philosophical approach to a particular issue in education: that of personal autonomy. The chapter surveys and extends the approach taken by James Marshall in his book *Michel Foucault: Personal autonomy and education*. After surveying Marshall's writing on the issue Olssen extends Marshall's approach, critically analysing the work of Rob Reich and Meira Levinson, two contemporary philosophers who advocate models of personal autonomy as the basis for a liberal education. As Olssen argues, yet another thing autonomy neglects is the strategic sense in which agency is exercised. For Foucault the game is a useful metaphor to express his sense of freedom. The game illustrates the political nature of freedom as pertaining to possibilities under specific conditions. In a game one is both free and constrained. Players find themselves at points where they must respond. In addition, movements in a game are infinitely variable and fluid. While players are confined by rules, indefinite numbers of possibilities and options exist within them. In addition, through effective strategies players can utilise the rules to their own advantage; they can invent and improvise; within a system of constraints, moves are numerous. Freedom and constraint co-exist. Such a view expressed Foucault's conception of freedom, as something political, expressed, or mobilised, through the exercise of power. The role of education is important here, for the exercise of power involves resources, capacities, skills, acumen, techne, eristic, and an understanding of rules. In Olssen's view, these are the tasks of education.

Introduction

Foucault has had a major impact on the social sciences and a smaller, yet growing, impact on educational studies. In 1989 James Marshall (1989, p. 98) could note that 'educationalists had little to say on the subject'. In reviewing the works influenced directly by Foucault, Marshall refers to studies by Jones & Williamson (1979), Hoskin (1979), as well as the critical psychology of Henriques, Hollway, Urwin, Venn, and Walkerdine (1984). In the few years after Marshall made this observation, the situation began to alter. Publications by Cherryholmes (1988), Ellesworth (1989), McLaren & Hammer (1989), Walkerdine (1989), Davies (1989), Marshall (1989, 1990), Ball (1990), Miller (1990), Pagano (1990), Anyon (1991), Aronowitz and Giroux (1991), Britzman (1991), Lather (1991), McLaren (1991), Giroux (1991), and Olssen (1993), to name just some, established a veritable explosion of works influenced by Foucault or by post-structuralism generally. Indeed, since 1993 the influence of Foucault and post-structuralism on education has continued to grow, affecting almost every area of study, although Marshall's (1989, p. 98) observation that 'it is far from clear that the theoretical radicalness of the work has been grasped' would still seem to be relevant. In addition, notwithstanding an increasing volume of literature, in many places Foucault's ideas are still marginalised within the mainstream discourses of educational scholarship.

Many of the works that appeared in the late 1980s and early 1990s relating Foucault to education simply sought to explain the relevance of Foucault's distinctive orientation to education, or of post-structuralism generally (e.g. Cherryholmes, 1988, or Marshall, 1989). Others sought some sort of integration of synthesis between post-structuralism and critical theory (Giroux, 1991; Aronowitz & Giroux, 1991; Lather, 1991; Ellesworth, 1989), proposing post-structuralism as a theory of emancipation towards a more equitable society. The appeal of Foucault, as of other post-structuralist writers, was that he problematised the meta-narratives of the enlightenment and advocated the possibility of treating all knowledge and forms of pedagogy as *contingent, specific, local* and *historical* (Aronowitz & Giroux, 1991, p. 81). It permitted too the realisation of historically constituted forms of knowledge and pedagogy as 'regimes of truth' (Gore, 1993, Ch. 6) without resorting to 'top-heavy' critical meta-narratives such as Marxism. More recent works in the last decade have sought to expand the horizon, applying Foucault's approach to both substantive and methodological issues (Biesta, 1998; Popkewitz and Brennan 1998; Olssen, 1999; Gale 2001; Peters, 2001; Popkewitz et al., 2001; Varela, 2001; Edwards, 2002; Edwards, 2003; Marshall, 2003; Baker and Heyning, 2004; Edwards and Nicoll, 2004; and Olssen, Codd and O'Neill, 2004).

In this paper I intend to limit my review and application of Foucault to the issue of personal autonomy, extending the work of James Marshall with that of my own 'Foucauldian-inspired' approach to the subject. In a number of papers and books spanning several years James Marshall (1989, 1990, 1995, 1996a, 1996b) has presented a Foucauldian analysis of liberal education principles focusing upon (1) personal autonomy, (2) notions of identity, (3) the adequacy of the liberal concept of authority, and (4) the notion of the improvement or progress of human beings through education or in society.

Maintaining the Foucauldian thesis that the autos or self has been constructed politically by power-knowledge, Marshall critiques the view that education is involved in the pursuit of personal autonomy, or that rational autonomy is the aim of education. For Foucault, says Marshall, the pursuit of personal autonomy in such Enlightenment terms is a social construction and is destined to fail because it masks the fact that any such persons have been constituted by political acts. As he puts it (1996a, p. 113), 'the notion of a self able to deliberate upon and accept laws so as to act autonomously as opposed to following laws heteronomously is a fiction, furnished upon the western world post-Kant as the basis for moral action but, for Foucault in the cause of governmentality'. Rather, for Foucault, says Marshall, our conception of ourselves as 'free agents' is an illusion, and he argues that liberal educators like Kenneth Strike, R. F. Dearden, Paul Hirst and R. S. Peters who advocated personal autonomy as a fundamental aim of education do not understand how modern power, through the technologies of domination and the technologies of the self, has produced individuals who are governable. As he states (1996b, p. 70):

> For [R.S.] Peters education becomes essentially the development of mind through the search for truth, essentially in the traditional academic disciplines . . . In thinking rationally a person thinks on their own, autonomously. This person, the autos, is the source of law, the nomos.

For Marshall, the very concepts which we use to construct our identities are such as to make independence and autonomy illusory. Hence education via governmentality effects the production of a new form of subject—one who believes they are free. Such an education simply introduces a new form of social control and socialisation and new and more insidious forms of indoctrination where a belief in our own authorship binds us to the conditions of our own production and constitutes an identity that makes us governable. In that 'selves' do emerge it is as 'pathologised' into certain types of human beings which are discursively constructed.

The human sciences have been pivotal here as technologies of the self in the construction of human subjects as autonomous. The human sciences have produced knowledge about man during the period of the Enlightenment. This, says Marshall (1996a, p. 120), entails a 'messy involvement':

> Man enters the scene as both speaking subject and as an object that is spoken about. As speaking subject, Man represents the very conditions of possibility of content knowledge about the object man. Foucault argues that Man as subject in the human sciences has a continuous messy involvement in knowledge about the object Man. Or, to put it another way, whereas the very conditions for the possibilities of knowledge should be separate from the contents of knowledge, or that there should be a dividing line between the transcendental and the empirical, Foucault believes that in the human sciences they are not and *cannot* be so divided.

In a related sense, utilising Foucault's concept of governmentality, Marshall (1995, 1996a, 1996b) and Peters & Marshall (1996) examine the neo-liberal notion of the autonomous chooser as embodying a particular conception of human nature, as a model of the security of the state, and as a particular model of surveillance and control. Focusing upon the massive changes in political policies regarding education, as well as other social services, which have taken place in countries such as America, Britain, Australia and New Zealand since the late 1970s, he develops a Foucauldian analysis of the reforms in terms of notions such as 'choice', 'quality', 'freedom', and 'autonomy'. In a way similar to his analysis of autonomy as a liberal educational goal, what is presupposed in the notion of the 'autonomous chooser', says Marshall, is that the notion of autonomy needed to make choices, and the notion of needs and interests entailed as a result, have not been manipulated or imposed in some way upon the chooser, but are the subject's own. A Foucauldian critique rejects such a possibility.

Problematising Autonomy

What I want to do in the rest of this paper is extend Marshall's Foucauldian critique of autonomy to contemporary work in the political philosophy of education. Two contemporary American liberals utilising the concept of autonomy are Rob Reich (2002) and Meira Levinson (1999). Both define autonomy as the end or goal of a liberal education. For Reich the prime task for the liberal state is the creation of political virtues, such as trust and reasonableness, and these in turn presuppose that each citizen is autonomous. Reich defines autonomy as:

> A person's ability to reflect independently and critically upon basic commitments, desires and beliefs, be they chosen or unchosen, and to enjoy a range of meaningful life options from which to choose, upon which to act, and around which to orientate and pursue one's life projects.
>
> (p. 46)

Unlike Kant or Mill, or many within the liberal tradition, Reich is at pains to point out that autonomy is not a natural quality of humans but is something that is learnt. In this he has clearly taken on board many of the communitarian criticisms of liberalism, regarding the importance of an 'embedded' conception of the self, and the need not to presume a natural 'already formed' view of the human being. In order to get citizens to be autonomous, the liberal state must educate them in the political virtues. So, says Reich (p. 43), the political virtues 'imply at least that citizens are autonomous'. Reich's conclusion at this point is that autonomy must be planned for, educated for, and is not culturally neutral.

The weight Reich gives to autonomy, or as he will eventually qualify it, 'minimalist autonomy', causes serious problems for much of multicultural political theory. Here he criticizes a long list of writers in what is an impressive survey of the field, including William Galston (1995), the more staunch multiculturalists Avishai Margalit and Moshe Halbertal (1994), and Chandron Kukathas (1995, 1997). While Reich is prepared to tolerate diversity, it is only on the basis that autonomy is not compromised. Arguments, and cultural groups, that fail to respect autonomy are thus not acceptable. William Galston, who celebrates diversity over autonomy, is criticized on the grounds that the value of autonomy remains central even to Galston's project, for 'Galston packs into his account a concern for autonomy which evinces itself specifically in his discussions about civic education' (p. 52). Yet, Galston sees autonomy as only one possible mode of existence. While it needs respecting and safeguarding, what is really important is the protection of social diversity. As he puts it (1995, p. 523) 'liberalism is about the protection of diversity, not the valorization of choice'. Because some cultures may not value choice, Galston, adopts the familiar tactic among multiculturalists of allowing for a 'right to exit'. Reich indicates he is unhappy with arguments of this sort for any 'right to exit' *presupposes autonomy,* for autonomy underlies such abilities as critical independent judgement which are necessary in order to make decisions about whether one wants to exit ones cultural group or not. In this way, Reich keeps coming back to his argument that because autonomy is central to the creation of the political virtues, it cannot be compromised, and must assume a fundamental role—for all cultural groups.

Theories of the liberal multiculturalists, and theories of group rights, are also criticized (Reich, Ch. 3). His objection to group rights is not on the usual grounds that group rights threaten common citizenship values, but rather that with regard to group rights, groups trump individuals, and hence individuals— frequently children—become sacrificed to the interests of the group. Although the 'right to exit' is usually held up as the bulwark of a minimal liberalism, in Reich's view, it can not perform the task required of it. Such arguments apply even against 'sophisticated' liberal multiculturalists like Kymlicka (1989, 1995) who also takes the concept of autonomy seriously. But group rights don't effectively give children a meaningful right of exit, even in Kymlicka's theory. In this sense, Kymlicka's conception of autonomy is unsatisfactory and his defense of rights to separate schooling for some cultural minorities is weak in that it constitutes a punitive restriction for children by confining them *within* a particular cultural group. Meaningful autonomy, as Reich will argue, presupposes *intercultural awareness,* which Reich maintains (in an unfair characterization of Kymlicka's views) Kymlicka's theory fails to acknowledge or resolve.

Clearly Reich's view of liberalism as a doctrine grounded in autonomy, based on the respect for individuals and the choices they make, has radical implications for multicultural theory of education. Recognising historical problems with autonomy as developed by writers like Kant and Mill, where it assumed the role as an overarching metaphysical postulate, Reich limits his conception to what he terms 'minimalist autonomy'. Minimalist autonomy, he claims, avoids the troublesome effects of the 'strong' conception, avoids being 'rarefied' or 'elitist', and doesn't assume an important role in the architecture of the political theory. As he tells us:

> Minimalist autonomy will not insist that an autonomous life be one that makes the person both author and subject of universal moral laws, nor will it insist that people create for themselves a life like any other. What is important

for a minimalist conception of autonomy is that autonomous persons are self-determining, in charge of their own lives, able to make significant choices from a range of meaningful options about how their lives will unfold.

(p. 100)

Reich then makes three important distinctions. The first concerns the fact that autonomy does not apply to reason, but to the 'a person's life or character'. As he states:

> When we ask whether or not people are autonomous actors or agents, we normally mean to ask about the extent to which they are able to lead the life they desire for themselves, to act upon the commitments, values, wishes and beliefs they deem worthy: we are asking whether they exhibit an autonomous character, a character that is exhibited in the way that a person adheres to his conception of the good life. Autonomous persons are discernable not on the basis of any particular act but on the basis of an overall shape they give to their lives, the freedom this has in making decisions for themselves that relate to fundamental aspects of their lives.
>
> (p. 92)

Reich's second point is that autonomy is a matter of degree, not an all or nothing state. People he observes are not born autonomous:

> Furthermore, the exercise of autonomy will vary by degree not only within each person and over a lifetime, but also by degree across persons. Individuals are variously capable of leading autonomous lives, some more so than others.
>
> (p. 93)

Reich's third distinction concerns the difference between autonomy and liberty. Central to autonomy is 'reflection' rather than 'the fidelity of tradition'. But being autonomous is not reducible to acting freely:

> Autonomy carries with it an implication of directing ones' life through choices made independently and reflectively. To be free or to have liberty involves on the other hand, an absence of constraints (negative liberty) or organisation of character (positive liberty) that enables choice making, but says little about the actual course and character of a person's life.
>
> (p. 95)

Meira Levinson (1999) also develops the notion of autonomy as central to her weak perfectionist brand of liberalism and claims this is essential to liberal education. According to Levinson, the problem with political liberals like Rawls is that they cannot argue convincingly from (1) the fact of pluralism over values and ideologies; to (2) fair and neutral criteria that justify liberal procedures, to (3) the substantive realisation of institutions that support constitutional democracy. Rawls, she says, radically underestimates the extent and depth of pluralism and reasonable disagreement, and seeks artificially to constrain it through his arguments concerning the 'burdens of judgement'.[1] The fact is, however, that there is no way to argue from pluralism to liberal proceduralism, and from there to constitutional democracy, unless one establishes liberal autonomy as a value the state must be committed to. Such a concept must indeed be 'thick' enough to justify state support for constitutional democracy, and 'thin' enough that the vast majority of people agree.

Levinson defines autonomy as 'the capacity to form a conception of the good, to evaluate ones values and ends with the genuine possibility of reviving them should they be found wanting' (p. 15). A few pages later (p. 19) she defines it as 'the capacity to evaluate one's values and ends self-critically with the possibility of revising and then realising them'. She claims that any liberal justification of substantive liberal institutions and freedoms rests on such a value. And, in parenthesis she notes (p. 33) '*incidentally*, that the achievement of autonomy requires that individuals basic needs be fulfilled, including the provision of food, shelter, clothing, affection, and self-esteem, to give a partial but representative list' (emphasis added). Clearly, neither Reich, nor Levinson, would see their support for autonomy as excluding support for a welfare state.

Levinson's justification for using the concept certainly indicates the seriousness of the cause, for as she explains it, there is need for a perfectionist principle if liberal institutions and values are to be justified. It is certainly correct, given the way she proceeds, that there is need for some principle or other, if the liberal state is to be justified, and the concept of autonomy builds in the idea that each individual will have an equal space and be in charge of their life. That individuals' rights to make decisions over their lives be recognised and respected and for such rights to be enshrined in law is the basis of the principle. This is important for liberals, and it is a worthy ideal, but we should note that the idea of justifying liberal institutions is not unimportant for Foucault, and for that matter, all non-totalitarians. What Foucault would suggest is that concepts other than autonomy can do this just as well, and with far fewer negative effects than use of the concept of autonomy brings with it. While the concept of autonomy may convey ideals that are important, it *misrepresents* at the same time. A Spinozist, for example, might suggest that 'self preservation and well-being' (*conatus*) could provide such a principle, where a concern for freedom and security are seen as integral to such a principle, and thus become important in justifying the types of institutions we live with. Spinoza, like Foucault, did not develop a specifically liberal philosophy, or not one commonly recognised as within the liberal tradition of political philosophy, but nevertheless was concerned ultimately with the values of democratic justice and freedom. 'The true aim of the republic is freedom', said Spinoza (1985, Chp. XX, p. 241). I mention this because Spinoza influenced Deleuze and Foucault, and (with some adaptation) can be used to supplement Foucault to provide scope for a normative political theory, and overcome the problems of epistemological and moral relativism.[2] It is as well to point out that liberals have no monopoly on a concern with such values. Indeed, the perfectionism of self preservation and well-being would surely be better, and one could argue, as I have endeavoured to do elsewhere (Olssen, *et al.*, 2004) that these dictate a conception of democracy which has multiple values including *freedom, security, equality* and *inclusion*. In such a conception, the concept of *autonomy* is not necessary. Not because autonomy does not, as a conception, contain values of importance, but rather for two reasons. Firstly, because the term contains too many ideas of importance, and yet fails to differentiate between them, i.e., because the term is too diffuse, too abstract, and in short too indeterminate; secondly, because it grounds political obligation to the individual's private arena, underemphasising the social relations, ethical duties and responsibilities, and the complexities of the individual-collective interaction. In this sense, utilisation of the concept in political philosophy has distorting effects of an ideological nature.

To start with the idea that the concept is too diffuse, let me point to a few possible meanings that it is not sensible to run together. First, as people are interdependent and inter-connected in the structures of social support, and to other people, the concept is—when applied to people, rather than city-states—technically inappropriate, as I will comment further below. Second, while autonomy is the basis of freedom, it is also the basis of the competitive market order. That is, it is the privileged and protected space in which competitive entrepreneurial conduct takes root, and one might say, is in this sense both the normative underpinning of *homo economicus*, and more generally of white Anglo Saxon protestant middle class values. In this sense, autonomy has served to link the freedom of individuals in the history of liberalism to natural law theories of property rights, to government strategies of laissez-faire, to arguments for a minimal state, and for support for policies of low taxation. While it is unfair to accuse Reich or Levinson of advocating these types of policies, it is difficult to dissociate these various ideals within the expansive semiotic possibilities of the concept, especially when considered in relation to the history of its usage. Third, it is also the model of *personal health* (for Levinson extremely needy people cannot be autonomous) and thus a political ideal is confounded with a psychological and medical one; Fourth, it is also the model, or principle of a *healthy polis*. By this, it refers to a political formula of legitimate as opposed to illegitimate state action, concerning the issue of individual freedom or liberty. Fifth, relatedly, the concept is also used to support a notion of individual rights as fundamental. The conception of rights supported by Reich and Levinson is implicitly a traditional one with connotations of self-ownership and exclusive sovereignty, which sees the self as existing in a natural arena with exclusive rights of ownership and control over private decisions, set against the artificiality of society, and the danger of the collective. Sixth, notwithstanding an explicit concern to distance autonomy from Kant, autonomy is invoked to refer to 'critical judgement', both in a cognitive and moral sense. As Reich (p. 95) says, '[a]utonomy carries with it an implication of directing one's life through choices made independently and reflectively'. This ability to make decisions which are assumed to be the individual's own, unrelated to the social and historical milieu is evident in both writers works. To some extent, this independence of judgement coalesces with the first point, concerning separateness or independence of a life, but it would seem to me that the first point contains an economic and political dimension while the second refers more directly to mind or consciousness. But, whether this is so or not, it would appear that the concept of autonomy is something of a Trojan horse that carries a number of different riders. When cultural groups such as the Amish wish to withdraw from public system of education, their rejection of the concept of autonomy may well be related to *the other work done in its name,* rather than any opposition to the development of independent thinking skills in its children. They might also claim that one's liberal freedoms, if taken literally within certain versions of the harm principle, sanction types of behaviour which liberals themselves do not permit their children to engage in.[3] They may claim that it carries unfortunate associations with traditional models of property rights and self-ownership, or that it allows for and promotes forms of behaviour which are arrogantly disrespectful of community traditions and norms. Or it may claim, as I will, that it implicates liberal underpinnings which are in contradiction to recent extensions of democratic theory in a global direction.

From a Foucauldian perspective, it should be noted at the outset, that the objections are not to the value of freedom, or of constitutional democracy, or to the value of rights. Rather, the objections are to the theoretical and methodological function of the concept of autonomy within liberal philosophers' theories. It is claimed that such a concept, in seeking to ground liberal polity, also misrepresents and distorts the character of social existence. Although it alludes to and identifies important qualities (freedom, control, rights, etc.), it does so in a way that distorts the overall frame of reference in a particular political direction. One of its drawbacks is the very expansiveness of the possible meanings such a concept conveys. Hence, while it identifies some values which many people hold to be important, it is also ideological. Further, I will argue that the methodological work such a concept does to justify democracy can better be done by other means—means which preserve what is valuable in 'autonomy', but are more specifically focused and include other important dimensions and values as well.

What can be noted from the outset is how the word is in many instances inaccurate when applied to individuals. Such a concept, originally applied to city-states, made sense in that the city-state *was* independent.[4] Kant used the term to apply to the fact that reason operated in the noumenal realm and was *unconditioned* by sensuous experience, hence, quite literally, *it was autonomous.*[5] Reich, as we have seen, criticizes the transcendental sense in which Kant uses the term. Both he and Levinson use the term in a different sense to refer to the overall quality or character of a life, and in the ability of individuals to engage in reflective critical thinking determining the overall form of a life. But lives do not develop in separateness, and independence from the world. People may be capable in dealing with the world, but this is a far cry from saying they are autonomous or separate from it. Indeed, it is not inaccurate to say that autonomy is precisely what people—who are interdependent as the empirically ascertainable condition of their being—*do not have*. As the word is commonly used, it is what many people—the disabled; the mentally impaired; the sick; the elderly, the young—cannot even aspire to. But I do not want to refer specifically to special groups, as I will maintain that nobody is autonomous in this sense. To define the perfection of the state in terms of such a value therefore will obviously short-change many groups. To make it the foundation value of the state also potentially exonerates the state from responsibility to assist its citizens when in need. It is not so much of a slippage, after all, from arguing that 'the state should assist people to become autonomous' to arguing that 'they expect all to *be* autonomous'.

Levinson, like Reich, can of course acknowledge that as a capacity autonomy is a matter of degree. It is not seen as a natural condition but as something to be achieved. Both have bought into, and acknowledged, most of the communitarian criticisms of the early Rawls, and see the self as 'embedded', and therefore concede that people are only partially autonomous. Reich sees the problem here in the following way: if autonomy is never fully realised and is only a potential to be achieved, it can hardly function as the locus of state respect for individuals. Hence, Reich states (2002, pp. 93–94) that as well as being a *capacity*, it must also be a *condition*. As a capacity it is partial. But as a condition it is total, and is always 'on'.

One is still left wondering why 'autonomy', rather than, say, 'respect' or 'dignity' or 'well-being', 'freedom', 'integrity' or even just plain simply 'rights'? While it makes sense to suggest that individuals should have rights to challenge or contest authority, and even that they have the freedom to do so, it is far from clear that they are ever 'autonomous' in the sense that is clearly conveyed in this term, of being 'self-sufficient', or 'independent'. While many people may aspire to become self-sufficient, not all groups have this aim, and those that profess to—including one suspects liberal philosophers—frequently mistake the ideology of the society for the reality, as the ideal. Even when we profess autonomy as ideal, we delude ourselves; people are far less independent that they feel, or claim. It is really that we suffer the myth of the 'self made' person, believing that we are far more independent than we are. As Hobhouse (1911) made clear there is a social factor in achievement which is frequently unacknowledged, and sometimes unrecognised. We start from a situation of non-autonomy, and end in one as well. Some of us attain what appears as reasonable partial autonomy, but is in fact more dependent on the structures of social support than possibly believed. Even for those who do so aspire, what is really meant in such an ideal is a degree of reasonable self-sufficiency, of mature judgement, and reasonable detachment of perspective, as they balance the interests of themselves and their families with those of the community, and the polis. In that it is autonomy, it is of a highly relative and qualified nature.

This last comment raises yet another concern about use of the concept, and this concerns the sense in which it functions *ideologically*. Are the skills that Reich and Levinson and others associate with it as residing under its banner really indicative of 'autonomy'? Or, to put it differently, are western liberal societies so independent and self-critical, self reflective about their lives and goals. Is it really true that certain minorities all follow tradition and we all think for ourselves? Do we really educate children for critical reflective selfhood? Certainly, individuals exercise free choices within specific constraints, and with varying degrees of success, they manage and control much of their own lives. Such freedom is exercised as choice over fairly ordinary options in day to day living, which are the same types of choices exercised in all cultures by all peoples. It's called living. Such freedom is also seen as the legitimate basis of the way societies in the west should be organised. But, as I will argue, one does not need a concept like autonomy to serve this function. It can be argued that the very use of the concept assumes a degree of 'self-reliance' which is illusory, however, for the very concept embodies the self-reliant and individualistic conception of the person that has been the hallmark of western liberalism, and which is avidly promoted through its popular forms of entertainment and media. It not only understates the degree of interconnectedness and interdependence that characterizes relations in societies; but it exaggerates the extent to which people are independent and self-legislating. Every individual depends far more than they probably imagine—and far more than liberal political philosophers have traditionally acknowledged—on the structures of social and institutional support. Even those few who finally end up being highly competent at achieving life's goals cannot really be said to be 'autonomous' in anything but a highly qualified sense. It is rather that their privileged capabilities depend on a whole network of complex structures and supports.

Related to this, citizens—both adults and children—are far more the products of normalization and socialization than they believe, or claim. But in individualistic cultures, the normalized representations are to models of 'choice', where the choices which are much of the time between the 'colours and the brands', are to a large extent illusory, or at least not significantly different from the choices made by people in all sorts of different cultures of the world. And in that people are socialized, they are 'responsibilized' through strategies of 'power-knowledge' to believe they are freer than they really are. The liberal middle classes manifest far more respect for the 'fidelities of tradition' than they believe, or at least claim. With relation to children, it can be claimed that education is structured not so much as to critically inform their minds, or to get them to engage in reflective practice, but rather to 'protect' their minds and adopt 'appropriate' middle class values. What is evident is that the very use of such a concept resonates the arrogance and self-deceiving nature of western phallocentricism, ethnocentrism and class-centrism. It helps create and perpetuate the illusion that we are more self-reliant than we are, that we are (solely/largely) responsible for our own achievements, and that we are the 'self-originating sources' of our values and goals. For contemporary liberals like Reich and Levinson, if this is no longer realistic as an originating idea, it is still operative as an end goal for education to pursue. Here I would claim they frequently seem to confuse autonomy with privilege.

In addition, and as a consequence of this, as both Reich and Levinson develop their case for autonomy-based liberalism, notwithstanding their denial, it assumes a metaphysical status within the theories they develop. Not only does it potentially harbour unacknowledged bedfellows such as market man, thus inadvertently contextualising autonomous critical development in an enterprise society, but it assumes an unhistorical and formal character which empties it of much significance. When Reich argues (p. 94) that as well as being a 'capacity', it must be respected as a (total, always 'on') 'condition', he is inserting it as a foundational ontic premis for which he has not a single scrap of evidence or support. It serves then a purely normative function within his theory, a matter I will address below.

Both may claim that in arguing for 'minimalist' autonomy, they themselves recognise the sociological objections I have raised above. If it is to do the important work in relation to both education and normative political theory it must be strong enough to justify a constitutional democracy, and yet 'thin' enough to apply to and appeal to almost all people. To support this they recognise the rights of groups to be 'non-autonomous' if they wish.[6] Another argument both maintain in order to support their arguments for 'minimal' autonomy is to draw a distinction between *self-determination* and *self-creation* or *self-authorship*. Individuals, they claim, are self-determining, but not self-creating. The inference is that self-determination is somehow 'less than' self-creation. Yet, I would argue that no real distinction can be made here, and they fail to justify grounds to differentiate the two. As most poststructuralist philosophers who have utilised the Nietzschean conception of self-creation maintain that every action has a *novel* aspect, self-determining actions *are* self-creating. The idea of self-determination, like that of self-creation, needs careful qualification, as it still implies *total control* of the individual over their environment. While the individual as a bearer of rights of citizenship is a vital stakeholder, any actual determinations reflect a complex balance of forces and strategies. As Foucault (1977a) explains, 'the man described for us, whom we are invited to free, is already in himself the effect of a subjection much more profound than himself'. Although he utilises practices of the self in the tasks of invention, 'these practices . . . are not something that the individual invents by himself. They are patterns that he finds in the culture and which are proposed, suggested, and imposed on him by his culture, his society and his social group' (1991, p. 11). Underpinning the determinations of individuals is a mix of shaping and conditioning forces and necessities. While this doesn't mean that freedom is not possible, and is possibly cumulatively successful over time, the agency of the self is intermittent and only one of a variety of factors affecting the course of a life.

A further related problem concerns the act of endeavouring to clarify what sort of personality-type 'autonomy' really describes. This is a problem that entangles Levinson, who disagrees with Dworkin (1988) over who is and who is not worthy of being called autonomous. Complaining that Dworkin's conception is purely formal, and not substantive, Levinson objects to Dworkin wanting to consider Harry autonomous when he is 'deeply psychologically dependant on his mother's approval' (p. 27), and similarly for people who 'abdicate control over the direction of [their lives]' (p. 28). A further point of contention emerges over 'Sister Susan' (p. 33) who devotes her life to the obedience to God. Whereas Dworkin would see Sister Susan as autonomous, Levinson doesn't see how she could be. She concludes that 'Dworkin's notion of autonomy is untenable as it currently stands, and further that it cannot provide a fruitful foundation for liberal freedoms' (p. 29). To his credit, Dworkin recognises the problems created when one considers the concept of autonomy in the light of basic human connectedness. As he puts it (1988, p. 21), 'the conception of autonomy that insists upon substantive independence is not one that has claims to our respect as an ideal . . . [it is] inconsistent with loyalty, objectivity, commitment, benevolence, and love'. Levinson (1999, p. 30) admits that 'such a notion of autonomy, if truly inconsistent with these virtues, is highly unappealing'. Yet, in contrast to Dworkin, her own more substantive conception ends by classifying only those who are psychologically independent, or as tending to independence, as being fit candidates for classification as autonomous. Although her tone is cautious when she notes that 'certain conditions, such as extreme neediness or dependence, can never be compatible with autonomous action' (p. 32) she creates the unfortunate 'sense', as a consequence of such a line of analysis (which coalesces with the general image of the Hollywood action-hero), of representing both social and psychological independence as the new figure of health in the brave new world of 'autonomy-based' liberalism.[7]

In relation to the issue of philosophical justification for the liberal state, and system of education, one real and important question that liberals wish to answer, and invoke autonomy to try to answer, is the issue of individual versus state discretion over jurisdiction. As Keynes (1931, pp. 312–313) put it in a different context, but one that highlights the real question being addressed here, the central issue concerns: 'what the state ought to take upon itself to direct by the public wisdom, and what it ought to leave with as little interference as possible to individual exertion?'. For John Stuart Mill (1859, p. 13), this was embodied in his formulation of the harm principle, which determined, in brief, that individuals are free to do anything they like, so long as their behaviour does not harm the interests of any other person, or group. Fundamentally, this concerns the issue of rights. In theory, to decide that individuals are, or ought to be, autonomous, means that the state has a duty to respect that autonomy.

That liberals utilise 'autonomy' to endeavour to solve this question is worthy. Both Reich and Levinson do a credible job in terms of the liberal philosophy they proffer. One suspects that this is the real reason that they seek to justify autonomy, not particularly because it has anything particularly to do with children, or psychological or cognitive independence, but because it defends *a way of life*. It's a particular form of 'rights-talk'. My argument is, however, that one does not need to 'invent' autonomy in order to safeguard individual rights and freedoms. Individual rights and freedoms are important to everyone's security and well being, even without autonomy. The concept of freedom, which is different to autonomy, is all that is required as far as John Stuart Mill's 'harm principle' is concerned. For Foucault, while rights are important, there are no rights antecedent to society. Moreover, Mill's presumption that some actions of individuals are 'self-regarding' and therefore of no concern to other people or society, as if individuals operated in some sort of 'nature-reserve', or exclusively private domain, would be untenable for Foucault. Given the self is social—by nature as it were—the issue of what a person can regard as their own, and claim 'rule' over is not directly what does not 'harm' others, but what may potentially harm others, what is even of concern to others in terms of its long-term, short-term, or even possible effects. In this sense, while Mill's principle may be a useful 'rule of thumb' given avowed goals of freedom and well being as the aims of the republic, as a principle it will always *underdetermine* any possible application in practice. What fills the gap is deliberation, contestation, and *public* arbitration made possible through a more expansive conception of democratic control.

In that Reich and Levinson invoke autonomy to defend a conception of rights however, it builds in a particularly liberal conception of individual rights as foundational. Hence Reich objects to Kymlicka privileging group rights over individual rights, on the grounds that 'individuals—frequently children—become sacrificed to the interests of the group'. Yet I find it problematic in Reich's account that individual and group rights are treated as mutually exclusive. There is an important sense again that we all live within groups, and our interests are to varying extents if not sacrificed, certainly effected by the groups within which we live. This is necessarily so, and that Reich objects to the influence of the group on individuals, simply reflects his liberal philosophical heritage. From Kymlicka's perspective, while he supports a conception of group rights, it had not occurred to me before reading Reich that he therefore excluded individual rights. In New Zealand certain group rights were given to Māori with reference to seats in Parliament, places in schools and higher education institutions, but these did not cancel the ordinary rights of citizens under the law. Reich says that acknowledging a 'right to exit' (which Kymlicka does) is not adequate, for prior to exercising an option of 'exit' a child would need to make a 'critical judgement', and this presupposes 'autonomy' as basic. Such an argument is fallacious on several grounds. First, children's ability to recognize abuse, or violence, or to think for themselves when confronted with unpleasant necessities, does not indicate 'autonomy', and the very application of this term—now in relation to children's mental faculties—shows clearly the paucity of the concept. Second, in that Kymlicka (as Reich concedes) acknowledges an 'exit' option, he clearly *is* recognizing the mutual co-existence of individual with group rights. The realistic issue is not concerning 'exit' of course, as children of all groups rarely have such an option in actual life. But the right is important, in that a right to 'exit' is also a right to complain, to appeal, to telephone a 'help line', to originate legal redress, and so on. In recognizing a right to 'exit' therefore, Kymlicka is not expressing a 'minimal liberalism' but acknowledging the importance of individual rights under the law as a general condition. Similarly, Reich criticizes Kymlicka for promoting group rights to the exclusion of inter-cultural awareness. But again, these two are not mutually exclusive. It is a case of both/and, not either/or. The more that one probes, the more such a conception of rights appears as a reinvention of traditional natural rights of the solitary (autonomous) individual of classical liberalism.[8] For Foucault, rights are important, not because any such foundation exists, but because they have proved historically important in protecting individuals and groups relative to the imperatives of well-being and survival. They save lives.

The real point here, however, is that while autonomy may well invoke some important values, to the extent it does so, it brings with it a number of other problems. Related to the points considered above, it may, indeed, seek ideologically to 'stack the deck' in advance, to expand the entitlements and responsibilities of the individual as against the collective, and one can suspect that liberal and neo-liberal arguments coalesce here. Such arguments historically have done a great deal to maximize individual and private entitlements to wealth, and understated the values of equality and collective determination. If the 'autonomy' of each is emphasised, one also, by definition as it were, underplays the responsibilities and duties which we owe to each other, individually and collectively. In fact, one could say that an emphasis upon 'autonomy' denies such responsibilities. If we are autonomous we are not interdependent; if we are not interdependent we do not owe each other anything. Such viewpoints have also been linked to campaigns to erode welfare state ('individual's should be responsible for themselves'); to argue for a reduction of state size and functions (laissez-faire) and to mobilise for free trade (which is what richer nations demand when their own economies are in order).

None of this, however, argues against rights, individual and group. That a constitutional democracy legislates a protected space, a system of rights and entitlements, is also important; that individuals require certain capabilities to function effectively in such a society can be acknowledged and accepted. But these are characteristics of the *political system* which defends and protects freedom and security. They concern the *socio-institutional* sense in terms of which freedom is exercised, and pre-suppose certain *institutional* and *political* arrangements. Autonomy in this sense is akin to the stability generated by a system of equal legal rights. In Kymlicka's usage, this seems understood, but with both Reich and Levinson there is a confusion of the personal with the political.

In this sense, rather than autonomy being privileged, inhering in the protection of individual against the demands of other individuals, or of society as a whole, it would be more appropriate to emphasis *democracy*, which by origin, attests to 'rule by the people', but which is better construed as a discourse which specifies rights, entitlements and obligations, and the protection of individuals and groups, both against each other and against their leaders, or those in power. In addition, as I have claimed, we must also balance the demands of freedom against those of equality, security, inclusion, participation, and social justice. While we can agree that societies exist for the individuals who make them up, it is unwise to reify any one term as a central ontological postulate. This is especially so in relation to education, for while children develop, and hopefully realise their potentials, what is needed to be understood is what freedom means, and how it can be expressed in the context of social, national and global *connectedness*. Rather than consider them as autonomous, or as potentially autonomous, it is preferable to consider what is owed them, and what they owe. In the educational context, my own preference is to speak of 'capabilities', such as critical reason, cognitive and cultural capital and resources, emotional and social capital, and so on. Capabilities also linked with needs, where resources and the structures of support are emphasised. Martha Nussbaum (1992) refers to such capabilities as constituting a 'thick vague' conception of the good. Such a conception comprises 'the most important functions of human beings in terms of which human life is defined' (p. 214) Such a conception is not metaphysical in the sense that it does not claim to derive from a source exterior to human beings in history, or to privilege a single term or concept as grounding educational development. Rather, such a conception is 'as universal as possible' and aims at 'mapping out the general shape of the human form of life, those features which constitute life as human wherever it is' (p. 216). This sort of approach also has the virtue of balancing freedom with equality and the concerns of justice. Now, if we are to educate for the political virtues required for democracy, in my view education must pursue a capabilities approach.

Towards a Foucauldian Conception

Ultimately, from a Foucauldian point of view, autonomy 'over-individualises' and confuses the effects of a certain form of power by which individuation takes place. By focusing on 'autonomy' as a personal trait, what the liberal philosophers do is to reduce the political domain as a trait of individuals (autonomous selves), thus perfecting the philosophical *interiorisation* that Foucaucalt (1997) traced to Descartes, and that Charles Taylor (1989) also traces in *Sources of the Self,* from the external to the internal; from Plato to modernity, involving both a *pyschologi-cization* and a *social amnesia,* not recognized in some cultures, possibly, inversely with the extent to which individualistic values have become sedimented into the deep structures of normalisation within the culture. What is being complained of here is a tendency to attribute what should be described at the level of the system or culture, to being a characteristic of individuals. What should really be meant by autonomy, is not a personal attribute of individuals with relation to their conduct, but *one* aspect of a democratic state. When, in other words, liberal philosophers talk of 'autonomy'; they are essentially speaking of democracy, with its implication of equal rights for all.

This is another way of saying that the concern with autonomy is a specifically modern exercise. During the seventeenth and eighteenth centuries morality and conduct was conceived in terms of obedience, which came to be increasingly contested and replaced with emerging conceptions of morality and life as an exercise in self-governance (Schneewind, 1998). This newly emerging individualism principally derived from four sources: (1) from the protestant reformation of the fifteenth and sixteenth centuries (2) from the scientific revolution of the sixteenth and seventeenth centuries, (3) from political and economic liberalism's emerging in the seventeenth century; and (4) from the industrial revolution of the eighteenth and nineteenth centuries. In each of these areas, specific proposals (religious worship, political obligation, scientific method) confounded various senses or forms of individualism—descriptive, moral, religious, political—asserting what in essence was a *metaphysic of individualism* against the more social and communitarian metaphysic of the *ancien regime*. The implication of this was to fashion a conception of the individual as 'owner and creator of his own capacities' (Macpherson, 1962). The ontological priority of the individual was reinforced by a broad spectrum of social and political theory and is closely tied to social, religious, economic and political changes from the sixteenth century onwards. The Reformation and the attendant Protestant religion gave rise to a new spirit of individualism whereby each individual could communicate directly with God and was solely responsible for his (or even her) salvation.[9] With the expansion of empire, the growth of science and the enlightenment belief in progress, the idea that the individual was master of their fate was further encouraged. Partly this was inspired by the successful methods of the physical sciences which employed mathematical laws, measurement quantification, and based itself on a metaphysic of atomism, reducing complex physical phenomena to its smallest component particle. Believing that the social world could be studied in the same way was to generally endorse the search for the truth of life in the individual.

Classical liberal individualism encompassed all aspects of life. In *The Wealth of Nations,* published in 1776, Adam Smith sought to explain laissez-faire capitalism as a consequence of the natural competition of the individual in very much the same way, with respect to basic postulates, that Darwin later sought to explain the processes of natural selection at work in the origins and evolution of species. In political philosophy John Stuart Mill was to frame a political conception of liberty to safeguard political freedom within a laissez-faire approach to capitalism. Others such as Jeremy Bentham and Herbert Spencer were to legitimise 'nonintervention', 'individual liberty' and 'unregulated competition' as being part of the *natural order of things,* reinforcing what was an ascendant view of society as a consequence of solely individual initiatives.

C. B. Macpherson has described the strain of thought in his book *The Political Theory of Possessive Individualism* (1962) and describes how, through a variety of thinkers from Thomas Hobbes to John Stuart Mill, English political and social thought from the seventeenth century to the nineteenth century is characterised by the idea of possessive individualism. This idea, says Macpherson, became axiomatic to liberal democratic thought and to scientific movements. In the nineteenth century it became an underlying and unifying assumption. Its 'possessive' quality is found in the condition of the individual as essentially the proprietor of his (or presumably her) own person or capacities, owing nothing to society for them. Thus for theorists such as Hobbes, Locke, Adam Smith, Herbert Spencer,

Bentham, Mill, Galton, the individual 'pre-figures' society and society will be happy and secure to the extent that individuals are happy and secure. Not only does the individual own his/her own capacities but also, more crucially, each is morally and legally responsible for him or herself. Freedom from dependence upon others means freedom from relations with others except those relations entered into voluntarily out of self-interest. Human society is simply a series of market relations between self-interested subjects. For Adam Smith it is guided by an 'invisible hand'. For John Locke society is a 'joint stock company' of which individuals are shareholders.

From a Foucauldian view this process of political individualism led to individualistic explanations at the level of the social and psychological sciences. Thus in his earliest published book, *Mental Illness and Psychology,* first published in 1954, Foucault (1987) traced how dysfunctions in the structure of societies, or environments, were represented as the pathologies of individuals—as 'conformity-disorders', 'behaviour problems' and the like.

With the liberal political philosophers there was a shift in the locus of political obligation from the community (obedience) to the individual (self-governance), although this transition was never as 'cut and dried' as it is often represented. From the time of Socrates individual rights have been argued about and violated, just as they have been from the seventeenth to the twenty-first centuries. What Foucault recognised was that the individual was never as autonomous or independent as modernity had represented them. The ideology of individualism may well have been useful in many arenas—science, religion, capitalist expansion—but it misrepresented the origins of identity, and the social and historical nature of selfhood. It obscured, also, the ontological independence of the social, as Wittgenstein (1953) had pointed out with his writing on 'forms of life' and our mistaken attributions regarding the private origins of language.

While the community defines identity through its objectified social practices, this doesn't deny the individual rights, however. But the rights of individuals do not emerge from nature, but through the common aim to survive. Thus, Foucault speaks of 'human rights' to 'confront governments' which is beyond the limits of nationality. As he puts it:

> There exists an international citizenship that has its rights and its duties, and that obliges one to speak out against every abuse of power, whoever its author, whoever its victims. After all, we are all members of the community of the governed, and thereby obliged to show mutual solidarity.
>
> (Foucault, 2001, p. 474)

International organisations have, says Foucault, 'created this new right—that of private individuals to effectively intervene in the sphere of international policy and strategy' (p. 475). The basis for such a cosmopolitan network, he perceived, was emerging, if only embryonically at the time he wrote, with the rise of NGOs and global conferences on trade, war, population and environment, which suggested the emergence of a new global public sphere. The emergence of public institutional forums, both national and global,[10] enabled deliberation and contestation, and ensured rights. Rather than educate children to be autonomous, one must give them the political capabilities to act in public and global arenas. It is by strengthening public institutions that democracy will work and that equal legal rights can be enforced.

In such a global system, new dimensions of democracy serve to transform traditional notions of rights, and freedom. *Transparency* is one such practice. As Anderson (2005, p. 9) observes:

> It was the principle of transparency, abolishing *arcana imperii* that had always characterized the foreign policies of democracies and tyrannies alike, under the pretext that affairs of state were too complex and delicate to broadcast to the public, and too dangerous to reveal to the enemy. Such secrecy could not but erode democracy itself, as innumerable actions—at home and abroad—as the national security services of contemporary states testified. Here a vicious circle was at work. States could only become fully democratic once the international system become transparent, but the system could only become fully transparent once every state was democratic.

Such transparency, extended as an operating principle of democracy at all levels—individual, national, global—interferes with, erodes and transforms, the very forms of sovereignty that traditionally defined 'privacy' and 'autonomy'. Both become undermined as a new relation of individual to collective is enacted. This recognises what has always been profoundly true: that nobody is autonomous; but that every one can have rights.

Democracy for Foucault does not rely on or need autonomy. Rights are given, and capabilities provided, in its absence. In fact, in Foucauldian terms autonomy is a strategy for decreasing the role of the state and increasing individual responsibility for welfare. As Jim Marshall (1996b, p. 83) puts it, 'to believe that personal autonomy in modern times is liberating is mistaken—according to Foucault . . . its pursuit leads to unfreedom'. According to Marshall, 'from Foucault's perspective the political has become *masked* and the true nature of this alleged autonomy and its role in governmentality hidden' (p. 85). In this sense, to advocate greater autonomy is to advocate greater individualisation in society and greater 'responsibilisation' of individuals and families.

In addition to expanding the public sphere, Foucault would encourage educational policies that represent it as a relation of power that develops agency and resistance. For Foucault, it is not autonomy, but *mature judgement* on the basis of existing terrain of forces. What are required are the arts of criticism. In a pluralistic universe, contradictory possibilities need to be analysed. They are analysed in relation to survival, from a particular point and place. They are mature, and not arbitrary. Discursive historical possibilities can be referenced to other mature discursive systems, that have generated confidence over time, as well as to practical issues and possibilities. Although through appeal to other mature discursive systems and rules of practice, one obtains a type of 'distance', of 'perspective', a perspective is nevertheless always historical, always expressed in relation to its relevance a particular time and place.

That education should intellectually and charactorlogically empower all individuals is a worthy ideal, and one that is important for the development of democratic values, but again, if power is the essence, in what sense is it accurate or meaningful to identify 'autonomy' as the foundation of the architecture to the neglect of other important goods and values, or social processes like social class.

If the concept of autonomy were to mean anything, it represents an equally balanced network of spaces, or points of reference, where the arts of criticism are safeguarded, and where freedoms can be exercised, and power relations enacted. As a particular strategy, it may have 'responsibilisation' as a developmental ideal to a certain extent, but its real value is that it ensures equalisation of power between people: that is an equalisation of entitlement to rights to live and develop. This theme of equalisation which ensured a distribution of power is what rights protect. It is what was argued for by Montesquieu (1900) in *The Spirit of the Laws*, and it is the essence of Foucault's relational approach.[11] It ensures conditions for the development of capabilities; for rights and entitlements to develop freely, without interference, and so on. But none of these qualities is it really helpful, or accurate to call 'autonomy'. The equalisation is not of 'autonomy' but of 'power', which renders agency effective. As Foucault states:

> One must observe also that there cannot be relations of power unless the subjects are free. If one or the other were completely at the disposition of the other and became his thing, an object on which he can exercise an indefinite and unlimited violence, there would not be relations of power. In order to exercise a relation of power, there must be on both sides at least a certain form of liberty. . . . That means that in the relations of power, there is necessarily the possibility of resistance, for if there were no possibility of resistance—of violent resistance, of escape, of ruse, of strategies that reverse the situation—there would be no relations of power.
>
> (Foucault, 1991, p. 12)

Yet another thing autonomy neglects is the strategic sense in which agency is exercised. For Foucault the game is a useful metaphor to express his sense of freedom. The game illustrates the political nature of freedom as pertaining to possibilities under specific conditions. In a game one is both free and constrained. Players find themselves at points where they must respond. In addition, movements in a game are infinitely variable and fluid. While players are confined by rules, indefinite numbers of possibilities and options exist within them. In addition, through effective strategies players can utilise the rules to their own advantage; they can invent and improvise; within a system of constraints, moves are numerous. Freedom and constraint co-exist. Such a view expressed Foucault's conception of freedom, as something political, expressed, or mobilised, through the exercise of power. Mind develops and works politically, i.e., *through power*.[12] In this view, there are constant necessities, but they are obstacles to 'got round', 'pushed against', 'maneuvered', 'fought', and 'tamed'. Freedom to be effective requires moral problematization. In a Foucauldian sense, what autonomy really constitutes is a form of power, or 'cultural capital' in Bourdieu's sense.

Ultimately, too, it requires individual and collective agency. To manifest effective agency is often a complex matter: it involves devising elaborate plans; implementing them through successive stages; and in many instances acting collectively (e.g., to achieve goals on climate change, or in relation to the community). On such a view necessity (rules, constraints) and freedom (agency, initiative, choices) co-exist. Thus, at critical junctures, in certain circumstances, given certain conditions, 'free' agency is rendered, in some instances more possible, and in others more effective in relation to goals. Ultimately, this is the view I think Foucault accepts. Freedom develops, and is difficult. It involves not just recognition of necessity, but a taming, of necessity.

What is clear is that neither freedom nor autonomy exists as a birthright prior to engagement in the historical process. The human subject is socially and historically constituted and develops a capacity for freedom and decision-making slowly, progressively, and with differential success. Freedom is a political skill to be exercised. But as a skill it holds out great promises. Like Spinoza, Foucault was ultimately an optimist. As he says (Martin, *et al.,* 1988, p. 10):

> My role is to show people that they are much freer than they feel, that people accept as truth, as evidence, some themes which have built up at a certain moment during history, and that this so-called evidence can be criticised and destroyed.

The role of education is important here for the exercise of power involves resources, capacities, skills, acumen, technē, eristic, and an understanding of rules. These are the tasks of education.

Notes

1 Rawls argument concerning the 'burdens of judgement' is presented in several places in his writing; see *Political Liberalism* (1993, p. 60). Also see Levinson (1999, pp. 18–22).
2 I cannot go into this relationship here except to say that the emphasis on power, on constitutive praxis, and on self-creation are all present within Spinosa. See Negri (1991) or my book Olssen (2005).
3 John Stuart Mill thought that taking drugs was within the private domain protected by the harm principle, in that such activity did no harm to others. Similarly, depending on how it is defined, gun-collecting or knife collecting could be so defined. The notion of autonomy seems to protect this idea of an exclusively private domain, which is frequently used by libertarians to defend an expansive understanding of private rights.

4 The idea of autonomy goes back to ancient Greece. The root meaning derives from the Greek word auto, which means self, and nomos, which means rule. Thus, autonomy was understood as 'self-rule or 'self-governance' and originally applied not to individuals but to Greek city-states (see Marshall, 1995; Reich, 2002, p. 90).

5 See Kant (1929, A5535/B562) where he says: 'There is in man a power of self-determination, independently of any coercion through sensuous impulses'. It was in the sense that it was independent of experience that determined it as autonomous, and it is in this sense that autonomy, for Kant, was tied to a 'pre-social', historical and metaphysical conception of the person. For in Kant's view an individual can reason independently of social and historical locatedness. Notice that for both Reich and Levinson, it is not reason but the overall character and course of a life that is 'autonomous'.

6 The policy, while noble, is clearly likely to depend upon repressive tolerance. For if the tolerated 'non-autonomous' groups become a majority, or hegemonic, then the viability for the support for autonomy would be 'questioned'.

7 This conclusion is strengthened by Levinson's language. She frequently qualifies her argument in a way that she may claim gives her an escape clause. For example, (p. 33) she claims that it is 'virtually impossible for Sister Susan to be thoroughly autonomous'. This tends to reinforce that there is a hierarchy of autonomy, and that 'thorough' autonomy represents the highest and most independent state of being.

8 To suggest, as Reich does, that children from different cultural groups should be as familiar with other groups as their own is of course impositional. It would be better to suggest open power relations and lines of communication as the solution to this problem.

9 Part of Luther's assertion in the *Ninety-Five Theses* was that the Bible, not the Church, was the final authority for belief and conduct in life. If this was the case then any individual who could read the Bible became the locus of interpretation and an independent authority in religion. Hence Luther's promotion of individualism was a factor supporting the general individualist surge in economics (the capitalist spirit) and in other areas of life.

10 Foucault's statement initially published in *Libération* in June 1984 was to mark the announcement in Geneva of the creation of an international Committee against Piracy. In the article, Foucault refers to Amnesty International, Terre des Hommes, and Médecins du monde. See Foucault (2001).

11 Charles Eisenmann (1933) maintained that the 'separation of powers' thesis was a myth, and that Montesquieu really advanced an 'equalisation of powers' theory, where he was concerned with issues of 'balance', of 'combination', rather than separation.

12 The analogy of the state works well in relation to mind: mind has its exchequer; its defensive arm; its home secretary; its consultative apparatus; and so on. The self *is* political.

References

Anderson, P. (2005) Arms and Rights: Rawls, Habermas and Bobbio in an age of war, *New Left Review*, 31, Jan.–Feb., pp. 5–42.

Anyon, J. (1991) The Retreat of Marxism and Socialist Feminism: Postmodern and poststructural theories in education, *Curriculum Inquiry*, 24:2, pp. 115–133.

Aronowitz, S. & Giroux, H. (1991) *Postmodern Education: Politics, Culture, and Social Criticism*. Minneapolis: University of Minnesota Press.

Baker, B. M. & Heyning, K. E. (eds), (2004) *Dangerous Coagulations: the use of Foucault in the study of education*. New York: Peter Lang.

Ball, S. J. (ed.) (1990) *Foucault and Education: Discipline and Knowledge*. London: Routledge.

Biesta, G. (1998) Pedagogy Without Humanism: Foucault and the Subject of Education, *Interchange*, 29:1, pp. 1–16.

Britzman, D. (1991) *Practice Makes Practice: A critical study of learning to teach* (Albany, SUNY Press).

Cherryholmes, C. (1988) *Power and Criticism: Post-structural investigations in education* (New York, Teachers College Press).

Davies, B. (1989) *Frogs and Snails and Feminist Tales: Preschool children and gender* (Sydney, Allen & Unwin).

Dworkin, G. (1988) *The Theory and Practice of Autonomy*. (Cambridge, Cambridge University Press).

Edwards, R. (2002) Mobilizing lifelong learning: governmentality in education practices, *Journal of Educational Policy*, 17:3, pp. 353–365.

Edwards, R. (2003) Ordering Subjects: Actor networks and intellectual technologies in lifelong learning. *Studies in the Education of Adults*, 35:1, pp. 55–67.

Edwards, R. & Nicoll, K. (2004) Mobilizing Workplaces: actors, discipline and governmentality. *Studies in Continuing Education*, 26:2, pp. 159–173.

Eisenmann, C. (1933) *L'Esprit des Lois et la Séparation des Pouvoirs* (Mélanges Carré de Malberg, Paris), pp. 163–92.

Ellesworth, E. (1989) Why Doesn't This Feel Empowering: Working through the repressive myths of critical pedagogy, *Harvard Educational Review*, 59:3, pp. 297–324.

Foucault, M. (1977) *Discipline and Punish* (trans. A. Sheridan). New York: Pantheon.

Foucault, M. (1987) *Mental Illness and Psychology* (trans. A. Sheridan). Berkeley: University of California Press.

Foucault, M. (1988) *Technologies of the Self* (L. Martin, H. Gutman, & P. Hutton eds) (London, Tavistock).

Foucault, M. (1991) The Ethic of Care for the Self as a Practice of Freedom: An interview (trans. J. D. Gauthier), in: J. Bernauer & D. Rasmussen, *The Final Foucault* (Cambridge, Mass., MIT Press).

Foucault, M. (1997) On the Genealogy of Ethics: An overview of work in progress, in: M. Foucault, *Ethics, Subjectivity and Truth: The essential works* (P. Rabinow ed., R. Hurley trans.) (Allen Lane, The Penguin Press), pp. 253–280.

Foucault, M. (2001) Confronting Governments: Human rights, in: James D. Faubion (ed.), *Michel Foucault: Power, the essential works 3* (Allen Lane, The Penguin Press), pp. 474–475.

Gale, T. (2001) Critical Policy Sociology: Historiography, archaeology and genealogy as methods of policy analysis, *Journal of Education Policy*, 16:5, pp. 379–393.

Galston, W. (1995) Two Concepts of Liberalism, *Ethics*, 61:3, pp. 516–534.

Giroux, H. (1991) Modernism, Postmodernism and Feminism: Rethinking the boundaries of educational discourse, in: H. Giroux (ed.), *Postmodernism, Feminism and Cultural Politics: Redrawing educational boundaries* (Albany, SUNY Press).

Gore, J. (1993) *The Struggle for Pedagogies* (New York, Routledge).

Henriques, J., Hollway, W., Urwin, C., Venn, C. & Walkerdine, V. (1984) *Changing the Subject: Psychology, social regulation, and subjectivity* (London, Methuen).

Hobhouse, L. T. (1911) *Liberalism* (London, Williams and Norgate).

Hoskin, K. (1979) The Examination, Disciplinary Power and Rational Schooling, *History of Education*, 8:2, pp. 135–46.

Jones, K. & Williamson, K. (1979) The Birth of the Schoolroom, *Ideology and Consciousness*, 5:1, pp. 5–6.

Kant, I. (1929) *Critique of Pure Reason* (trans. N. K. Smith) (London, Macmillan/ St. Martin's Press).

Keynes, J. M. (1931a) [orig.1926]. The End of Laissez-Faire, in: John Maynard Keynes, *Essays in Persuasion* (London, Macmillan).

Kukathas, C. (1995) Are There Any Cultural Rights?, in: Will Kymlicka (ed.), *The Rights of Minority Cultures* (Oxford, Oxford University Press).

Kukathas, C. (1997) Cultural Toleration, in: Ian Shapiro and Will Kymlicka (eds), *NOMOS 39,* (New York, New York University Press).

Kymlicka, W. (1989) *Liberalism, Community, Culture* (Oxford, Clarendon).

Kymlicka, W. (1995) *Multicultural Citizenshiip* (Oxford, Oxford University Press).

Lather, P. (1991) *Getting Smart: Feminist research and pedagogy within the postmodern* (New York, Routledge).

Levinson, M. (1999) *The Demands of Liberal Education* (Oxford, Oxford University Press).

McLaren, P. & Hammer, R. (1989) Critical Pedagogy and the Postmodern Challenge: Toward a critical postmodernist pedagogy of liberation, *Educational Foundations*, 3:3, pp. 29–62.

McLaren, P. (1991) Schooling and the Postmodern Body: Critical pedagogy and the politics of enfleshment, in: Henry Giroux (ed.), *Postmodernism, Feminism and Cultural Politics: Redrawing educational boundaries* (Albany: SUNY Press).

Macpherson, C. B. (1962) *The Political Theory of Possessive Individualism* (Oxford, Clarendon Press).

Margalit, A. & Halbertal, M. (1994) The Right to Culture, *Social Research*, 61:3, pp. 491–510.

Marshall, J. (1989) Foucault and Education, *Australian Journal of Education*, 2, pp. 97–111.

Marshall, J. (1990) Foucault and Educational Research, in: S. J. Ball (ed.), *Foucault and Education: Discipline and knowledge* (London, Routledge).

Marshall, J. (1995) Skills, Information and Quality for the Autonomous Chooser, in: M. Olssen & K. Morris Matthews (eds), *Education, Democracy and Reform* (Auckland: New Zealand Association for Research in Education/Research Unit for Maori Education).

Marshall, J. (1996a) Personal Autonomy and Liberal Education: A Foucauldian critique, in: M. Peters, W. Hope, J. Marshall & S. Webster, *Critical Theory, Poststructuralism and the Social Context* (Palmerston North, The Dunmore Press).

Marshall, J. (1996b) *Michel Foucault: Personal autonomy and education* (Dordrecht, Kluwer Academic Publishers).

Marshall, J. (ed.) (2003) *Postructuralism, Philosophy, Pedagogy* (Dordrecht, Kluwer Academic Publishers).

Mill, J. S. [1859] (1956) *On Liberty* (Currin V. Shield, ed.) (Indianapolis, Bobbs Merrill Library of Liberty Arts).

Miller, J. (1990) *Creating Spaces and Finding Voices: Collaborating for empowerment* (Albany, SUNY Press).

de Montesquieu, C. (1900) *The Spirit of Laws* (Thomas Nugent, trans.) (New York, The Colonial Press).

Nussbaum, M. (1992) Human Functioning and Social Justice: A defence of Aristotelian essentialism, *Political Theory*, 20:2, pp. 202–46.

Olssen, M. (1993) Science and Individualism in Educational Psychology: Problems for practice and points of departure. *Educational Psychology*, 13:2, pp. 155–172.

Olssen, M. (1999) *Michel Foucault: Materialism and education* (Westport, Bergin and Garvey).

Olssen, M., Codd, J., & O'Neill, A.M. (2004) *Education Policy: Globalisation, citizenship, & democracy* (London, Sage).

Olssen, M. (2005) (forthcoming) *Michel Foucault: Materialism and education*. (Second enlarged ed.) (Boulder, Paradigm Publishers).

Pagano, J. (1990) *Exiles and Communities: Teaching in the patriarchal wilderness* (Albany, SUNY Press).

Peters, M. & Marshall, J. (1996) *Individualism and Community: Education and social policy in the postmodern condition* (London, The Falmer Press).

Popkewitz, T. S., Franklin, B. M. & Pereyra, M. A. (eds) (2001) *Cultural History and Education: Critical essays on knowledge and schooling* (New York, Routledge/Falmer).

Rawls, J. (1993) *Political Liberalism* (New York, Columbia University Press).

Reich, R. (2002) *Bridging Liberalism and Multiculturalism in American Education* (Chicago, Chicago University Press).

Schneewind, J. B. (1998) *The Invention of Autonomy: A history of modern moral philosophy* (Cambridge, Cambridge University Press).

Spinoza, B. (1985) *Collected Works* (Edwin Curley, trans.) (Princeton, Princeton University Press).

Taylor, C. (1989) *Sources of the Self. The making of modern identity* (Cambridge, Mass., Harvard University Press).

Varela, J. (2001) Genealogies of Education: Some models of analysis, in: T. S. Popkewitz, B. M. Franklin & M. A. Pereyra (eds) *Cultural History and Education: Critical essays on knowledge and schooling* (New York: Routledge/Falmer).

Walkerdine, V. (1989) *Counting Girls Out* (London, Virago).

Wittgenstein, L. (1953) *Philosophical Investigations*. (G. E. M. Anscombe, trans.) (Oxford, Blackwell).

Index

Page numbers in *italics* refer to figures. Page numbers in **bold** refer to tables. Page numbers with "n" refer to notes.